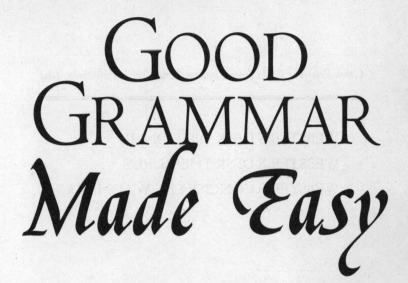

# GOOD GRAMMAR
## Made Easy

# GOOD GRAMMAR
# *Made Easy*

*Martin Steinmann*

*Michael Keller*

GRAMERCY BOOKS
NEW YORK

This 1999 edition is published by Gramercy Books™,
an imprint of Random House Value Publishing, Inc.,
201 East 50th Street, New York, New York 10022,
by arrangement with NTC/Contemporary Publishing Group, Inc.

Gramercy Books™ and design are trademarks of Random House Value Publishing, Inc.

Printed in the United States of America

(Originally published as *Grammar Without Grief*)

Random House
New York • Toronto • London • Sydney • Auckland
http://www.randomhouse.com/

**Library of Congress Cataloging–in–Publication Data**

Steinmann, Martin, 1915-
    [NTC's handbook for writers]
    Good grammar made easy / Martin Steinmann, Michael Keller.
        p.      cm.
    Originally published: NTC's handbook for writers. Lincolnwood,
Ill. : NTC Pub. Group, 1995
    ISBN 0-517-20497-5
    1. English language—Rhetoric Handbooks, manuals, etc.   2. English
language—Grammar Handbooks, manuals, etc.   3. Report Writing
Handbooks, manuals, etc.   I. Keller, Michael (Michael A.)
II. Title.
PE1408.S7275    1999
808'.042—dc21                                           99-29884
                                                          CIP


9 8 7 6 5 4 3 2 1

# Introduction

The chief purpose of this book is to give you information and advice about how to write Standard American Written English (SAWE) *correctly, clearly,* and *persuasively.* SAWE is the variety, or dialect, of English that almost all college-educated citizens of the United States and Canada strive to write, especially in business letters, applications, academic papers, and anything for publication.

To write SAWE *correctly* is to do three things:

1. to choose words and phrases that conform to SAWE *usage;*
2. to put these words and phrases into sentences that conform to SAWE *grammar;* and
3. to make these words, phrases, and sentences conform to SAWE conventions of spelling, punctuation, capitalization, and the like—matters never at issue in speaking, only in writing.

To write SAWE *clearly* is to write it so that your readers understand your assertions, questions, and requests.

To write SAWE *persuasively* is to write it so that your readers believe your assertions, answer your questions, and grant your requests.

But this handbook has yet another purpose: to give you some basic information about language, its uses, and its diversity. Though this information is perhaps only indirectly useful to you in writing SAWE, it can satisfy your curiosity, not only about what language is and what you do when you write or speak any language, but also about varieties of English other than SAWE. What is a noun? A verb? A preposition? What is a subject? What is a grammatical rule? How does writing differ from speech? What is Black English? WASP language?

## ENTRIES

To achieve its purposes, *Good Grammar Made Easy* provides two kinds of entries: word entries and topic entries.

### Word Entries
Word entries (in lower case) answer questions about words and also about phrases, prefixes, and suffixes. These questions arise, not when you are planning what to write, but when you are actually writing or rewriting. Should you write *He inferred he was suspicious* or *He implied he was suspicious*? (See **imply, infer.**) *The cat laid there* or *The cat lay there*? (See **lay** (**laid, laying**), **lie** (**lay, lying, lain**).) *The universe is comprised of atoms* or *The universe is composed of atoms*? (See **comprised of.**) *Suppose to* or *supposed to*? (See **-ed, -d.**)

### Topic Entries
Topic entries (in capital letters) answer a greater variety of questions than do word entries.

First of all, though no topic entry is devoted to an individual word, phrase, prefix, or suffix, many topic entries answer questions about individual expressions. **CLICHÉS,** for instance, provides an alphabetical list of clichés; **CONCISION,** of wordy expressions and concise substitutes; **EUPHEMISMS,** of euphemisms and corresponding taboo words; **IDIOMS,** of troublesome idioms; **MALAPROPISMS,** of malapropisms and the words they are confused with. And many other topic entries give information and advice about choosing words and phrases: **AGREEMENT: VERBS WITH SUBJECTS,** for example, and **ALLUSIONS AND REFERENCES, DESCRIPTIVE AND EVALUATIVE**

WORDS, ELEGANT VARIATION, HYPERCORREC-
TION, LATINISMS, POLITICAL CORRECTNESS, and
SEXIST LANGUAGE.

Second, many topic entries answer questions about the conventions of SAWE: among them, **CAPITALIZATION, COLONS,**
and **COMMAS.**

Third, many entries answer questions, not about choices of
expressions or conventions—questions arising when you are actually writing or rewriting—but about questions arising when you
are planning or organizing or when you are making large-scale
revisions: **ARGUMENT AND PERSUASION,** for example,
and **FALLACIES** and **READERS, COMMUNICATION,
AND PERSUASION.**

Some topic entries help you understand SAWE: the language,
its uses, and its diversity: among them, **ANTONYMS, BLACK
ENGLISH, FIGURES OF SPEECH, FORMS AND FUNC-
TIONS, GRAMMATICAL RULES, NOUNS, VERBS,** and
**WASP LANGUAGE.**

Finally, some of the topic entries have been set off by highlight-
ing for one or both of two reasons. First, they are of special
importance to understanding or producing all good writing—for
example, **CLARITY, COHERENCE,** and **CONCISION.** Second, they are rarely or inadequately discussed in handbooks—for
example, **ASSUMPTIONS AND PROPOSITIONS, CON-
TRADICTIONS,** and **READERS, COMMUNICATION,
AND PERSUASION.**

## GUIDING PRINCIPLES

In choosing and writing both word and topic entries, we have
been guided by four principles:

1. For effective writing—writing that is correct, clear, and
   persuasive—there are no recipes, only guidelines. For
   writing effectively or ineffectively is a creative act, like

painting a picture, composing a symphony, or inventing a spacecraft. Every piece of writing, effective or ineffective, is unique. Never before in the history of the language have those very words in that very order been set on paper.

2. Like every other language or dialect, Standard American English, written (SAWE) or spoken, is not a static system of heaven-sent rules. It is always changing. (See, for instance, **GRAMMATICAL RULES** and **SEXIST LANGUAGE**.) Its rules, moreover, are made and changed, not by English teachers or handbooks, but by writers writing and speakers speaking. If language did not change, modern English would be identical with the English that King Alfred wrote and spoke in the ninth century. In any case, what you ought to write depends not just upon rules but upon context: time, place, genre or occasion, your purpose, and, above all, your readers. (See **AUDIENCE**.)

3. Your readers are supremely important to your writing. How your writing affects them is the sole test of its effectiveness.

4. In using a handbook, you often can profit vastly more from examples, illustrations, and analogies than from definitions or formulations of rules or principles, however necessary these often are. (See, for instance, **USE AND MENTION**, which, depending solely upon examples, defines neither *use* nor *mention*.)

And, in writing word entries, we have been guided by yet another principle:

5. In choosing a word or a phrase, you need answers to four questions:

- Does the word or phrase you are considering mean exactly what you intend it to mean?
- Is it well established in SAWE usage?
- Is it—besides being well established in SAWE usage—accepted by your readers? Word entries often point out (in a **Caution**) that some or even many readers object to a word or phrase well established in SAWE usage, even readers in whose own writing it occurs. Use of *flaunt* to mean "treat with contempt," for example, is now well established in SAWE usage. But, if some readers object to this use, why not use *flout*, to which no readers object? (See **flaunt, flout.**)
- Is the word or phrase you are considering formal (appropriate in business and professional writing and in any writing for publication) or informal (appropriate in letters to friends and relatives or perhaps in a light-hearted spoof written for *Vanity Fair*)?

## HOW TO USE *GOOD GRAMMAR MADE EASY*

If you have a question about an individual word, phrase, prefix, or suffix:

1. Check word entries to see whether it is there.
2. If it is not, try to think of a category to which it may belong (clichés, euphemisms, or malapropisms, for example), and then check the topic entries to see whether that category is there (**CLICHÉS, EUPHEMISMS, MALAPROPISMS,** and so on).
3. If neither word nor topic entries answer your question, consult your dictionary. Of the thousands of words, phrases, prefixes, and suffixes in English, only a selection of the most troublesome can be included in this handbook.

If you have a question about several issues related to argument, clarity and style, the conventions of writing, grammar, language, or the writing process, check the following Topical Guide to the Handbook for listings of entries that relate to those categories.

# Topical Guide to the Handbook

**Conventions of Writing**

**Language**

**Writing Process**

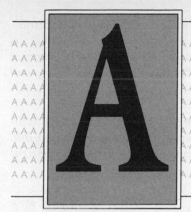

**a, an** Use *a* before a consonant (*a bird, a hamburger, a NATO official, a youth*), **an** before a vowel (*an engine, an onion, an accent*). **Exception:** You may use *an* before an unstressed *h*: *an historical* (but *a history*). **Caution:** Consonants and vowels are sounds, not letters. Therefore, in choosing between *a* and *an,* be guided by your ear, not your eye: *a European* (because *European* sounds like *yeuropean*), *a once-over* (*wonce-over*), *a university* (*yuniversity*), *an FBI* (*ef-be-i*) *official, an honor* (*onor*).

**a, an; per** In the sense "by each" or "for each," both *a* (or *an*) and *per* are SAWE: *40 miles an hour* (or *per hour*); *fifteen cents a slice* (or *per slice*). The Anglo-Saxon *a* or *an* is less formal than the Latin *per* and perhaps more natural. *Per* tends to be preferred in scientific or technical writing: *20 seconds per revolution.*

**abdicate, abrogate**  Sometimes confused. *Abdicate* as an intransitive verb means "give up a throne" (*Edward VII abdicated*); as a transitive verb, it means "give up" (*He abdicated his right to counsel*). *Abrogate* means "annul," "nullify," or "revoke": *The rival factions abrogated their treaty.*

**abjure, adjure**  Sometimes confused. *Abjure* means "abstain from," "recant," or "renounce solemnly": *He abjured liberalism. Adjure* means "order or urge solemnly": *She adjured her patient to quit smoking.*

**above**  As an adjective meaning "mentioned above" or as a noun meaning "topic mentioned above," *above* is SAWE. **Caution:** Some readers object to both uses as awkward, commercial, or both.

> NOT THIS:    The **above** argument is not very persuasive.

> BUT THIS:    The argument **referred to earlier** is not very persuasive.

**absent**  Avoid use of this adjective as a preposition, because non-SAWE.

> NOT THIS:    **Absent** a father, the child is unhappy.

> BUT THIS:    **Without** a father. . . .

**ABSOLUTE CONSTRUCTIONS**  (1) An **absolute construction,** typically a noun or pronoun followed by a participle, is an expression that bears no grammatical relationship to any other expression in its sentence: *The concert having ended, we left the theater. The concert having ended* is not a modifier, for example, or the subject or an object. If it is deleted, the rest of the sentence can stand alone.

(2) In such a phrase, never insert a comma (or any other mark of punctuation) between the noun and the participle.

NOT THIS:    The concert, having ended, we left the theater.

BUT THIS:    The concert having ended, we left the theater.

**academic**  In the sense "of little or no practical importance," *academic* is SAWE but may offend some readers.

NOT THIS:    The question (or issue) is **academic.**

BUT THIS:    The issue is **of little practical importance.**

**ACCENT MARKS**  **Accent marks** (or diacritics) are little used in American English nowadays. Words borrowed from other languages sometimes retain their original accent marks—the acute accent mark in *passé,* for instance, and the grave accent mark in *à la mode.* Quotations of passages in other languages should, of course, preserve accent marks: *He said, "Señor* [the tilde] *Alvarez esta aqui."*

**accept, except**  Sometimes confused. *Accept,* a verb, means "receive willingly" or "agree to": *accept responsibility. Except* as a preposition means "excluding (*everyone except Stephen*); as a verb, it means "exclude" (*We excepted Stephen*).

**account, count**  Sometimes confused. As a noun, an *account* is either a credit arrangement at a place of business or a description or explanation: *an account of the disaster.* A *count* is either a charge (*guilty on all counts*) or a synonym for *respect* (*unsatisfactory on two counts*).

NOT THIS:    I prefer this car on at least two **accounts.**

BUT THIS:    . . . on at least two **counts.**

**acoustics**   In SAWE, it is either singular or plural, whether meaning (1) "science of sound" or (2) "sound qualities of a space." In (1), however, it is usually construed as singular (*Acoustics is a relatively new science*); in (2) as plural (*The acoustics of the concert hall are good*).

**acquiesce**   The idiomatic preposition after *acquiesce* is *in*: *We acquiesced in their proposal.* (See **IDIOMS**.)

**ACRONYMS**   An **acronym** is a word formed from the initial letters of the words in a compound term. Usually an acronym consists of capital letters (*NATO*) but not always (*radar*). Use an acronym only if you supply the corresponding compound term or are sure that your readers know what it is.

**ACTIVE VS. PASSIVE VOICE**   See **VOICE**.

**actual, actually**   Often, though not always, a source of wordiness (see **CONCISION**).

> NOT THIS:   The **actual** cause of death was cancer.

> BUT THIS:   The cause of death was cancer.

For contrast, however: *Though the **reported** cause of death was cancer, the **actual** cause was congestive heart failure.*

**ad**   Now SAWE to mean "advertisement."

**additionally**   Prefer *also* because shorter.

**address**   For the verb, prefer more specific synonyms, such as *deal with, direct attention to, direct efforts to,* and *treat.*

**AD HOMINEM**   An argument **ad hominem** (meaning "to the man" or "to the person" in Latin) is a fallacy. (See **FALLACIES**.)

You commit this fallacy whenever you attack an argument by finding fault with the person who made it:

PREMISES: (1) The President, in his last broadcast, argued that all Americans ought to carry organ-donor cards.
(2) But the President himself does not carry an organ-donor card.

CONCLUSION: The President's argument is bad.

Perhaps the President is bad not to practice what he preaches, but the only relevant question in evaluating his argument is whether *it* is good or bad, not whether he is.

**ADJECTIVAL CLAUSES** See **RELATIVE CLAUSES.**

**ADJECTIVES** **Adjectives** are a part of speech that, like adverbs, can perform only one function—modification—and that, unlike nouns, pronouns, and verbs, never change form. (See **FORMS AND FUNCTIONS** and **MODIFIERS AND MODIFICATION.**) Most adjectives have no distinctive ending (*alone, big, thin, high, nice, small*), but many end in *-able* (*lovable*), *-al* (*normal*), *-ful* (*thoughtful*), *-ish* (*lavish*), *-ly* (*lovely*), *-worthy* (*praiseworthy*), and *-y* (*sandy*). An adjective (ADJ) can modify only a noun or a noun phrase and can occupy a position either just before the noun (NOUN) or noun phrase (NP) it modifies or just after it or after a verb such as *appear, be, look,* or *seem* (VERB):

ADJ   NOUN
The beautiful house is on Elm Street.

NOUN   ADJ
The Breakers is truly the house beautiful.

VERB   ADJ
The house on Elm Street is beautiful.

Adjectives have three degrees: positive, comparative, and superlative (*good, better, best; fine, finer, finest; bad, worse, worst*).

**adjust salaries, benefits, etc.** Often a euphemism for *reduce* (see **EUPHEMISMS**).

**administrate** Prefer the shorter *administer.*

NOT THIS:   Hamilton **administrates** the fund.

BUT THIS:   Hamilton **administers** the fund.

**adult** As an adjective, frequently a euphemism for *pornographic: an adult bookstore.*

**advance reservations** Wordy. All reservations are, by definition, made in advance. (See **CONCISION**.)

**advance warning** Wordy. All warnings are, by definition, made in advance. (See **CONCISION**.)

**ADVERBIAL CLAUSES** An **adverbial clause** is a dependent, or subordinate, clause that begins with a subordinating conjunction such as *after, as, because, before, if, in order that, lest, once, provided that, since, so that, though, unless, until, whether,* and *while* and that can function as an adverb can, chiefly to modify a verb. Some examples: *After he finished, he collapsed; As the plot unfolded, the audience grew tense; Because the dam broke, the town was flooded; Since the general manager left, the firm has prospered; Bill turned on the lights so that he could see; Unless we try, we may fail; While Rome burned, he fiddled.* (See **CLAUSES**.)

**ADVERBS** Adverbs are a part of speech that, like adjectives, can perform only one function—modification—and that, unlike nouns, pronouns, and verbs, never change form. (See **FORMS AND FUNCTIONS** and **MODIFIERS AND MODIFICATION**.) Most adverbs end in *-ly* (*completely, organically*), but not all (*often, seldom, very, well*). Many, though not all, adverbs can modify not only verbs (VERB), but adjectives (ADJ) and other adverbs (ADV):

    ADV       VERB
It completely encloses the area.
    ADV       ADJ
It is completely original.
    ADV       ADV
It is completely organically grown.

As these examples suggest, the typical position of an adverb is just before the word it modifies. But some adverbs can occupy a variety of positions:

**Heartily** I endorse the candidate.

I **heartily** endorse the candidate.

I endorse the candidate **heartily.**

Like adjectives, adverbs have three degrees: (*far, farther* or *further, farthest* or *furthest; slowly, more slowly, most slowly*).

**adverse, averse**  Sometimes confused. *Adverse* means "unfavorable": *Adverse winds delayed the sailing. Averse* means "against": *I am averse to loud music.*

**advice, advise**  (1) Sometimes confused. *Advice* is a noun meaning "recommendation about what to do": *My advice is to sell this stock. Advise* is a verb meaning "give advice": *I advise you to sell this stock.*
  (2) Avoid using *advise* to mean "inform," "say," or "tell."

    NOT THIS:   Let me **advise** you that your account is overdue.

    BUT THIS:   Let me **tell** you that your account is overdue.

    OR BETTER:   Your account is overdue.

**affect, effect**  Often confused. Each word is both a verb and a noun. **Verbs**: *Affect* means either "influence" (*Unemployment affects sales*) or "display ostentatiously" (*Algernon affects indifference*). *Effect* means either "produce" or "result in" (*The negotiations effected a compromise*). **Nouns**: *Affect* is a technical term in psychology rarely used elsewhere meaning "a feeling or emotion" (*He is depressed and displays little affect*). *Effect* means "result" (*The effect of the negotiations was a compromise*).

**affiliated or associated with**  Usually pretentious for *belongs to* or *works for.*

NOT THIS:  She is **affiliated with** the wholesale supermarket.

BUT THIS:  She **works for** the wholesale supermarket.

**aforementioned, aforesaid**  Wordy (see **CONCISION**).

NOT THIS:  The **aforementioned** crisis. . . .

BUT THIS:  **The** (or **this**) crisis. . . .

**African-American**  Now the preferred expression for reference to an American of black African ancestry. It has largely replaced *black,* which long ago replaced *Negro.* A frequently favored alternative is *person of color* (but never *colored person*). (See **POLITICAL CORRECTNESS.**)

**aftermath**  Use only when what follows or followed is unpleasant: *the aftermath of the infection was paralysis.*

**afterward, afterwards**  Synonymous in SAWE.

**agenda**  In Latin, *agenda* is plural (singular: *agendum*). But in SAWE it is almost always singular (*a hidden agenda*) though occasionally plural (*our agenda are numerous*).

**aggravate**  In conversation and informal writing, *aggravate* often means either "annoy" (*The loud music aggravated me*) or "irritate" (*That deodorant aggravates Leslie's skin*). **Caution:** In formal writing it means "make worse": *The cold weather aggravated Ralph's cough.*

**AGREEMENT: PRONOUNS WITH ANTECEDENTS**  In general, a pronoun agrees with its antecedent noun or indefinite pronoun in gender and number (see **ANTECEDENTS** and **NUMBER**):

Jack **himself** has **his** problems.

Jane **herself** has **her** problems.

Jack and Jane **themselves** have **their** problems.

**AGREEMENT: VERBS WITH SUBJECTS**  In general, a verb agrees with its subject in number and person. In three situations, a writer whose native language is English is likely to have difficulty in making a verb agree with its subject in number.

One situation is a sentence or clause that begins with a pseudo-subject (*there*) and places the real subject (here: *flaws*) after the verb: *There are* (not *is*) *flaws in Smith's solution.* For this situation, see **there is ('s), are ('re), was, were, etc.**

The second situation is a sentence or clause whose subject is a noun phrase (see **NOUN PHRASES**) consisting of, among other things, a singular head noun followed by one or more plural nouns or pronouns:

SUBJECT: NOUN PHRASE

| HEAD NOUN | | PLURAL NOUN | | PLURAL NOUN | PLURAL NOUN |
|---|---|---|---|---|---|
| The list | of | problems | sick | people encounter in seeking cures | |

VERB

**is/are** enough to discourage them.

The rule is that the verb must agree with the head noun—in a noun phrase like this one, whatever noun has one or more premodifiers (here: *the*) and one or more postmodifiers (here: the prepositional phrase *of problems sick people encounter in seeking cures*) but is not itself a modifier. The danger is that the writer may make the verb agree, not with the singular head noun, but with the plural nouns between it and the verb.

> NOT THIS:    . . . **are** enough to discourage them.

> BUT THIS:    . . . **is** enough to discourage them.

The third situation is a sentence or clause with a compound subject consisting of two or more noun phrases joined, not by *and*, but by *or, either . . . or*, or *neither . . . nor: Either the door or the hinge causes/cause the trouble; Either the door or the hinges causes/cause the trouble; Either the doors or the hinge causes/cause the trouble; Either the doors or the hinges causes/cause the trouble.* The rule is that the verb must agree with the head noun of the noun phrase closest to it. The danger is that the writer, confusing *or, either . . . or*, or *neither . . . nor* with *and*, may make the verb plural whether the head noun of the closest noun phrase is singular or plural.

> NOT THIS:    Either the door or the hinge **cause** the trouble.

> BUT THIS:    Either the door or the hinge **causes** the trouble.

> NOT THIS:    Either the doors or the hinge **cause** the trouble.

> BUT THIS:    Either the doors or the hinge **causes** the trouble.

(See **NUMBER.**)

**a half a/an**    NonSAWE for *a half* or *half a/an*

> NOT THIS:    **a half an** hour.

> BUT THIS:    **a half** hour.

> OR THIS:    **half an** hour.

**aid, aide**  Now synonymous in SAWE, but prefer *aide* to mean "assistant": *the president's* **aide**.

**ain't**  Though the only contraction of *am not* (no one says *am't*) and sometimes used in SAWE humorously, it is otherwise non-SAWE as a contraction for *am not, is not, are not, has not,* and *have not.*

> NOT THIS:   She **ain't** in college.

> BUT THIS:   She **isn't** (or **is not**) in college.

**alibi**  From Latin *alibi* ("elsewhere"), *alibi* is SAWE for a legal defense that the accused was not at the scene of the crime. Avoid using to mean "excuse."

> NOT THIS:   His **alibi** was that he was busy.

> BUT THIS:   His **excuse** was that he was busy.

**all-around, all-round**  These synonyms are both SAWE.

**all during**  Wordy for *during*. (See **CONCISION**.)

> NOT THIS:   **all during** the night.

> BUT THIS:   **during** the night.

**alleged**  Sometimes wordy. (See **CONCISION**.)

> NOT THIS:   He was convicted of an **alleged** crime.

> BUT THIS:   He was convicted of a crime.

**all is not . . .**  Ambiguous. Prefer either *Nothing is . . .* or *not all is. . . .*

**ALLITERATION**  Repetition of an initial sound in successive words: *Peter Piper picked a peck of pickled peppers.*

**all of**  Usually wordy for *all*. (See **CONCISION**.)

> NOT THIS:    **All of** the judges agreed.

> BUT THIS:    **All** the judges agreed.

**all ready, already**  Often confused. *Already* means "by a speci-fied or implied time": *By noon, the players were **already** there*. In *all ready, all* means either (a) "completely" or (b) "every one of," and *ready* means "prepared." *The players were **all ready***, for example, can mean either (a) *The players were completely prepared* or (b) *Every one of the players was prepared*.

**all right**  See **alright, all right**.

**all that**  See **that (all that, not all that, not that)**.

**all the farther, all the faster**  NonSAWE for *as far as, as fast as*.

> NOT THIS:    Forty is **all the faster** this old car will go.

> BUT THIS:    Forty is **as fast as** this old car will go.

**all together, altogether**  Often confused. *All together* means either "all in one place" (*The swimmers were **all together** in the pool*) or "all in a group" (*The swimmers went **all together** to see the coach*). *Altogether* means "wholly" or "completely": *Mack was **altogether** unqualified for the job*.

**allude, elude**  Often confused. *Allude* means "refer indirectly": *Marie frequently **alludes** to her husband's stinginess*. *Elude* means either "evade" (*The terrorists **eluded** the police*) or "escape the notice of" (*The details of American history **elude** Tom*).

**allusion, illusion**  Often confused. *Allusion* means "indirect ref-erence": *"The melancholy Dane" is an **allusion** to Shakespeare's*

*Hamlet. Illusion* means "false belief": *Tim had the illusion that Sue loved him. Illusion* also means "something deceptive or misleading": *The magician produced the illusion of sawing a woman into halves.*

**ALLUSIONS AND REFERENCES**   A **reference** picks out or points to someone or something either by name (*Bill Clinton*) or by chief claim to fame (*the President of the United States*). An **allusion** is an indirect reference (*the White House saxophone player*). References, of course, are indispensable in all writing; allusions are not. Allusions do, however, please (by flattering) readers who recognize and comprehend them. Never use a reference or an allusion that you are not fairly certain your readers will get, unless you wish to shame them or educate them. (See **MEANING AND REFERENCE.**)

**almost**   SAWE as an adverb meaning "nearly" (*He almost died*), but avoid as an adjective meaning "near."

NOT THIS:   an **almost** collision.

BUT THIS:   a **near** collision.

**alot**   *Alot* is a misspelling of *a lot* (two words: *a + lot*).

NOT THIS:   **alot** of trouble.

BUT THIS:   **a lot** of trouble.

**already**   See **all ready, already.**

**alright, all right**   Both spellings are now generally considered SAWE, but many readers object to the spelling *alright.*

NOT THIS:   Route 63 is **alright.**

BUT THIS:   Route 63 is **all right.**

**also** Avoid using as a substitute for *and*.

> NOT THIS:   She is my teacher, **also** my friend.

> BUT THIS:   She is my teacher **and** (or **and also**) my friend.

**altar, alter** Sometimes confused. *Altar* is a noun designating a part of a church: *kneel at the altar. Alter* is a verb meaning "change": *alter your views.*

**alteration, altercation** Sometimes confused. *Alteration* means "change"; *altercation* means "a quarrel."

**alternate, alternative** Sometimes confused. *Alternate* is either a verb meaning "cause to go by turns" (*alternate the performers*), an adjective meaning "arranged by turns" (*alternate performances*), or a noun meaning "substitute" (*an alternate to receive the prize*). *Alternative* is either an adjective meaning "that may be chosen in place of something else" (*an alternative route*) or noun meaning "something that may be chosen in place of something else" (*an alternative to life in prison*).

**altho** This abbreviated spelling of *although* has found favor only in a few newspapers and should be avoided in formal writing.

**although, though** These synonyms are both SAWE, but *although* is a bit more formal.

**altogether** See **all together, altogether.**

**alumna, alumnae, alumni, alumnus** All four words mean "graduate(s) or former student(s), member(s)," and so on. In strictest SAWE usage, *alumna* refers to one female; *alumnae,* to more than one; *alumnus,* to one male; *alumni,* to more than one. In general SAWE usage, *alumnus* refers to one person of either sex; *alumni,* to more than one.

**AMBIGUITY** Multiplicity of meaning. The noun *board,* for instance, has at least three meanings (or senses): (1) "Wooden plank" (*replace a floor board*), (2) "meals" (*room and board*), (3) "governing body" (*board of education*). And the sentence *He wants to marry a rich woman* has two meanings: (1) *There is a certain rich woman whom he wants to marry;* (2) *He wants to marry a woman who is rich but has no particular one in mind.*

Context—neighboring words or sentences—usually eliminates ambiguity. For example, preceded by *room and, board* means "meals."

**amend, emend** Sometimes confused because similar in both sound and meaning. *Amend* means either "improve" (*amend his ways*) or "change phraseology" (*amend the proposed bill*). *Emend* means "correct or revise" (a text): *emend the first edition.*

**America** It can refer to North, Central, and South America, taken together, or to the United States. Unless qualified, it refers to the latter.

**amiable, amicable** Virtually synonymous in SAWE. But *amiable* may suggest that there is little other than good nature to recommend the person so described.

**among, between** The object of *among* refers to at least three things or persons: **among** *the members of the club,* **among** *the rich.* The object of *between* refers to at least two: **between** *you and me.* **Caution:** Some readers object to use of *between* with an object referring to more than two.

NOT THIS:   The will divided his estate **between** his four grandchildren.

BUT THIS:   The will divided his estate **among** his four grandchildren.

**amoral, immoral**  An *amoral* person violates a moral code unknowingly; an *immoral* person, knowingly.

**amount, number**  Often confused. *Amount* refers to a quantity, something that cannot be counted: *amount of pleasure, amount of sugar, amount of work. Number* refers to things that can be counted: *number of cookies, number of pleasures, number of jobs.*

**AMPERSANDS**  In SAWE, an **ampersand** (&) is used for *and* only in names of businesses that so use it: *H. A. Walker & Co.*

**a.m., p.m.**  Used only after numerals.

> NOT THIS:    At four in the **p.m.**, the game ended.

> BUT THIS:    At 4:00 **p.m.**, the game ended.

> OR THIS:    At four in the afternoon, the game ended.

**an**  See **a, an.**

**ANALOGIES**  An **analogy** is a figure of speech in which two unlike things are compared to one another. For example: *"A meeting of a committee of the United States Senate is like a circus: the senators are like clowns. . . . "* (See **FIGURES OF SPEECH.**)

**ANAPHORA**  Either the repetition of a word or words at the beginning of two or more clauses or sentences (*We cannot dedicate, we cannot consecrate, we cannot hallow this ground*) or the use of a word as a substitute for another one (*Joe plays better than Al does; Bob hates himself*).

**and etc.**  See **etc.**

**and in addition**  Wordy for *and.* (See **CONCISION.**)

**and/or**   Prefer *or* to the awkward *and/or*. The conjunction *or* is taken to be inclusive (that is, to mean "and/or") unless preceded by *either: Choose either chocolate or vanilla.*

**and, so**   Be sparing in your use of these conjunctions to connect independent clauses and sentences. Don't overlook other conjunctions (*but, for*), conjunctive adverbs (for example: *however, moreover, nevertheless, notwithstanding, therefore*), and other transitional words and phrases. (See **TRANSITIONS**.)

**and, to**   Prefer *to* to *and* in sentences such as *Try to be on time.*

**and which, and who, and whom**   Used in SAWE only after a relative clause (see **RELATIVE CLAUSES**).

> NOT THIS:   Riley is an honest man **and who** obeys the law.

> BUT THIS:   Riley is a man who is honest **and who** obeys the law.

> OR:   Riley is honest and obeys the law.

**annual yearly**   Wordy for *annual* or *yearly*. (See **CONCISION**.)

**ante-, anti-**   Often confused. The prefix *ante-* means either "before" (*antebellum, antecedent*) or "in front of" (*antechamber, anteroom*). The prefix *anti-* means "against": *anticlimax, antiestablishment.* **Caution:** Use a hyphen after *anti-* when the next letter is either *i* (*anti-independence*) or a capital (*anti-Marxist*).

**ANTECEDENTS**   An **antecedent** is an expression for which another expression is a substitute, to which it refers, and from which it gets most of its meaning. The antecedent of a typical pronoun (see **PRONOUNS**) is another nominal (see **NOMINALS**); the antecedent of a pro-verb (see **PRO-VERBS**) is either a verb (see **VERBS**) or a verb phrase (verb + auxiliaries or objects or modifiers):

ANTECEDENT: NOMINAL          PRONOUN
The meals are terrible. I can't stand them.
ANTECEDENT: VERB          PRO-VERB
He dithers; sometimes I do too.

**ANTONYMS**  If two words are opposites in meaning, they are **antonyms.** In their opposition, antonyms may be either negational, scalable, or symmetrical. If negational (*on/off, true/false*), antonyms are negations of one another: *on = not off, off = not on; true = not false, false = not true.* If scalable (*brightness/darkness, long/short*), antonyms name opposite ends of a scale: in between *brightness* and *darkness,* for example, is *dimness;* in between *long* and *short* is *medium-length.* If symmetrical (*physician/patient, teach/learn*), antonyms have a symmetrical relationship to one another: *if X is Y's physician, then Y is X's patient; if X teaches something to Y, then Y learns that thing from X.* (See **SYNO-NYMS.**)

**anxious, eager**  Use of either *anxious* or *eager* to mean "enthusiastically or impatiently desirous" is now SAWE: *Nancy was anxious* or (*eager*) *to see our new house.* **Caution:** Some readers object to this use of *anxious.*

NOT THIS:   Bill was **anxious** to begin his vacation.

BUT THIS:   Bill was **eager** to begin his vacation.

But no one objects to *anxious* to mean "worried": *Mary is anxious about her job interview.*

**any**  SAWE counts *any* as singular when it means "any one" (*Any of the suspects is sure to have been in trouble before*), but as plural when it means "some" (*Any of the cookies are delicious*).

**any and all**   Wordy (see **CONCISION**). Choose *any* or *all*.

NOT THIS:   **Any and all** efforts failed.

BUT THIS:   **Any** (or **all**) efforts failed.

**any, anyone, anyone else, any other**   Be sure to include *else* or *other* to avoid a contradiction.

NOT THIS:   Barrymore runs faster than **anyone. (Anyone** includes Barrymore, which is a contradiction: Barrymore cannot run faster than himself.)

BUT THIS:   Barrymore runs faster than **anyone else.**

NOT THIS:   Senator Smothers got more votes than **any** senator. (**Any** includes Smothers, which is a contradiction: Smothers cannot have gotten more votes than he got.)

BUT THIS:   Senator Smothers got more votes than **any other** senator.

**any more, anymore**   Often confused. *Any more* is an adverb (*any*) plus an adjective (*more*): *I don't want **any more** trouble. Anymore* is an adverb meaning "now": *Herbert isn't in college* **anymore. Note:** Use both only with a negative.

**any one, anyone; every one, everyone; some one, someone**   *Any one, every one,* and *some one* always come before a prepositional phrase:

PREPOSITIONAL PHRASE
**Every one** of the suspects may be guilty.

But *anyone, everyone,* and *someone* never do: *Everyone may be guilty.*

**anyplace, anywhere**  Synonymous in SAWE, but some readers object to *anyplace*.

> NOT THIS:   She couldn't find it **anyplace**.

> BUT THIS:   She couldn't find it **anywhere**.

**anyways, anywheres**  NonSAWE for *anyway* and *anywhere*.

> NOT THIS:   **Anyways,** I don't like physics.

> BUT THIS:   **Anyway,** I don't like physics.

**a period of**  Wordy (see **CONCISION**).

> NOT THIS:   He worked in Detroit for **a period of** ten years.

> BUT THIS:   He worked in Detroit for ten years.

**APOSTROPHES**  Use an **apostrophe** ('):

(1) To form the possessive case of a noun or an indefinite pronoun (see **CASE**):

> one boy's bat        two boys' bats        anyone's guess

(2) To mark a missing letter or letters, word or words in a contraction:

> can't (cannot)        o'clock (of the clock)

(3) To form with *s* the plural of a word, a letter, or a numeral mentioned (that is, referred to as such) rather than used:

> two *of*'s              four *3*'s

**apparent, apparently**  Sometimes misused.

> NOT THIS:   Cecil died of an **apparent** heart attack.

> BUT THIS:   Cecil **apparently** died of a heart attack.

What is apparent is not the heart attack but that Cecil died of it.

**apparent, evident, obvious** Almost synonymous. But *apparent* leaves more room for doubt than *evident,* and *evident* more than *obvious.*

**APPOSITIVES** One of the twelve functions that a part of speech can perform in a clause. (See **FORMS AND FUNCTIONS.**)

An **appositive** is a word or phrase referring to (but rarely meaning—see **MEANING AND REFERENCE**) the same thing that a word or phrase just before it refers to: *John, my brother; my brother, John; Washington, the capital of the United States.* An appositive may be either restrictive (*my brother John*) or nonrestrictive (*my brother, John*). (See **RESTRICTIVE AND NONRESTRICTIVE.**) An appositive must be in the same case (see **CASE**) as its appositor: *The committee, John and I, will reconvene tomorrow. The secretary will reconvene the committee, John and me.*

**appraise, apprise** Often confused. *Appraise* means "evaluate": *The real-estate agent **appraised** the condominium. Apprise* means "inform": *Her roommate **apprised** Sue that her father had called.*

**appreciate** Avoid using to mean "like," especially in negative constructions.

NOT THIS:  I don't **appreciate** having my honesty questioned.

BUT THIS:  I don't **like** having my honesty questioned.

**ARCHAISMS** Words no longer used in the language: *eftsoons, methinks, quoth, whilom.* Avoid them, even in verse, except perhaps in historical novels.

**area, field** Often sources of wordiness (see **CONCISION**).

NOT THIS:  the **area** (or **field**) of computer design.

BUT THIS:  computer design.

**ARGUMENT AND PERSUASION**   One purpose in writing is to persuade your readers to believe something or do something. Indeed, in a way it is the only purpose.

Two means of persuasion are available to you. One is appeals to reason by use of good arguments. The other is appeals to feelings—appeals to emotions, attitudes, desires, affections, loyalties, values, and the like. You are not likely to persuade thoughtful readers by appealing solely to their feelings: they will expect good arguments as well. But you are not likely to persuade them solely by using good arguments either. Indeed, an appeal to feelings—in particular, to readers' values—is an essential ingredient of some good arguments. You are unlikely, for instance, to persuade readers to give up alcohol solely by arguing that it is a leading cause of heart disease and therefore death. They must value a long life more than the pleasures of the bottle.

One way to appeal to your readers' feelings is to tell them how you intend them to feel: tell them what to approve or disapprove of, tell them when to feel enthusiasm or indignation, joy or sorrow, delight or horror, sympathy or antagonism. Telling can take the form of using evaluative words: *the housing bureau's shameful treatment of minority students*.

The other way is to show your readers why they should feel the way you intend them to feel: show them what caused you to feel that way. Showing is giving the facts—facts you need in any case to construct a good argument. It is, for instance, saying, *With few exceptions, the housing bureau puts minority students in the old, drafty, damp, badly furnished wing of the dormitory*.

Which is better—telling or showing? A balance between them is best. The disadvantage of telling, especially in the absence of showing, is that your readers may find it strained, feel their arms twisted, even feel insulted. "Let the showing speak for itself," they may think. The disadvantage of showing is that the same fact may speak differently to your reader than it does to you. Or it may speak differently to different readers. How people feel about a fact depends not only upon the fact but upon what their experiences have been—upon their religious upbringing, for example, or where they grew up. What makes one person cry may make another laugh. Consequently, your readers usually need some telling. Otherwise they may fail to see what your persuasive intention is. But a little telling goes a long way. When in doubt, weight the balance on the side of showing, as does the following passage from *Matchbox*, the newsletter of Amnesty International:

> In many countries, political killings are carried on as a routine means of eliminating political opposition or frightening the population into submission. Often the attendant cruelty ranges far beyond the actual killing. Among the ghoulish methods of executing prisoners in Ugandan prisons during the 1970s was that of forcing them to stand in line and beat each other to death with a hammer. The process continued until the last one in line was shot. In Indonesia, killers had banquets with their bound victims looking on. After the meal each guest was invited to decapitate one of them.

(See also TELLING AND SHOWING.)

Persuasion by means of argument is so large a subject that many entire books have been devoted to it. Here we can only highlight some distinctions and principles.

**What is an argument?** An argument (good or bad) consists of (1) one or more premises and (2) a conclusion and follows a pattern of argument (good or bad). The premises are reasons for believing or accepting the conclusion. The conclusion is drawn from the premises. The pattern of argument is a means (good or bad) for drawing the conclusion from the premises. Here is an example:

ARGUMENT:       Like all victims of famine, the people of the Sudan are worthy of our help.

PREMISES:       (1) All victims of famine are worthy of our help.
                (2) The people of the Sudan are victims of famine.

CONCLUSION:     The people of the Sudan are worthy of our help.

PATTERN OF ARGUMENT:  What is true of all members of a group (here: all victims of famine) is true of some (here: the people of the Sudan) or of any one of them.

**What's the difference between a good argument and a bad one (a fallacy)?** A good argument has two characteristics: (1) Every premise in it is true (or probably true); (2) the argument is valid. A valid argument follows a valid pattern of argument. A valid pattern of argument guarantees that, if the premises of an argument are true (or probably true), then the conclusion also is true (or probably true). An invalid pattern of argument—a fallacy (see FALLACIES)—does not guarantee this.

An example of a valid pattern of argument is the pattern followed by the argument concerning famine given above.

An example of a fallacy is the pattern followed by this bad argument concerning the same subject:

PREMISES: (1) All victims of famine are worthy of our help;

(2) The people of the Sudan are worthy of our help.

CONCLUSION: The people of the Sudan are victims of famine.

FALLACY (INVALID PATTERN OF ARGUMENT): If a group of things (here: the people of the Sudan) is associated with another (here: victims of famine) in some way (here: in being worthy of our help), then it is included in the other.

At a glance, the invalid and the valid arguments look much alike. Each argument consists of two premises and a conclusion, for instance, and each has the same first premise. But, when you stop to think about the invalid argument, you begin to notice that something is wrong. And, when you detect that the second premise (*The people of the Sudan are worthy of our help*) is identical with the conclusion of the valid argument, you take an important step towards identifying the problem. The only connection that the two premises of the invalid argument can establish between all victims of famine and the people of the Sudan is that both groups are worthy of our help. These premises cannot establish that the latter group is included in the former.

An argument is a network, usually fairly elaborate. The main argument (A) is supported by second-rank arguments

(B and C); each of these arguments is, in turn, supported by third-rank arguments (E and F, for example); and so on.

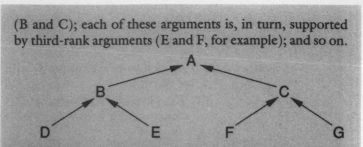

**Each argument in this network has its own premises and conclusions.** But—with certain exceptions—at least one premise of each argument is also the conclusion of another argument. The exceptions, of course, are the arguments farthest away from the main argument (D and E, and F and G, in the diagram above).

With your knowledge of your readers in mind, you must decide how elaborate your network of arguments should be. Begin by examining each premise of your main argument. Are your readers likely to accept it without any argument? If not, you should construct a second-rank argument that has this premise as its conclusion. Once you have constructed a second-rank argument, construct a third-rank argument, and so on.

And you may go on elaborating your network of arguments until you believe that you can base a paper upon it persuasive enough to make your readers accept the conclusion of your main argument.

**Organizing and presenting your network of arguments.** Your network is the logical structure of your paper. It is not an outline (see **OUTLINES**). You may well decide, for example, to begin your paper not with your own argument, but with a second-rank or even a third-rank argument. Within a given argument, you may decide to put your conclusion before your premises, after them, or in both places. Put it before if you believe that your readers will welcome it; after, if you believe that they are likely to resist it. And you may organize the premises supporting a conclusion in a variety of ways. Perhaps the best way is to organize them in the order of increasing persuasiveness, saving your most persuasive premise till last. In short, while there are many possibilities, there are no absolute recipes for organizing premises or arguments.

Above all, don't let your paper look like your network: formal and stiff. Occasionally, you may wish to label a premise (*One reason is* . . . ) or label a conclusion (*I concluded, then, that* . . . ). These are ways of achieving coherence (see **CO-HERENCE**). Ordinarily, however, you should announce a premise by *because, for,* or *since,* and a conclusion by a word like *consequently, hence, therefore,* or *thus* or by a phrase like *implies that, it follows that,* or *which shows that.* Often a clause or a sentence is so obviously a premise or a conclusion that it needs no announcement.

**Factual versus policy arguments.** Based upon the distinction between an *is* statement and an *ought-to-be* statement, every argument is either a factual argument or a policy argument. In a *factual argument,* both the conclusion and every statement is an *is* statement, a statement that something is (or is not) the case: that Jack the Ripper was a member of the British royal family; that, at a concert of The Who on 3 December 1980, eleven people were trampled to death. The point is not, of course, that these *is* statements are true—only that the writer claims them to be true. In a *policy argument,* both the conclusion and at least one premise are *ought-to-be* statements, statements that something ought to be (or not to be) the case: that the people of the Sudan ought to (or should or deserve to or are worthy to) get our help.

**Deductive versus inductive arguments.** Based upon the distinction between a necessarily true statement and a more or less probably true statement, every argument is either a deductive argument or an inductive argument. The difference between these two kinds of arguments lies in their guarantees. A good deductive argument guarantees that, if its premises are true, then its conclusion is true. But a good inductive argument does not. It guarantees only a conclusion that is more or less probably true and hence maybe false; thus, the more probable the conclusion, the better the argument. In other words, the conclusion of a good deductive argument follows *necessarily* from its premises, but the conclusion of a good inductive argument does not.

If, for instance, the following deductive arguments have true premises, their conclusions necessarily follow from their premises:

PREMISE: Some Baptists are plumbers.

CONCLUSION: Some plumbers are Baptists.

PREMISES: (1) Either the butler or the victim's chiropractor is the murderer.
(2) The victim's chiropractor is not the murderer.

CONCLUSION: The butler is the murderer.

How can a good deductive argument guarantee that, if its premises are true, then its conclusion is true? There are two complementary answers.

First, if we rephrase a good deductive argument as a statement, we will see that the statement is necessarily true. For example:

> If either the butler or the victim's chiropractor is the
> murderer [premise 1], and the chiropractor is not the
> murderer [premise 2], then the butler is the murderer
> [conclusion].

This statement is like the statement that all mothers are
women or that you recover from every illness that is not
fatal. If you know what it means, you know that it is
necessarily true—that it cannot be false. In other words, if
you know what this argument about the murderer means,
you know that its conclusion is necessarily true.

To know this, you need know nothing about the butler,
the chiropractor, or the murderer. All you need know is the
English language. Indeed, if you know English, you know
that the conclusion of any argument in the same *if . . . then*
pattern is necessarily true. Substitute any phrase you like
for *the butler* and for *the victim's chiropractor*. What you
substitute doesn't matter: the conclusion necessarily follows from the premises.

The second, and complementary, answer is that, if you
accept the premises of a good deductive argument, then
you cannot reject its conclusion without contradicting
yourself and thereby constructing a *bad* deductive argument with a necessarily false conclusion:

> If either the butler or the victim's chiropractor is the
> murderer [premise 1], and the chiropractor is not the
> murderer [premise 2], then the butler is *not* the
> murderer [conclusion: necessarily *false*].

Obviously, it is contradictory to say both that either the
butler or the chiropractor is the murderer and that neither
is the murderer.

A final point about deductive arguments: their guarantee of necessarily true conclusions seems very attractive. But it is, alas, worth about as much as a guarantee that, as long as you are alive, you will not be dead. The catch in this guarantee, of course, is that the premises of deductive arguments must be true for the guarantee to hold. And they can be only more or less probably true and quite possibly false, because—directly or indirectly—they can be supported only by *in*ductive arguments. Consequently, the conclusion of a deductive argument can be only more or less probably true and quite possibly false.

In short, if a deductive argument is likely to persuade your readers, it must be a part of a network of arguments that includes some inductive arguments.

Just what is induction? Just what is a good inductive argument? Here we can do no more than to analyze one very humble, but fairly good inductive argument. For the theory of induction is vast and technical, including the theory of sampling. Moreover, there are many kinds of inductive argument: argument by generalization, for example, and argument by analogy. Induction, finally, is the basis of all scientific research and of all historical research. Nevertheless, induction is also the basis of the most humble everyday activities. Without it, we could not cope in the world; indeed, we could not survive.

INDUCTIVE ARGUMENT:

PREMISES:   (1) The shirts I sent to Acme Launderers two weeks ago came back wrinkled.

(2) The shirts I sent there last week came back wrinkled.

(3) The shirts my cousin sent there a months ago came back wrinkled.

(4) The shirts my brother sent there two months ago came back wrinkled.

CONCLUSION:    Shirts sent to Acme Launderers always come back wrinkled.

Rephrased as a statement—not a necessarily true statement, but only a more or less probably true statement—this inductive argument reads as follows:

If shirts sent to Acme Launderers on *four* different occasions came back wrinkled [premises 1–4], then shirts sent there *always* come back wrinkled [more or less probably true conclusion].

The first thing to notice about this argument is that its conclusion would be more probable if its premises cited more cases of the laundry wrinkling shirts. The second thing to notice is that, if you accept its premises, you can still reject its conclusion without contradicting yourself.

NO CONTRADICTION:    Though shirts sent to Acme Launderers on four different occasions came back wrinkled, shirts sent there do not always come back wrinkled.

After all, it is surely possible that the shirts that hundreds of other people have sent to Acme Launderers have come back unwrinkled, that the shirts that hundreds of others will send there will come back unwrinkled, and that, if you send shirts there next week, they will come back unwrinkled. In other words, it is surely possible that your conclusion is false.

This argument, like every other inductive argument, makes what is known as in inductive leap. It leaps from observation of *some* cases to a conclusion about *all* cases.

This inductive leap is the argument's virtue as well as its defect. The defect, of course, is that the conclusion may be false and therefore give you no knowledge. The virtue is that, when an inductive argument has a true conclusion, the argument is either a shortcut or the only route to the knowledge the conclusion embodies.

The inductive argument about Acme Launderers, for instance, is a shortcut. It saves you the almost endless labor of examining (if you can find them) all the shirts that have ever or ever will come back from that laundry.

And, if you want knowledge of some group of people, things, or events that dates back to antiquity or is indefinitely expanding, an inductive argument is the only route to knowledge of the group.

**ARGUMENT: APPEALS TO BOTH REASON AND FEELINGS**  See **ARGUMENT AND PERSUASION.**

**ARGUMENT BY ASSOCIATION**  An **argument by association** is a fallacy. (See **FALLACIES.**) You commit this fallacy whenever you conclude that, because one thing is associated with another in some way, it is identical with or part of that other thing.

PREMISES:  (1) Representative Karth favors abortion upon demand.

(2) Feminists favor abortion upon demand.

CONCLUSION:  Representative Karth is a feminist.

This argument certainly establishes that one thing (*Karth*) is associated with another (*feminists*) in some way (*in favoring abortion upon demand*). But it does not establish any other connection between Karth and feminists. You might as well argue that, if Barbra Streisand likes ice cream (Premise 1) and so do Boy Scouts (Premise 2), then she is a Boy Scout (Conclusion).

**ARGUMENT: CONSTRUCTING A GOOD ONE**  See  **ARGUMENT AND PERSUASION.**

**armed with**  Avoid using this military metaphor to mean "having," "possessing," or "prepared with."

> NOT THIS:   The prosecutor was **armed with** conclusive
>           evidence.

> BUT THIS:   The prosecutor was **prepared with** conclusive
>           evidence.

**around, round**  Synonymous either as adverbs (*sat around, round*) or as prepositions (*around, round three o'clock*).

**artful, artistic**  Sometimes confused. *Artful* means "crafty" or "ingenuous": *an artful lawyer.* *Artistic* means "skilled in some art": *an artistic illustrator.*

**ARTICLES**  Though not every noun phrase begins with an article, every article begins a noun phrase and determines its use (see **NOUN PHRASES**). (Indeed, another word for article is *determiner.*)

English has two **articles.** The indefinite article, *a* or *an* (see **a, an**), begins a noun phrase used to open a discourse (*A funny thing happened to me yesterday*) or as a subject complement (*Louise is a nice person*). The definite article, *the,* begins a noun phrase used either to refer to something known to readers or listeners (*The house next door is for sale*) or to assert the existence of something

(*The tallest man in Topeka* [which implicitly asserts that there are at least three men in Topeka and that one of them is taller than the others] *has red hair*).

**artifact**   By definition, a physical object, usually small (a tool, for instance), created by a human. Do not, therefore, write sentences such as *Obsolescence is an **artifact** of marketers.*

**artisan, artist, artiste**   Sometimes confused. An *artisan* is a craftsperson (a carpenter, for example). An *artist* is a painter, a sculptor, a print-maker, a poet, or a novelist (consider Joyce's *A Portrait of the Artist as a Young Man*). An *artiste* is a singer, a dancer, or possibly an artist.

**as**   (1) Sometimes wordy.

> NOT THIS:   He was appointed **as** a judge.

> BUT THIS:   He was appointed a judge (*or* judge).

**(See CONCISION.)**
(2) Sometimes commits writers to endorsing what they paraphrase or quote.

> NOT THIS:   (unless you intend to endorse Smythe's view): **As** Smythe says, the administration is deceitful.

> BUT THIS:   Smythe says that the administration is deceitful.

**as anyone, as anyone else**   Sometimes confused.

> NOT THIS:   I was as happy **as anyone** about the outcome.

> BUT THIS:   I was as happy **as anyone else** about the outcome. (*Anyone,* but not *anyone else,* includes the writer.)

**as follow, as follows**   Only the latter is SAWE, whatever the context.

NOT THIS:    The contestants are **as follow.**

BUT THIS:    The contestants are **as follows.**

**as how**   Not SAWE as a substitute for *that.*

NOT THIS:    She told me **as how** she had seen the accident.

BUT THIS:    She told me **that** she had seen the accident.

**Asian, Asiatic, Oriental**   For reference to a person of Asian ancestry, *Asian* is now the preferred word. *Asiatic* and *Oriental* are considered derogatory. (See **POLITICAL CORRECTNESS.**)

**as if, as though**   (1) Synonymous in SAWE.
  (2) If the verb in the following clause is a form of *be,* that form must be the subjunctive *were.*

NOT THIS:    He looked **as if** he **was** dead.

BUT THIS:    He looked **as if** he **were** dead.

(See **MOOD** and **were.**)

**as, like**   (1) Use of *as* either as a conjunction (*As the train began to move, he got off*) or as a preposition (*As a student, he is not very good*) is SAWE. **Caution:** Some readers object to use of *as* as a preposition meaning "similarly to" or "similar to."

NOT THIS:    Herbert, **as** his father, is bald.

BUT THIS:    Herbert, **like** his father, is bald.

(2) Use of *like* either as a conjunction (*Do like I do*) or as a preposition (*Her room is like a pig pen*) is SAWE. **Caution:** Some readers, however, object to use of *like* as a conjunction.

NOT THIS: The swindler took him **like** the Vandals took Rome.

BUT THIS: The swindler took him **as** the Vandals took Rome.

Use of *like* as an adverb meaning "rather" or "completely" is nonSAWE.

NOT THIS: He was **like** crazy.

BUT THIS: He was **rather** crazy.

(3) Use of *like* as an auxiliary verb meaning "come near to" is nonSAWE.

NOT THIS: He **liked** to have died when he saw her.

BUT THIS: He **almost** died when he saw her.

**assassin** A murderer whose victims are famous (or infamous).

NOT THIS: The grocery clerk was **assassinated.**

BUT THIS: The grocery clerk was **murdered.**

**assay, essay** As verbs, synonymous in SAWE to mean "try" except that *assay* also means "determine the components of" (a drug or an ore, for instance).

**as, so** Prefer *so* to *as* in negative comparisons: *He is not so smart as Robert.* But: *He is as smart as Robert.*

**associate** Often part of a euphemism. (See **EUPHEMISMS.**)

NOT THIS: a sanitation **associate.**

BUT THIS: a garbage collector.

NOT THIS: a sales **associate.**

BUT THIS: a clerk, a salesman, a saleswoman, *or* a salesperson.

**as such**   Often wordy. (See **CONCISION.**)

NOT THIS:   The bank **as such** was insolvent.

BUT THIS:   The bank was insolvent.

**assume, presume**   Synonymous in SAWE to mean "believe without evidence": *I assume* (or *presume*) *that he is trustworthy.* But *presume* also means "do something without permission or warrant": *He presumed to call her by her first name.*

**ASSUMPTIONS AND PROPOSITIONS**   An assumption (or presupposition) is a proposition whose truth a speaker or writer takes for granted rather than asserting or arguing. Use of an assumption can divert attention away from one issue and focus it upon another. For example, the infamous question *When did you stop beating your wife?*—by assuming that the man used to beat his wife—diverts attention away from the issue of whether he ever beat her to the issue of when (if he ever did beat her) he stopped.

But what is a proposition? A **proposition** is an expression a speaker or writer uses to refer (R) to one or more persons or things and to predicate (P) either one or more qualities of them or one or more relationships between or among them:

   R        P
(a) Charles has a computer.

      P    R
(b) Does Charles have a computer?

   R        P
(c) Charles, have a computer.

R        P
(d) Charles and Ann have a computer.

R      P   R
(e) Charles loves Ann.

(a), (b), and (c) express the same proposition; they have the same reference (to Charles) and the same predication (the quality of having a computer). The sole difference is that they put this proposition to different uses: (a) asserts that Charles has a computer, (b) asks whether he has, and (c) requests that he have one. (d) expresses another proposition, and (e) expresses yet another. (d) and (e) refer, not just to Charles, but to both Charles and Ann. The difference between them is that, while (d) predicates the quality of having a computer, (e) predicates the relationship of lover to loved one.

Instead, however, of using a proposition as an assertion, a question, or a request, a speaker or writer may use it as an assumption of such a proposition, a ghost of a proposition within a proposition:

R            P
(f) What Charles has is a computer.

P R                              R
(g) Is the person who has a computer Charles?

R       P                   R
(h) Charles, buy a computer for the person who needs one.

(f), while asserting that Charles has a computer, assumes that he has something. (g), while asking whether the person who has a computer is identical with Charles, assumes that some person has a computer. (h), while requesting that Charles buy a computer for the person who needs one, assumes that some person needs one.

Notice how each of the following examples diverts attention away from what is assumed and focuses it upon what is asserted:

(i)  It was Fred who got drunk at the party last night.
     (Assumptions: there was a party last night, and someone got drunk at it.)

(j)  It was getting drunk that Fred did at the party last night.
     (Assumptions: there was a party last night, and Fred did something at it.)

(k)  It was at the party last night that Fred got drunk.
     (Assumptions: there was a party last night, and Fred got drunk at it.)

Compare (i), (j), and (k) with (l) and (m):

(l)  Fred got drunk at the party last night.
(m)  At the party last night, Fred got drunk.

(l) and (m) make only one assumption: there was a party last night. (Nevertheless, (l), by putting *Fred* first, calls more attention to Fred than to the party, while (m) does just the opposite.)

What should a writer do about assumptions? Be aware of them and use them to advantage.

**as to**  Use of *as to* to mean "about" is SAWE. **Caution:** Some readers object to this use.

NOT THIS:  The teachers asked the principal **as to** guidelines.

BUT THIS:  The teachers asked the principal **about** guidelines.

But no one objects to the use of *as to* to mean "according to": *We sorted the books out **as to** color.*

**astronomical** Avoid in the sense "extremely large" because over-stated and imprecise.

> NOT THIS: Her vocabulary is **astronomical.**

> BUT THIS: Her vocabulary is **extremely large** (or **immense**).

(See **SUPERLATIVES.**)

**as well as** See **both . . . as well as.**

**ASYNDETON** Typically, deletion of *and* or *or* before the last word or phrase in a series: *Marshall is aloof, autocratic, [and] unpleasant.* A stylistic device that some readers find mannered or affected.

**at about** Unobjectionable when used to mean "at approxi-mately": *He drove at about that speed.* **Caution:** Wordy when used to mean "approximately" or "about."

> NOT THIS: He drove **at about** fifty miles an hour.

> BUT THIS: He drove **about** fifty miles an hour.

**atheist, agnostic, positivist** *Atheists* say that there is no God; *agnostics,* that they don't know whether there is; *positivists,* that the question of whether there is is a pseudo-question. (See **PSEUDO-QUESTIONS.**)

**a, this** Prefer *a* (or *an*) in sentences like *I saw this* (better: *a*) *man running away.*

**at present, at the present time** The latter is wordy for the for-mer. Avoid it. (See **CONCISION.**)

**attacked** Still sometimes a euphemism for *rape.* (See **EUPHE-MISMS.**)

**attend to, tend to**  Prefer *attend to* in the sense "look after" or "take care of."

NOT THIS:   Murphy will **tend to** the catering.

BUT THIS:   Murphy will **attend to** the catering.

**at the rear (or in the back of), in front of**  Wordy for *behind* and *before,* respectively.

**at this (that) point in time**  Wordy for *now* (or *then*). Coined in the Watergate hearings.

**attorney general**  In conservative usage, the plural is *attorneys general;* in liberal usage, *attorney generals.*

**attorney, lawyer**  Prefer lawyer in the sense "one admitted to the practice of law." *Attorney* is pretentious for *lawyer.* Moreover, in one sense, an attorney is simply someone authorized to act for someone else (such an authorization is called *power of attorney*).

**attractive**  Not always synonymous with *beautiful* or *good-looking.* A person not beautiful may be attractive for charm or wit, for example.

**at your earliest convenience**  Once a fixture of many business letters but now little used. Prefer *at once, immediately, soon,* or *as soon as possible.*

**AUDIENCE**  The readers a writer is writing for (see **READERS, COMMUNICATIONS, AND PERSUASION**).

**au naturel**  A euphemism for *naked* (see **EUPHEMISMS**).

NOT THIS:   They swam **au naturel.**

BUT THIS:   They swam **naked.**

**authentic, genuine**  Synonymous is SAWE. But there are some differences in usage: *an authentic* (but not *genuine*) *portrayal of Victorian England; a genuine* (but not *authentic*) *pearl.*

**author**  Avoid as a verb. It is SAWE, but some readers object to it.

NOT THIS:  She **authored** a novel.

BUT THIS:  She **wrote** a novel.

**AUXILIARIES**  An **auxiliary** (or helping) verb—such as *can, could, may, might, ought, shall, should, will, would,* or any form of *be, do,* or *have*—combines with an infinitive or a participle for the following purposes:

(1) To form the present-perfect tense:

I **have** watched.

(2) To form the past-perfect tense:

I **had** listened.

(3) To form the future-perfect tense:

I **shall** (or **will**) **have** waited.

(4) To form the progressive tense:

I **am** dozing.

(5) To form the conditional mood:

I **should** (or **would**) sleep.

(6) To form the passive voice:

I **was** hit by a bicycle.

(7) To give emphasis:

I **do** want to go.

(8) To express possibility:

I **may** (or **might**) join.

(9) To express permission:

You **may** (or **might**) join.

(10) To express capability:

I **can** sing.

(11) To express obligation:

I **ought** to contribute.

(See **INFINITIVES** and **PARTICIPLES**.)

**average, mean, median, mode**  All measures of central tendency. An *average* (or a *mean*) of a set of values is their sum divided by their number. If, for example, the values are 12, 24, 24, 36, 48, 60, 72, then the average is 39.43 (276 divided by 7). The *median* is the middle value (or, when there is more than one middle value, the average of them)—for the set of values above: 36. The *mode* is the most frequently occurring value, if any value occurs more than once—for the set of values above: 24. A set may be bimodal (two values occurring the same number of times), trimodal, and so on.

Use these terms precisely; and, if you believe that your readers may be unfamiliar with them, define them.

**awaked, awakened, awake, wakened, wake (up)**  Synonymous in SAWE.

**awesome**  Avoid in the sense of "surprising," "astounding," or "spectacular." (See **SUPERLATIVES**.)

**awful, awfully**  (1) Avoid using *awful* as a vague expression of disapproval.

NOT THIS:     His checked polyester pants are **awful**.

BUT THIS:     His checked polyester pants are **ugly**.

(2) *Awful* or *awfully* for *very* is SAWE and often used in conversation and informal writing. **Caution:** But it is rarely used in formal writing.

NOT THIS:     The minister's manner was **awful** (or **awfully**) formal.

BUT THIS:     The minister's manner was **very** formal.

**awhile, a while**   Often confused. *Awhile* is an adverb: *We jogged awhile. A while* is an article (*a*) plus a noun (*while*): *We jogged for a while.* In other words, *awhile* can modify a verb (*jogged*), and *a while* can be the object of a preposition (*for*), but not vice versa.

# B

**BACK-FORMATION** A word coined by subtraction of an affix (real or, more often, imagined) from a longer work (*burgle* from *burglar*). No one objects to back-formations that have been around for a long time (*diagnose* from *diagnosis*), but many object to more recent coinages (*enthuse* from *enthusiasm; reminisce* from *reminiscent*). (See **enthuse.**)

**back of, in back of** Prefer *behind*. (See **CONCISION.**)

**bad, badly** (1) Use of *bad* as an adverb is nonSAWE.

NOT THIS: The mugger beat Al up **bad.**

BUT THIS: The mugger beat Al up **badly.**

(2) Use of *badly* as an adjective is SAWE. **Caution:**  Many readers object to this use.

NOT THIS:    Everyone felt **badly** about losing the game.

BUT THIS:    Everyone felt **bad** about losing the game.

**balmy, bananas, batty, bonkers**  Such delightful adjectives for a mildly eccentric or neurotic person are SAWE but very informal.

**base, bass**  Sometimes confused. *Base* means "foundation"· *the base of a building.* As an adjective, *bass* (pronounced like *base*) means "low-pitched"; as a noun, "person with a low-pitched voice" or "a musical instrument" or (pronounced to rhyme with *lass*) "species of fish."

**based on**  Beware of making this a dangling modifier. (See **MODIFIERS AND MODIFICATION.**)

NOT THIS:    **Based on** new information, he changed his mind. (Is *he* based on new information?)

BUT THIS:    His change of mind was **based on** new information.

**basic**  Sometimes a euphemism for *incompetent* or *poor* (see **EUPHEMISMS**).

NOT THIS:    **basic** students.

BUT THIS:    **incompetent** students.

**basis**  Avoid wordy uses.

NOT THIS:    They perform on a regular **basis.**

BUT THIS:    They perform **regularly.**

**bazaar, bizarre** Sometimes confused. A *bazaar* is a sale or a market—typically, in the Middle East, Near East, or India or in a church basement. *Bizarre* means "outrageous" or "very peculiar": *His behavior at the party was bizarre.*

**be advised that** To *Be advised that such and such is the case,* prefer (because less pretentious) *Let me say that such and such is the case.* Or better, *Such and such is the case.*

**beauty** SAWE in the sense "excellent feature": *the beauty of the new software.* **Caution:** Some readers object to this use.

> NOT THIS:  the **beauty** of the new contract.

> BUT THIS:  an **excellent feature of** (or **the best thing about**) the new contract.

**because** (1) Use of *because* to introduce an adverb clause is SAWE: *Because I'm addicted to chocolate, I'm getting fat.*
  (2) Use of *because* to introduce a noun clause is also SAWE. **Caution:** Many readers object to this use.

> NOT THIS:  The reason the dam broke is **because** it was poorly designed.

> BUT THIS:  The reason the dam broke is **that** it is poorly designed.

> NOT THIS:  **Because** a boat has a deep draft does not mean it is seaworthy.

> BUT THIS:  **That** a boat has a deep draft does not mean it is seaworthy.

  (3) A sentence such as (a) containing both *not* (or *n't*) and *because* may be ambiguous: (a) *I did not become a lawyer because of family pressure.* The reason that (a) is ambiguous is that it is synonymous with both (b) *Family pressure caused me not to become*

*a lawyer* and (c) *Family pressure did not cause me to become a lawyer (something else did),* though (b) and (c) are not synonymous with one another and though neither (b) nor (c) is ambiguous. Prefer (b) or (c) to (a), your choice depending upon your intended meaning. (See **VAGUENESS** and **AMBIGUITY**.)

**because, for**   *Because* is a subordinating conjunction (see **CONJUNCTIONS**) introducing a clause stating the cause of a state or an event described in the main clause: *He returned because he was in bad health.* *For* is a coordinating conjunction sometimes synonymous with *because* but typically introducing a clause giving a reason for believing the preceding clause to be true: *He attempted suicide, for he was weary of life.*

**because of**   See **due to.**

**BEGGING THE QUESTION**   **Begging the question** is a fallacy. (See **FALLACIES**.) You commit this fallacy whenever you assume the truth of the very conclusion whose truth you are arguing. The question at issue in any argument is whether its conclusion is true. But, by assuming that it is true, you beg (or avoid) that question. You make this assumption whenever one of your premises is identical with your conclusion in meaning, though not perhaps in wording.

PREMISES:  (1) People who support the proposed freeway are not working in the best interests of the city.

(2) The freeway would fill one of our oldest and finest neighborhoods with noise and exhaust fumes.

(3) The freeway would, for many residents of this neighborhood, cut off easy access to schools, churches, and shopping.

CONCLUSION:  No one who favors this freeway has the best interests of the city at heart [ = Premise 1].

This argument begs the question of the truth of its conclusion by assuming its truth (in Premise 1).

**BEGINNING A PAPER** There is no best way to begin a paper. There are only many good ways, varying with subject, purpose, and audience. Every good beginning, however, does two things for readers: interest them and inform them, give them some inkling of what the paper is about. The most direct, economical way of beginning is with a thesis statement—stating in one or a few sentences the main point of your paper and perhaps indicating as well how the paper is organized (see **ORGANIZATION**). Other good ways to begin are with a question, with background information, with a definition of a key term (see **DEFINITIONS**), and with an example (see **EXAMPLES**).

**behalf** In SAWE, *on behalf of* means either "acting for" (*on behalf of my client*) or "for the benefit of" (*on behalf of all widows and orphans*).

**being as, being that** NonSAWE for *because* or *since*.

NOT THIS:   **Being as** (or **being that**) she was tired, she stayed home.

BUT THIS:   **Because** (or **since**) she was tired, she stayed home.

**belabor, labor** Either is SAWE to mean "talk lengthily and tiresomely about": *belabor* (or *labor*) *a point*.

**benefactor, beneficiary** Complementary terms sometimes confused. A *benefactor* provides a benefit; a *beneficiary* receives one.

**beside, besides** (1) Both *beside* and *besides* are prepositions meaning "in addition to": *Beside* (or *besides*) *working hard, there is nothing you can do. Beside* also means "next to" (*the house beside the road*), "in comparison with" (*Beside Lincoln, Grant was a weak president*), and "on a par with" (*To rank Grant beside Lincoln is a mistake*).

(2) *Besides* is also an adverb meaning "in addition" or "moreover" (*Besides, I can't afford a Cadillac*) and "otherwise" or "else" (*He is nice but very little besides*).

**best, better** (1) *Best* is superlative, said of one of three or more things. *Better* is comparative, said of one of two.

NOT THIS:    The **best** of the two hotels is the Ritz.

BUT THIS:    The **better** of the two hotels is the Ritz.

(2) But *had best* or *had better* are synonyms: *You had best* (or *better*) *go home.*

**be sure and, come and, try and**   SAWE for *be sure to, come to, and try to*. **Caution:** Some readers object to this usage in formal writing.

NOT THIS:    ". . . they should not **try and** dress like the upper classes" (Oscar Wilde).

BUT THIS:    . . . they should not **try to** dress like the upper classes.

**better**   *Better* for *had better* is SAWE and often used in conversation and informal writing. **Caution:** But it is rarely used in formal writing.

NOT THIS:    You **better** leave guns alone.

BUT THIS:    You **had better** leave guns alone.

**better than**  In the sense "more than" prefer *more than*.

>NOT THIS:  a salary **better than** $100,000.

>BUT THIS:  a salary **more than** $100,000.

**between**  See **among, between.**

**Between . . . to**  NonSAWE for *between . . . and*.

>NOT THIS:  To treat a drug abuser in a hospital costs **between** $300 **to** $400 a day.

>BUT THIS:  To treat a drug abuser in a hospital costs **between** $300 **and** $400 a day.

**between you and I/he/she**  NonSAWE for *between you and me/him/her*.

>NOT THIS:  Everything is over **between you and I.**

>BUT THIS:  Everything is over **between you and me.**

(See **HYPERCORRECTION.**)

**bid**  In all senses of this verb, SAWE permits either *bade* or *bid* for the simple past tense and either *bade, bid,* or *bidden* for the past participle. **Caution:** Some readers expect conservative discrimination among senses, best explained by examples. (1) In the sense "make an offer": *Yesterday, I **bid** $2,000. I have **bid** as much as $3,000.* (2) In the sense "command" or as part of a greeting: *Yesterday I **bade** you to leave or **bade** you farewell. I have often **bidden** you to leave or **bidden** you farewell.*

**bisect, dissect**  Sometimes confused. To *bisect* is to cut into two equal parts. To *dissect* is to cut up into any number and size of parts.

**bi-, semi-** The prefix *bi-* is so ambiguous that you should avoid it. *Biweekly,* for example, can mean either "occurring once every two weeks" (once the only meaning) or "occurring twice a week." If you mean "occurring once every two," write *once every two* (*weeks, months,* and so on). If you mean "occurring twice a," write either *twice a* (*week, month,* and so on) or *semi-* (*weekly, monthly,* and so on).

**BLACK ENGLISH** A variety, or dialect, of American English spoken (but rarely written) by many, though by no means all, African-Americans. In vocabulary, it is much like Standard American English. The chief differences are in pronunciation, in grammar, and in the meanings of a few words. *Ask,* for example, is pronounced like *axe,* and *tuber* like *tuba.* Grammatically, it is less redundant and otherwise simpler than Standard. The sentences *I have three book; He go yesterday;* and *They cooking for me last night,* for instance, are in every way grammatical. Because *three* signifies "more than one," and because *yesterday* and *last night* signify the past, use of the plural suffix (*-s*) and of the past tense (*went, were*) is redundant. (An exception is the use, in *They be cooking for me every night,* of both *be* and *every night* to signify habitual action.) Another grammatical example: unlike Standard, Black English allows an indirect question (*I don't know can she do it*) to be identical with a direct question (*Can she do it?*). Two examples of differences in meaning: in some contexts, Black English, unlike Standard, allows *bad* to mean "good" (*a bad book* can be synonymous with Standard *a good book*) and allows *evil* to mean "grumpy" (*Why you so evil today?*).

To say that Black English is ungrammatical English makes no more sense than to say that French is ungrammatical English. Like every other variety of English, and like every other language, Black English has its own grammar. (See **GRAMMATICAL RULES.**)

**boat, ship**  In the Navy and among seagoing people generally, a *boat* is small enough to be carried on a *ship*. But SAWE permits boat to designate a larger vessel in informal writing.

**born, borne**  In the sense "give birth to," use *born* to indicate the point of view of the child (*He was **born** blind in 1924*); use *borne* to indicate the point of view of the mother and also in the sense "endured" (*She had **borne** him in 1924; she had **borne** so much sorrow*).

**born in . . .**  Avoid the use of such past participial phrases, in which the phrase has little relevance to the main clause: ***Born in Peoria, he is president of the World Bank***. Either omit the phrase or change it to make it relevant: *though born in Peoria, because born in Peoria*. (See **PARTICIPLES** and **PARTICIPIAL PHRASES.**)

**borrow, lend**  Because *borrow* and *lend* are antonyms, they are sometimes confused. *Borrow* means "receive temporarily": *I **borrowed** bus fare from Millie*. *Lend* means "give temporarily"; *Millie **lent** me bus fare*. (See **ANTONYMS.**)

**both . . . as well as**  NonSAWE for *both . . . and*.

NOT THIS:    Jerry was **both** a guide **as well as** a friend.

BUT THIS:    Jerry was **both** a guide **and** a friend.

**both, each**  As an antecedent, *both* is plural; *each* is singular. (See **ANTECEDENTS.**)

NOT THIS:    **Both** said that the **other** is guilty. (*Other* is
             singular.)

BUT THIS:    **Each** said that the **other** is guilty.    .

**boys, girls**   *Boys* for *men* and *girls* for *women* are SAWE and often used in conversation and informal writing. **Caution:** They are rarely used in formal writing and are offensive to some readers in any writing.

NOT THIS:   The **girls** at the office gave a party for the **boys** there.

BUT THIS:   The **women** at the office gave a party for the **men** there.

**BRACKETS**   The chief uses of **brackets** [ ] are:

(1) To enclose explanatory words inserted into a quotation—

According to Smith, "The former postmaster [Lionel Jones] embezzled the funds."

(2) To enclose the word *sic* (Latin for "thus") inserted into a quotation to indicate that the writer is aware that an error exists either in the language or the content of a quotation—

According to one textbook, "Columbis [*sic*] discovered America in 1592 [*sic*]."

**bring, take**   Often confused, because antonyms. (See **ANTO-NYMS.**) The appropriate choice between them depends upon a reference point established by the context—that is, upon a place from which the action (bringing or taking) is being regarded. *Bring* means "go *toward*" the reference point (with something): *Joe* [who was *not* at the reference point] ***brought*** *Mary* [who was there] *the book. Take* means "go *away from*"the reference point (with something): *Joe* [who was at the reference point] ***took*** *Mary* [who was *not* there] *the book.*

**broke**  NonSAWE for *broken.*

NOT THIS:    The Ming vase was **broke.**

BUT THIS:    The Ming vase was **broken.**

**broken, burst, bust, busted**  A pipe *bursts,* not *busts;* and a lamp is *broken,* not *bust* or *busted.* But *bust* and *busted* are SAWE to describe arrests: *Federal agents* **busted** *a narcotics ring last night; this* **bust** *was long anticipated.*

**brother-in-law, etc.**  Plural: *brothers-in-law.* Possessive case singular: *brother-in-law's.* Possessive case plural: *brothers-in-law's.*

**bug**  Slang when used either as a verb meaning "pester" or as a noun meaning "devotee" or "fan."

NOT THIS:    His constant calls **bugged** her.

BUT THIS:    His constant calls **annoyed** her.

NOT THIS:    Bert is a video **bug.**

BUT THIS:    Bert is a video **fan.**

**building, edifice**  *Edifice* is pretentious.

NOT THIS:    a four-story **edifice.**

BUT THIS:    a four-story **building.**

**bulk of**  Use *bulk of* to refer only to things that cannot be counted.

NOT THIS:    the **bulk of** the members.

BUT THIS:    the **bulk of** the coffee.

**bunch**  *Bunch* for *cluster* or *group* is SAWE and often used in conversation and informal writing to refer not only to bananas and grapes but to people. **Caution:** In formal writing, it is rarely used to refer to people.

NOT THIS:   The protesters were a **bunch** of radicals.

BUT THIS:   The protesters were a **group** of radicals.

**burglary, robbery**   Sometimes confused. *Burglary* is theft from within a building illegally entered. *Robbery* is theft by use of threat or force.

**business, line, occupation**   Prefer *business* or *occupation* to *line*: *My occupation is pharmacologist.*

**but, hardly, scarcely**   Since "not" is part of the meaning of each of these words, use of them with *not, n't, nothing,* or *without* is wordy. It is also nonSAWE because it makes a double (or multiple) negative.

NOT THIS:   I couldn't **but** laugh.

BUT THIS:   I could **but** laugh.

NOT THIS:   **Hardly nothing** matters now.

BUT THIS:   **Hardly anything** matters now.

NOT THIS:   **Without scarcely** any delay, the plane took off.

BUT THIS:   **Without** any (or **with scarcely any**) delay, the plane took off.

See also **never, no, none, not, n't, nothing, nowhere.**

**but however, but nevertheless, but yet**   Wordy for *but*.

NOT THIS:   She hated him **but nevertheless** married him.

BUT THIS:   She hated him **but** married him.

**but, however, nevertheless**   *But* is less emphatic than *however; however,* less than *nevertheless.* Because *but* is a coordinating conjunction (see **CONJUNCTIONS**) and *however* and *nevertheless* are conjunctive adverbs, they require different punctuation when joining independent clauses: *The weather is unfavorable, **but** we are going anyway. The weather is unfavorable; **however** (or **nevertheless**), we are going anyway.*

**Note:** *But* combined with *however* or *nevertheless* is wordy (see **CONCISION**).

> NOT THIS:    He is unreliable; **but, however** (or **nevertheless**), I like him.

> BUT THIS:    He is unreliable, **but** I like him.

> OR THIS:    He is unreliable; **however** (or **nevertheless**), I like him.

**but that, but what**    Often wordy.

> NOT THIS:    I don't question **but that** (or **but what**) he is guilty.

> BUT THIS:    I don't question **that** he is guilty.

**by definition**    Sometimes a useful phrase in an argument: *This "red-tag" sale, advertised as an auction, is not one. **By definition**, an auction is a sale of goods to the highest bidder.* **Caution:** Check a dictionary to make sure that your definition is correct.

**by means of**    Ordinarily, prefer *by* as less wordy (see **CONCISION**).

> NOT THIS:    I went **by means of** bus to Houston.

> BUT THIS:    I went **by** bus to Houston.

**by nature**    Avoid because always wordy. (See **CONCISION**.)

> NOT THIS:    Archer is **by nature** thrifty.

> BUT THIS:    Archer is thrifty.

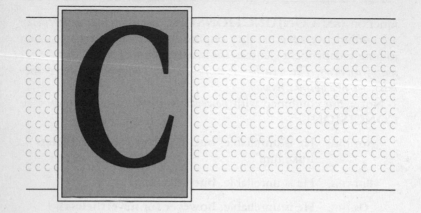

**calculate, guess, reckon, suppose** All mean "believe." But *guess* signals only marginal belief; *calculate* and *reckon* are old-fashioned and informal; and *suppose* often carries a tinge of sarcasm: *I suppose that we can count on Merriweather to be on hand for the festivities.*

**Calvary, cavalry** Sometimes confused. *Calvary* was the site of Christ's crucifixion. A *cavalry* is a military unit using horses or armored vehicles.

**can, can't** Though *can* is positive and *can't* negative, they are sometimes used synonymous as in *Ask whether they can* (or *can't*) *go.*

**can, may** In SAWE, *can* means "have the ability to" (*Mary can ride a horse*); *may* means either "have permission to" (*You may leave whenever you please*) or "possibly will" (*You may encounter some bad weather.*)

But these distinctions are breaking down. In particular, *can* often means "have permission to": *In these permissive times, children, it seems, can do whatever they like.*

**can't hardly, can't scarcely** Wordy and, because a multiple negative, nonSAWE. (See **but, hardly, scarcely** and **MULTIPLE NEGATIVES.**)

**can't help but** Wordy and informal.

> NOT THIS: I **can't help but** like Shirley.

> BUT THIS: I **can't but** like Shirley.

**can't scarcely** See **but, hardly, scarcely** and **can't hardly, can't scarcely.**

**capital, capitol** Sometimes confused. A *capital* is a city; a *capitol,* a building.

**CAPITALIZATION** Capitalize:

(1) The first word of a sentence or a sentence fragment, of a direct question within a sentence, of a direct quotation, of a line of verse (except for verse that is purposely not capitalized), and the salutation and the complimentary close of a letter:

The best was yet to come.

Just a word more.

The question is this: Will the peace last?

Patrick Henry said, "Give me liberty. . . ."

Oh there is a blessing in the gentle breeze
That blows from the green fields and from the clouds
And from the sky . . . (Wordsworth, "The Prelude").

Dear Ms. Balfour,
Yours Sincerely,

(2) Proper names:

| | |
|---|---|
| Air Force One | the *Santa Maria* |
| the French Revolution | the Supreme Court |
| German | the Swiss |
| Germany | the Treaty of Ghent |
| the Ice Age | the Trinity |
| the Mobil Corporation | George Washington |

(3) Words derived from proper names:

| | |
|---|---|
| Chicagoan | New Yorker |
| Keatsian | Parisian |

(4) The pronoun *I*

(5) The names of the days of the week and months

(6) Titles preceding proper names:

| | |
|---|---|
| Mother Cabrini | President Truman |
| Pope Pius IX | Secretary of State Christopher |

(7) Words in titles of works (except for internal articles, conjunctions, and prepositions):

*The Adoration of the Magi*
*The Sound and the Fury*

(8) Personifications

Beauty is Truth

(9) Names of botanical and zoological genera:

Hyacinthus (hyacinth)
Giraffa Camelopardalis (giraffe)

**Note:** Do not capitalize a word solely because it designates something you think important—for example, clergyman, senior citizens, sociology.

**case, line** Often a cause of wordiness.

NOT THIS:   **In the case of** pneumonia, death often results.

BUT THIS:   Pneumonia often causes death.

NOT THIS:   I am looking for a job **in the line of** (or **along the lines of**) computer programming.

BUT THIS:   I am looking for a job **in** computer programming.

**CASES** The **cases** of a noun or a pronoun are the different forms it takes when it performs different functions in a clause or a sentence (see **FORMS AND FUNCTIONS**).

A *noun* has two cases: the possessive case, for modification (see **MODIFIERS AND MODIFICATION**), and the common case, for all other functions.

| Cases | Singular | Plural |
|---|---|---|
| Possessive | boy's | boys' |
| Common | boy | boys |

An *indefinite pronoun* has two cases: the possessive case, for modification, and the common case, for all other functions.

| Cases | Indefinite Pronouns |
|---|---|
| Possessive | anyone's, everyone's, someone's |
| Common | anyone, everyone, someone |

A *personal pronoun* has four cases: the subjective case, for subjects and predicate nouns; the objective case, for direct objects, indirect objects, and objects of prepositions; the dual case, for functions that can be either subjective or objective; and the possessive case, for modification.

### FIRST PERSON

| Cases | Singular | Plural |
|---|---|---|
| Subjective | I | we |
| Objective | me | myself |
| Dual | myself | ourselves |
| Possessive | my, mine | our, ours |

### SECOND PERSON

| Cases | Singular | Plural |
|---|---|---|
| Subjective | you | you |
| Objective | you | you |
| Dual | yourself | yourselves |
| Possessive | your, yours | your, yours |

### THIRD PERSON

| Cases | Singular | | | Plural |
|---|---|---|---|---|
| | Masculine | Feminine | Neuter | |
| Subjective | he | she | it | they |
| Objective | him | her | it | them |
| Dual | himself | herself | itself | themselves |
| Possessive | his | her, hers | its | their, theirs |

A *relative pronoun* has four cases: the subjective case, for subjects of relative clauses; the objective case, for direct objects; the dual case, for subjects and direct objects; and the possessive case, for modification of subjects.

| Cases | Relative Pronouns |
|---|---|
| Subjective | who |
| Objective | whom |
| Dual | that, which |
| Possessive | whose |

**Note 1:** *Whom* and, when it is a direct object, *that* may be deleted.
**Note 2:** *Which* as subject always introduces a nonrestrictive clause
(see **RESTRICTIVE AND NONRESTRICTIVE**).

**casual, causal**   Sometimes confused. *Casual* means "occasional,"
"haphazard," "happenstantial," or "informal": *a casual meeting, casual dress. Causal* means "of or pertaining to cause": *a
causal relationship between consumption of alcohol and delirium
tremens.*

**Caucasian**   Prefer *white* as the racial designation because it is
more widely understood.

**cause, reason**   A *cause* is a necessary (and sometimes sufficient
as well) condition for the occurrence of an event: *The cause of
the fire was carelessly stored oily rags.* A *reason* is a purpose or a
motive for doing something: *My reason for working hard was to
earn more money.* Occasionally, cause and reason coincide: *The
reason for* (or *the cause of*) *my scream was a needle stuck beneath a
fingernail.*

**censer, censor, censure**   Often confused. A *censer* is an incense
lamp. *Censor* means "ban" (*The government censored the newspaper*) or "delete" (*Before showing the film, the parents censored one
scene*). *Censure* means "find fault with": *The supervisor censured
the clerk.* Something may be both *censored* and *censured: The
parents censored the scene because they had censured it.*

**center about/around**   SAWE for *center at/in/on*. **Caution:**
Some readers object to it as illogical.

NOT THIS:   Discussion **centered around** divorce.

BUT THIS:   Discussion centered **on** divorce.

**certain, particular**   Usually sources of wordiness. (See **CONCISION.**)

> NOT THIS:   A **certain** (or **particular**) man named Allen Thompson said. . . .
>
> BUT THIS:   Allen Thompson said. . . .

**chain reaction**   Not a synonym for *reaction*. A *chain reaction* is a series of reactions each caused by a predecessor.

**chair, chairman, chairone, chairperson, chairwoman**   Usage is pretty well divided between *chair* and the traditional *chairman,* though the latter is sometimes thought sexist (see **SEXIST LANGUAGE**). *Chairone,* though it had a brief vogue, won't do because it sounds like an obscure Greek word *(kyronee),* and *chairperson* is awkward. *Chairwoman* will do only for a woman.

**challenged**   Often a component of euphemisms (see **EUPHEMISMS**):

| NOT THESE: | BUT THESE: |
|---|---|
| auditorally challenged | deaf, hard of hearing |
| cognitively challenged | feeble-minded |
| financially challenged | hard up, poor |
| mobility challenged | feeble, handicapped |
| visually challenged | blind, far-sighted, near-sighted |

**challenging**   A cliché in the sense "demanding" or "stimulating" (see **CLICHÉS**).

> NOT THIS:   My new job is **challenging.**
>
> BUT THIS:   My new job is **demanding.**

**chaotic, inchoate**   Sometimes confused. *Chaotic* means "extremely disorganized": *a chaotic message. Inchoate* means "developing" or "immature": *an inchoate plan.*

**cheap prices, expensive costs, warm temperatures, etc.** Avoid. Goods or services, not prices or costs, are cheap or expensive. The weather or the day is warm, not the temperature. (See **METONYMY**.)

**chemical dependence** A euphemism for *drug addiction*. (See **EUPHEMISMS**.)

**Christian name** Prefer *first* or *given name*, especially if the person is not Christian.

**cite, sight, site** Sometimes confused. *Cite* means either "to summon to appear in court" (*cited for a traffic violation*) or "refer to" or "quote" (*cite a passage from the Bible*). *Sight* means "ability to see" (*lost his sight*). *Site* means "place" (*the site of the battle*).

**CLARITY** Your writing is clear—achieves clarity—only if it conveys to your intended readers the meaning you have in mind and *intend* to convey (see **LANGUAGE OF THOUGHT**).

Unlike spelling correctly and putting an apostrophe in the proper place, achieving clarity is much more than a minor virtue cherished by teachers of composition and editors. As the philosopher Karl R. Popper observes:

> . . . the search for truth is only possible if we speak clearly and simply and avoid unnecessary technicalities. In my view, aiming at simplicity and lucidity is a moral duty of all intellectuals; lack of clarity is a sin and pretentiousness is a crime.

Your sole problem in writing clearly is to choose the right words and put them into the right orders. But what words and orders are right?

To decide, you must first keep an eye on your intended readers. The success of your writing depends more upon them than upon all other factors put together. You can write a paper without considering your readers, but not an effective paper. You write it, but they must read and, reading it, react to it. The more you know about them, the better. Writing a paper is an act of collaboration—an act of cooperation—between you and them.

Another way of thinking of your paper is as a stimulus: your readers read it and react, or respond, to it:

Your paper → Your readers' reaction and response

Your paper, however, is just one stimulus competing with a great barrage of stimuli in your readers' environment: other things to read, like books, magazines, newspapers, junk mail; television; telephones; sports; and other distractions.

Will your potential readers read your paper at all? If they do, will they respond to it in the way you intend?

Your readers' response to your paper, moreover, like their response to any other stimulus, depends more upon them than upon the stimulus. Each reader's response is conditioned by a lifetime of responding to other stimuli:

Your paper

⟶ Readers' response
to your paper

Readers' earlier
responses

You need to know at least three things about your intended readers:

(1) **What is their knowledge of the subject?** Writing about nuclear physics to physicists should be very different from writing about it to the general

public, say, in a popular magazine. Writing about Greek drama to professors of classics should be very different from writing about it to professors of animal husbandry.

(2) **What is their vocabulary and their reading proficiency?** Writing about a crisis in the Middle East for adults won't do for second-graders.

(3) **What is their nationality or ethnicity?** A paper about a regional conflict between the Tories and the Labor Party in Britain might be ideal for readers of the London *Times* but puzzle readers of a newspaper in Mexico City.

But, whatever their knowledge of the subject, their vocabularies, their reading proficiency, and their nationality or ethnicity, virtually all readers will find the following sentence too opaque to comprehend:

Entrepreneurs who hope to reach the top of the ladder of success, in terms of consumer demand, must sponsor merchandise or services that have a positive image and fill a long-recognized gap.

It is not easy to say just what this sentence means, but perhaps this is a fair translation:

To succeed, sellers must offer goods or services that consumers like and need.

For some obstacles to clarity, see **AMBIGUITY; CLICHÉS; CONCISION** (for wordiness); **ELEGANT VARIATION; EUPHEMISMS; GOBBLEDYGOOK; JARGON (2); MALAPROPISMS; NONSENSE; PRETENTIOUS WORDS; VAGUENESS;** and **VOICE** (for inappropriate use of the passive voice). See also the numerous entries in this book about words confused with other words.

**CLASSIFICATION** To *classify* is to sort a group or class of things (people, objects, ideas, facts—whatever) into subgroups or subclasses upon some basis (size, weight, color, use) relevant to your purpose. A teacher classifies students upon the basis of academic achievement into A students, B students, and so on. A poker player classifies chips on the basis of color (or value) into blue chips, red chips, and so on. A good classification is relevant, complete (every member of the class is assigned to some subclass), and discrete (no member is assigned to more than one subclass).

Classification is fundamental to coping with the world and fundamental to writing coherently. (See **COHERENCE** and **ORGANIZATION**.)

A crossclassification, a classification neither complete nor discrete, results when the basis of classification shifts—from weight to hair color, for example.

NOT THIS: People are either overweight or blond. [Some people, of course, are neither overweight nor blond, and some are both overweight and blond.]

BUT THIS: People are either overweight or underweight or somewhere in between.

OR THIS: People are either blond or brunet or red-headed.

**CLAUSES** A **clause** is a string of words that has a subject (S) and a predicate (P) (see **SUBJECTS** and **PREDICATES**).

A **dependent,** or subordinate, **clause** begins with either a subordinating conjunction (SC) or a relative pronoun (RP):

SC     S
When   I   think about it

RP     S
Whom   I   admire

An **independent,** or main, **clause** does not begin with a subordinating conjunction or a relative pronoun; sentences, for example, are independent clauses.

P S

Then I thought about it.

S P

I admire Laura.

P S

Laura I admire.

(See **ADVERBIAL CLAUSES; NOUN CLAUSES;** and **RELATIVE CLAUSES.**)

**CLICHÉS** A cliché is a trite, stereotyped expression—an expression endlessly repeated, an expression with no originality: *bottom line, cruel hoax, make a long story short, nip in the bud, slick as a whistle.* But it takes more than repetition to make an expression a cliché. Though such expressions as *the girl, of course,* and *I'm fine* have been repeated millions of times and therefore can't be original, they are not clichés. In addition to being trite or stereotyped, a cliché calls attention to itself—usually by being a figure of speech (*jump the gun*), often by being pretentious verbiage (*in any manner, shape, or form*), sometimes by being a euphemism (*generate income* for *make money*), always by somehow pretending to have the originality it lacks. (See **FIGURES OF SPEECH.**)

Because no expression can become a cliché without much repetition, every cliché was once fresh and original. Many enduring clichés have their source in Shakespeare, Milton, and other famous writers. How many things have been said "more in sorrow than in anger" (*Hamlet*)? How many females have been invited to "trip . . . the light fantastic" ("L'Allegro")? How often has "all hell broke loose" (*Paradise Lost*) when something "rotten" was discovered "in the state of Denmark" (*Hamlet*)?

The leftovers of discourse—stale and unappetizing but ready to use—clichés are hard to avoid. Conversation, of course, is full of them, and excusably. Speakers rarely have time to coin fresh and original phrases. But writers have time for second thoughts, and considering them is well worth the effort. Clichés are seldom forceful. Besides, readers may take stereotyped expressions as evidence of stereotyped ideas.

Among the many clichés to be avoided like (as the cliché goes) the plague are

abysmal ignorance
ballpark figure
bridge the gap
can ill afford
dangerous precedent
dialogue (between Egypt and Israel, say)
few and far between
firm belief in
forward-looking
go full swing
heart-rending
ill-conceived
input
integral part
keep your eyes peeled
loved one
make a statement (*The new skyscraper fails to make a statement.*)
meet our needs
minding the store
more heat than light

needless to say

new lease on life

no way, manner, shape, or form

ongoing

open the floodgates

painfully obvious

pay off in rich dividends

pin the blame on

put your finger on

reign supreme

rubber stamp (a proposal, say)

rue the day

run the gauntlet

sadder but wiser

selling your ideas

sell someone short

significant strides

take for granted

task force (on education, say)

that's what it's all about

thorn in one's side

trials and tribulations

trouble shoot

warmly receive

**climactic, climatic**  Often confused, because similar in sound. *Climactic* means "relating to a climax"—that is, the highest point of dramatic tension: *The **climactic** scene of* Othello *is the death of Desdemona. Climatic* means "relating to a climate"—that is, the typical weather at a certain place: *Several climatic changes occurred during the Paleozoic Period.*

**close proximity to**   Wordy. Prefer *close to.* (See **CONCISION.**)

**clout**   SAWE but informal to mean "influence."

**coach**   SAWE as a verb with the name of a sport as object: *coach football, coach tennis.*

**COHERENCE** A paper or a developmental paragraph (see PARAGRAPHS AND PARAGRAPHING) has unity if it sticks to its subject or topic. It is **coherent** as well if it makes clear to readers how the things it says stick together or cohere. Among the chief means of making a paper or a paragraph coherent are an informative title; a topic sentence or a thesis statement; good organization; consistency; repetition of key terms, or a reference, or an idea; parallelism; and transitions. (See **TOPIC SENTENCES; ORGANIZATION; CONSISTENCY; SHIFTS; PARALLELISM, CLIMAX, AND RHYTHM;** and **TRANSITIONS.**)

**coiffeur, coiffure**   Sometimes confused. A *coiffeur* (feminine: *coiffeuse*) is a hairdresser; a *coiffure*, a hairdo.

**COLLECTIVE NOUNS** A **collective noun** is either a common noun or a proper noun naming a group of individuals. For example, both the common noun *army* and the proper noun *the United States Army* are collective nouns, because each names a group of individuals—a military organization consisting of many individual soldiers. Similarly, both the common noun *committee* and the proper noun *the Senate Foreign Relations Committee* are collective nouns, because each names a group of individuals—a deliberative or investigative body consisting of several individual members.

When a singular collective noun (*team,* say) is the subject of a verb or the antecedent of a pronoun, treat it as singular if you are thinking of the group it names (*The team has its problems*); treat it as plural if you are thinking of the members of the group (*The team have their problems*).

(See **ANTECEDENTS; COMMON AND PROPER NOUNS; NOUNS; NUMBER; PRONOUNS; SUBJECTS;** and **VERBS.**)

**collusion**    Use only to describe cooperation you disapprove of: *collusion among corrupt officials.*

**COLONS**    Use a **colon** [:]:

(1) To introduce one or more nominals (nouns, pronouns, noun phrases, noun clauses, and so on) referring to whatever a previous nominal refers to:

The letter shared **one common idea: all saw Post-Impressionism as a foreign threat to native English art and essential English morality.**—Samuel Hynes (The noun clause after the colon and *one common idea* refer to the same thing.)

**Other stars of the fabled Bauhaus** arrived about the same time: **Breuer, Albers, Maholy-Nagy, Bayer, and Mies van der Rohe.** . . . —Tom Wolfe (Taken together, the nouns after the colon and *Other stars of the fabled Bauhaus* refer to the same people.)

**Caution:** Do not use a colon to separate a verb from what follows it.

NOT THIS:    Other stars of the fabled Bauhaus are: Breuer,
Albers. . . .

BUT THIS:    Other stars of the fabled Bauhaus are Breuer,
Albers. . . .

(2) To separate two main clauses (not joined by *and, or, but,*
and so on) when the second gives a reason either for
believing the first, for doing what it requests, or for the
state of affairs it describes:

The balancing act seemed to work: the mayor was greeted
with equal warmth in the city's white and black
neighborhoods.

Eat the skin: it's the best part of the potato.

Smith was dead: he had taken an overdose of sleeping pills.

(3) To introduce a quotation, especially a set-off quotation:

The main idea of Friedman's essay is worth quoting at length:
Our schools, I submit, ill prepare us to make sober
appraisals of experimental sculpture, painting, literature,
or architecture in the context of history.

(4) To identify speakers in a dialogue:

**Socrates:** He ought not to speak of the name, but of the
thing which is contemplated under the name.
**Theaetetus:** Right.

(5) To replace *is* or *are:*

The cause: overwork.

(6) To follow the salutation in a formal letter:

Dear Ms. Slattery:

(7) To separate the hour from the minutes after the hour:

10:20

(8) To separate a title from a subtitle:

*Betrayal: A History of the Plains Indians*

(9) To separate a book's place of publication from publisher and year in a footnote:

New York: Harcourt, Brace, 1953

(10) To separate an article's date of publication from the page numbers in a footnote:

2 Jan. 1994: 21–7

(11) To separate a book's volume number from the page number in a footnote:

4: 91–100

**colossal**  Avoid using as a synonym for *great* or *very large*.

NOT THIS:   a **colossal** success.

BUT THIS:   a **great** success.

(See **DESCRIPTIVE AND EVALUATIVE WORDS**.)

**come and**  See **be sure and, come and, try and.**

**COMMA FAULT OR SPLICE**  Incorrect joining of two independent clauses with a comma (rather than a semicolon or a comma plus a coordinating conjunction [*and, but, for, nor, or*]). (But see **COMMAS, 3.**)

NOT THIS:   New York is the most populous city in the country, it is not the capital.

BUT THIS:   New York is the most populous city in the country; it is not the capital.

OR THIS:   New York is the most populous city in the country, **but** it is not the capital.

(See **CLAUSES; COMMAS; CONJUNCTIONS;** and **SEMI-COLONS.**)

**COMMAS** Use a **comma** [,]:

(1) To set off an introductory adverbial clause or long adverbial phrase:

If the knob is loose, tighten it.

(2) To separate independent clauses joined by *and, but, either . . . or, for, neither . . . nor,* or *or* if there is little or no punctuation within them:

At dawn, the party ended, and everyone left.

(3) To separate very short independent clauses not joined by conjunctions:

He came, he saw, he conquered.

(4) To set off a transitional expression from the rest of the sentence:

|  | finally | |
| | furthermore | |
| The matter was, | moreover, | settled. |
| | nevertheless | |
| | of course | |

(5) To separate words or phrases in a series:

The books, the magazines, and the files were lost.

(6) To set off a nonrestrictive modifier (appositive, phrase, relative clause) from the rest of the sentence (See **RESTRICTIVE AND NONRESTRICTIVE**):

My only sister, Nancy, is a teacher.

The President, who took office in December, is a bachelor.

(7) To introduce a direct quotation and, if it is not a question or an exclamation, and does not end its sentence, to end it:

He said, "I won't," curtly.

(8) To set off an expression used in direct address:

You know, Sanford, what the problem is.

(9) To set off an absolute construction:

Their work done, they left.

They knew that, their work done, they could leave.

(10) To set off a tag question:

He understands that, doesn't he?

(11) To indicate deletion of a word or words that readers can readily supply:

He chose exile; she, prison.

(12) To separate the two parts of a double-comparative sentence:

The more, the merrier.

The duller the evening, the greater the excuse.

(13) To group numerals into units of three:

>           35,000                    1,250,000

But not always:

>     the year 1066    1325 Forest Avenue        page 2730

(14) To separate a person's name from an abbreviation of a title or an honorific:

Mary Sanders, D.D.

Horace Rumpole, O.E.B.

Langston Bart, Esq.

(15) To separate the parts of inverted proper names as in an index:

Kennedy, John F.

(16) In informal usage, to end the salutation of a letter and, in any usage, the complimentary close:

Dear Ms. Harper,
Sincerely,

(17) To punctuate dates and addresses:

Tuesday, 23 March [or March 23,] 1994
716 Chicago Avenue, Evanston, Illinois [or IL]

**COMMON AND PROPER NOUNS**   A **common noun** names every individual belonging to a class or group. The common noun *president,* for example, names every person who ever has been or ever will be a president. Similarly, the common noun *city* names every place that ever has been or ever will be a city. A common noun can also name a quality shared by individuals (*boyishness, honesty, redness*) or a relationship between individuals (*equality, superiority, identity*).

A **proper noun** names only one individual, much in the way a social security number identifies one individual person or a license number identifies one individual car. For instance: it names one individual place (*Detroit*), organization (*Exxon*), or play (*Hamlet*). A phrase naming one individual is also considered a proper noun: *the American Revolution, Mount Rushmore, the White House.*

A proper noun is capitalized (except for *the* in such a proper noun as *the White House*). But capitalization is not a sure sign that a noun is proper, because some common nouns are capitalized, especially common nouns that are brand names. Though capitalized, *Chevrolet,* for example, is a common noun. It names, not one individual car, but every car belonging to a class of cars (all the cars that bear the name *Chevrolet*). Similarly, *Kleenex* is a common noun. (See **NOUNS.**)

**community**   Don't use *community* to refer to a group of people if it is not a community—unless you want to suggest that the group exemplifies such community values as mutual support.

NOT THIS:   the business (or civil-rights) **community.**

BUT THIS:   **business people** (or **civil-rights activists**).

**COMPARATIVES AS ABSOLUTES**   Avoid use of a comparative as though it were an absolute.

NOT THIS:   found at **better** stores everywhere.

BUT THIS:   found at the **best** stores everywhere.

NOT THIS:   a comfort to **older** Americans.

BUT THIS:   a comfort to **old** Americans.

**compare to, compare with**   Use of either is SAWE to mean either (a) "liken (something) to (something else)" (*You can't compare a Volkswagen to a* [or *with*] Rolls-Royce) or (b) "observe similarities and differences between (something) and (something else)" (*Comparing a Volkswagen to* [or *with*] *a Rolls-Royce, you notice a big difference in price*). **Caution:** Many readers object to use of *compare to* to mean (b) and of *compare with* to mean (a).

## COMPARISON OF ADJECTIVES AND ADVERBS
English adjectives and adverbs have three degrees of comparison: the positive, the comparative, and the superlative. If the positive (or unmarked) degree is one syllable (*fine*) or two syllables (*gentle*)—but does not end in *-al, -ed, -en, -ent, -ful, -ic, -id, -il, -ile, -ing, -ive, -on, -ose, -ous, -que, -st*, or *-ure*—the comparative is formed by the suffix *-er (finer, gentler)* and the superlative by the suffix *-est (finest, gentlest)*. Otherwise, the comparative is formed

by *more (more understanding)* and the superlative by *most (most understanding)*. Special cases are (a) *good, better, best* and (b) *bad, worse, worst*.

**COMPARISONS: AMBIGUOUS, INCOMPLETE**    Such comparisons as *I like Sarah better than Phyllis* are ambiguous because incomplete.

UNAMBIGUOUS:    I like Sarah better than I **like** Phyllis.

OR:    I like Sarah better than Phyllis **does.**

**COMPARISONS AND CONTRASTS**    To compare and contrast two or more things—institutions, for instance, or professions—with one another is a way of clarifying the meaning of the nouns or noun phrases used to refer to them (see **CLARITY**).

Compare and contrast a college with a university, for example, and thereby clarify the meanings of the nouns *college* and *university*. Each is an institution of higher learning, a school that a student may attend after completing high school. But, though a college may be independent of a university (Carleton College, Kenyon), it may, along with such professional schools as law, medicine, and nursing, be part of a university (Columbia University, the University of Texas).

**compatible**    Always designates a relationship between two people or things: *Harriet and John are compatible* (they can get along with one another); *love is compatible with hate* (they can coexist); *the pumpkin and the summer squash are compatible* (they can cross-fertilize). **Caution:** *Compatible* never means "agreeable" or "easy to get along with."

NOT THIS:    Charles is a very **compatible** person.

BUT THIS:    Charles is a very **agreeable** person.

**COMPETENCE AND PERFORMANCE** Your **competence** in a language is what you know about it (usually tacitly, implicitly, and inarticulately); your **performance,** what you do with it. Your performance may fail to match your competence for a variety of reasons. You may be tired or ill or even incapacitated. You cannot speak at all if you have laryngitis. You cannot write at all if your arm is in a sling. You may know perfectly well that the superlative of *well known* is *best known,* yet you write *most well known*—or that the past tense of *forbid* is *forbade,* yet write, *He forbid me to do it.*

**complement, compliment; complementary, complimentary** (1) *Complement* and *compliment* are often confused, because identical in sound. As a verb, *complement* means "fill out" or "complete" (*Her brains complement her athletic ability*); as a noun, it means "something that fills out or completes" (*Her brains are the complement to her athletic ability*). As a verb, *compliment* means "offer an expression of admiration to" (*They complimented her upon her victory*); as a noun, it means "expression of admiration" (*They paid her a compliment upon her victory*).

(2) **Caution:** *Complementary* and *complimentary* are often confused, because identical in sound. *Complementary* means "supplying each other's lack": *Her wit and his tact are complementary. Complimentary* means either "given free" (*complimentary tickets*) or "favorable" (*complimentary remarks*).

**comprised of** Now SAWE. **Caution:** Some readers object to it because of its origins as a blend of *is composed of* and *comprises.*

NOT THIS:   Our club **is comprised of** bowlers.

BUT THIS:   Our club **is composed of** (or **comprises**) bowlers.

**conceive, conceive of** Sometimes confused. To *conceive* is to create: *the couple conceived a child.* To *conceive of* is to imagine: *I cannot conceive of any circumstances in which I could do that.*

**concerned about, concerned with**  Sometimes confused. To be *concerned about* someone or something is to worry about it: *I am concerned about my brother's safety.* To be *concerned with* is simply to be somehow involved with: *I am concerned with computers of all makes.*

**concerns**  Avoid using as a euphemism for *complaints* or *worries.* (See **EUPHEMISMS.**)

NOT THIS:    Parents expressed **concerns** about the curriculum.

BUT THIS:    Parents **made complaints** (or **complained**) about the curriculum.

**concertize**  NonSAWE as a synonym for *perform in concert.*

NOT THIS:    The famous soprano often **concertized.**

BUT THIS:    The famous soprano often **performed in concert** (or **gave concerts**).

**CONCISION**  To write concisely is to express meaning in as few words as possible: the fewer words, the greater concision. Concise writing, of course, is not necessarily effective. Effectiveness sometimes requires more words than concision permits—for emphasis, say, as in Lincoln's Gettysburg Address ("we cannot dedicate, we cannot consecrate, we cannot hallow this ground"). On the whole, however, clear writing is concise; and unclear writing is often wordy, hiding meaning rather than expressing it. There are six good ways of being concise.

(1) **Using the Shortest Synonym.** When two or more expressions have the same meaning (are synonymous) but differ in number of words, use the shortest:

WORDY:    Reagan was the most effective president in terms of rhetoric.

| | |
|---|---|
| CONCISE: | Reagan was the most effective president **rhetorically.** |
| WORDY: | Commissioner Schweik **expressed himself to the effect that he believed** that cooperation is essential. |
| CONCISE: | Commissioner Schweik **said** that cooperation is essential. |
| WORDY: | There is **literally a shortage of** enough money. |
| CONCISE: | There is **not** enough money. |
| WORDY: | We are now **in the process of making plans** for 1996. |
| CONCISE: | We are now **planning** for 1996. |

| WORDY: | CONCISE: |
|---|---|
| at all times | always |
| at no time | never |
| at some point in time | some time |
| at the present time | now |
| at the same time as | while |
| comes to the conclusion | concludes |
| due to the fact that | because |
| economically disadvantaged | poor |
| has the ability to | can |
| has the belief | believes |
| in the event that | if |
| in the highest income bracket | rich |
| is an authorization for | authorizes |
| is an exaggeration of | exaggerates |
| prior to | before |
| the present writer | I/me |

(2) **Avoiding Ineffective Repetition of Words.**

WORDY:    The **intelligence** that has this profound effect on politics is not political **intelligence**, but scientific **intelligence** and technical **intelligence**.

CONCISE:    "The **intelligence** that has this profound effect on politics is not political, but scientific and technical."—Bertrand Russell

WORDY:    At the last auction, a plaster bust of Henry Kissinger **brought** $205, a Russian silver tea set **brought** $2,300, and a soiled Gucci handbag **brought** $175.

CONCISE:    At the last auction, a plaster bust of Henry Kissinger **brought** $205; a Russian silver tea set, $2,300; and a soiled Gucci handbag, $175.

**Caution:** In avoiding ineffective repetition, do *not* use equally ineffective elegant variation (see **ELEGANT VARIATION**): *At the last auction, a plaster bust of Henry Kissinger brought $205, a Russian silver tea set was sold for $2,300, and a soiled Gucci handbag fetched $175.*

(3) **Avoiding Ineffective Repetition of Meaning.** One kind of repetition of meaning occurs when two expressions in a sentence are synonyms and serve the same purpose. In the following example, *once a year* and *annual* are synonyms and serve the same purpose (to indicate that the festival is yearly):

WORDY:    **Once a year** they have an **annual** festival.

CONCISE:    They have an **annual** festival.

The other, more common kind of repetition of meaning occurs when the meaning of a modifier is part of the meaning of the expression it modifies. In the following example, the meaning of the modifier *in advance* is part of the meaning of *predict*, the word it modifies (*predict* means "declare in advance"):

WORDY:     Meteorologists **predicted** the cyclone **in advance.**

CONCISE:     Meteorologists **predicted** the cyclone.

More examples of both kinds of repetition of meaning:

| WORDY: | CONCISE: |
| --- | --- |
| accidental slip | slip |
| advance forward | forward |
| advance reservations | reservations |
| assorted varieties | varieties |
| basic fundamentals | fundamentals |
| binary in nature | binary |
| combined into one | combined |
| commissioned in advance | commissioned |
| contemporary world of today | contemporary world |
| cooperate together | cooperate |
| false illusion | illusion |
| few in number | few |
| field of chemistry | chemistry |
| finish completely | finish |
| flaming inferno | inferno |
| forecast in advance | forecast |
| free gift | gift |
| large in size | large |
| lucrative profits | profits |

| | |
|---|---|
| mutual cooperation | cooperation |
| mysterious puzzle | puzzle |
| natural instinct | instinct |
| new innovation | innovation |
| old poems of long ago | old poems |
| ongoing process | process |
| past history | history |
| personal belongings | belongings |
| personal friend | friend |
| plans for the future | plans |
| preprepared | prepared |
| qualified expert | expert |
| rational reason | reason |
| return back | return |
| sad tragedy | tragedy |
| warn beforehand | warn |

(4) **Eliminating Nearly Meaningless Expressions.**
Eliminate any expression with too little meaning
to justify the space it takes:

WORDY:    "When a great number of people cannot
find work, unemployment
results."—attributed to President
Coolidge (Hardly news to readers who
know what the word *unemployment*
means, this statement is at best a
roundabout definition of that word.)

WORDY:    The manager's decision may or may not
turn out to be a disaster. (Like all other
decisions?)

WORDY:

all things considered

for all intents and purposes

in any manner, shape, or form

in the last analysis

so far as I'm concerned

when all is said and done

(5) **Avoiding Wordy Jargon.** Jargon need not be
wordy. (See **JARGON (1)** and **(2)**.) Indeed, one
reason to use jargon is to be concise. In the
jargon of bridge players, for instance, *bid* is a
one-word substitute for an eight-word phrase:
*announcement of what a player proposes to
undertake.* But another reason is to impress and
exclude outsiders. And this is often wordy.
Unfortunately, outsiders often imitate it. (See
**GOBBLEDYGOOK.**)

WORDY:     Your child manifests difficulty in
distinguishing between imaginary and
factual material and needs guidance in
learning to adhere to rules and standards
of equitable social relationships.

CONCISE:     Your child lies and cheats.

WORDY:     The degree of mitigation of risk with
asbestos is uncertain.

CONCISE:     Asbestos may be risky.

(6) **Combining Sentences.** A good way to avoid
some kinds of wordiness is to combine sentences:

WORDY:     Heresy was not a social act. It was not a biological condition. It was a state of mind. Therefore, the crime of witchcraft could never have been established if recognized judicial procedures had been followed.

CONCISE:   "Since heresy was neither a social act nor a biological condition but a state of mind, the crime of witchcraft could never have been established if recognized judicial procedures had been followed."—Thomas Szasz (The concise version is easier to read not only because it is more concise, but also because it better expresses the relationships among the writer's ideas—making clearer, for example, the structure of his argument.)

WORDY:     Almora took the town by storm. He installed a mayor. The mayor was a journalist.

CONCISE:   Almora took the town by storm and installed a journalist as mayor.

**conclude, decide**  Sometimes synonymous. But to *decide* is always to choose among alternatives (*He decided to go to Florida rather than California*), while to *conclude* is to make an inference even though it may not affect choice (*He concluded that Florida is warmer than California*).

**CONCLUSIONS**  See **ARGUMENT AND PERSUASION.**

**CONCRETE AND ABSTRACT NOUNS**  A **concrete noun** is either a common noun or a proper noun that names something tangible (real or imaginary)—something that can be or could have been seen, smelled, tasted, heard, or touched: *battle, unicorn, scientist; the Battle of Waterloo, the Waldorf-Astoria, Albert Einstein.*

An **abstract noun** is a common noun that names something intangible—an idea or a system (*belief, democracy, harmony, ideology, justice, principle, racism*), a quality (*bravery, fidelity, hardness, brashness*), or a relationship (*dependency, difference, jealousy, opposition, pity*).

(See **COMMON AND PROPER NOUNS** and **NOUNS.**)

**condition**  Avoid using it as a synonym for disease.

NOT THIS:    She has a heart **condition.**

BUT THIS:    She has heart **disease.**

**conflicted**  NonSAWE as a substitute for *in doubt, of two minds,* or *torn (between alternatives).*

NOT THIS:    Judson is **conflicted** about whether to marry.

BUT THIS:    Judson is **in doubt** about whether to marry.

**congenial, genial**  Sometimes confused. *Congenial* means "easy to get along with"; *genial* means "pleasant." Doubtless, most genial people are congenial, but they need not be.

**CONJUNCTION AT BEGINNING OF SENTENCE**  To begin a sentence with a coordinating conjunction—*and, but, for, nor, or, so, yet*—is SAWE. (See **CONJUNCTIONS.**)

**CONJUNCTIONS**  **Conjunctions** are a part of speech that relate expressions (words, phrases, clauses, or sentences) to one another. Coordinating conjunctions (CC) connect like expressions (nouns, verbs, or sentences, for example) to one another: *and, but,* *neither, nor, or,* and *so.* The correlative conjunctions *either . . . or, neither . . . nor,* and *not only . . . but also* also are coordinating conjunctions. Subordinating conjunctions (SC) preface subordinate clauses: *because, before, if, since, so that, that, though, unless, until, when, whenever, where, wherever, whether, while.*

<pre>
SC                      CC              SC
</pre>
When summer has come and gone, I know that winter is near.

**Note:** *That* is a subordinating conjunction when, as in this example, it prefaces a noun clause. When it does not, it is a relative pronoun and therefore has a function within the clause—for instance, subject (*the dog **that** saved me*) or direct object (*the dog **that** I saved*).

**CONJUNCTIVE ADVERBS** Words that modify verbs and that relate sentences or independent clauses to one another: for example, *furthermore, however, moreover, nevertheless: Smith denies the charge. The facts, however, are clear.* Or this: *Smith denies the charge; the facts, however, are clear.* SAWE generally embeds them into sentences as in these examples.

NOT THIS:   **However,** the facts are clear.

BUT THIS:   The facts, **however,** are clear.

**CONNOTATIONS** What a word or phrase suggests, as contrasted with what it means. The word *nurse,* for instance, means "one who cares for the ill." But its connotations include such things as white uniforms and devotion to duty.

**conscience, conscious** Sometimes confused. *Conscience* is a noun meaning "awareness of guilt or innocence": *Joan's conscience told her it was wrong to lie to Bill. Conscious* is an adjective meaning "aware" or "capable of feeling, thought, and willing": *Though severely injured, Joan was **conscious.***

**CONSISTENCY**   Ralph Waldo Emerson once wrote, "A foolish consistency is the hobgoblin of little minds. . . ." But not all consistency is foolish. Within a given piece of writing, absolute consistency is a great virtue. Any variation in the way you write—variation in tone (familiar in one place, formal in another), in point of view (yours in one place, your readers' in another), in reference (*this journalist, this newspaper reporter, this writer*), in voice (*I believe, it is believed*) can confuse your readers and thereby decrease their comprehension. (See **ELEGANT VARIATION; TONE;** and **VOICE.**)

**consultant**   Often a euphemism for *clerk*. (See **EUPHEMISMS.**)

NOT THIS:   a floral **consultant.**

BUT THIS:   a florist's **clerk.**

**contact**   SAWE for "get in touch with." **Caution:** Some readers object to this use of *contact*.

NOT THIS:   **Contact** your insurance agent for rates.

BUT THIS:   **Get in touch with** your insurance agent for rates.

**contemporary**   *Contemporary* means "existing at the same time." That time is often now (*Clinton and Yeltsin are contemporaries.*) but need not be (*Jonson and Shakespeare were contemporaries.*)

**contemptible, contemptuous**   Often confused. *Contemptible* means "deserving contempt": *a contemptible assault. Contemptuous* means "feeling or expressing contempt": *I am contemptuous of most politicians.*

NOT THIS:   a **contemptuous** slander.

BUT THIS:   a **contemptible** slander.

**CONTEXT** Either (1) the words surrounding a word, phrase, or a clause in a discourse or (2) the circumstances surrounding creation of a discourse—notably, the writer or speaker, the time, the place, current events, and the intended audience or listeners. In both senses, the context is usually crucial to interpretation. *Bank,* for example, means one thing in the context *The bank is steep;* another in the context *The bank is insolvent.* For a different example, the salt referred to in *Please pass the salt* can be identified only by the context.

**continually, continuously** Often confused. *Continually* means "again and again": *He calls me **continually**. Continuously* means "without stopping": *He talks **continuously** whenever I see him.*

**CONTRACTIONS** Contractions—in particular, *n't* for *not*— are SAWE in all but the most formal contexts (charters, constitutions). **Caution:** Many readers object to them in all formal contexts, especially in business correspondence, cover letters, and so on.

**CONTRADICTIONS** A contradiction is a statement that something both possesses and does *not* possess a certain characteristic. In other words, it is a statement that something A is both B and *not* B (whatever A and B may be)—for example, that cigarette smoking (A) is both harmful (B) and *not* harmful (*not* B). Because it both asserts and denies that A is B, it is necessarily false. In effect, it combines two statements that contradict or negate each other: *A is B* and *A is not B.*

Very few contradictions are explicit: few, that is, take one of the following forms:

A is both B and *not* B.
An angel [A] is both blue [B] and *not* blue [not B].

A is B, and A is *not* B.
An angel [A] is blue [B], and it is *not* blue [not B].

B A is *not* B.
A blue [B] angel [A] is *not* blue [not B].

Here, however, are two real-life examples of explicit contradictions—the first from a committee report, the other from D. H. Lawrence's *Selected Letters:*

Clearly, the final [B] version [A] is *not* final [not B].

They [A] have become detestable [B] . . . and yet they [A] are*n't* detestable [not B].

Of course, if Lawrence meant one thing by *detestable* the first time and a different thing the second—as President Coolidge did by *business* when he said, "The business of America is business"—then his statement is not a contradiction.

Explicit contradictions occur infrequently; they are easy to avoid. But implicit contradictions—contradictions that reveal themselves in less obvious ways—are so common that avoiding them requires vigilance. Let's analyze one:

"Generally, the victim will always be unconscious."
—*First Aid for Soldiers*
**Analysis:** The victim [A] will both always [B] and—because generally—*not* always [not B] be unconscious. (The words *generally* and *always* are responsible for the contradiction. *Generally* means "at *almost* all—and therefore *not* at all—times"; *always* means "at all times." In effect, part of the meaning of *generally* is "*not* always." And to say that something occurs both always and *not* always, or at all times and *not* all times, is a contradiction.)

Here are a few other implicit contradictions:

"There is some unanimous support for him."
—Politician's statement

"Most of the immigrants are often illiterate."
—Newspaper story

"Santorini is possibly the site of mythical
Atlantis."—Advertisement

**convince, persuade**   *Convince* means "cause to believe": *They convinced him that loyalty comes first; They convinced him of the preeminence of loyalty. Persuade* means either "cause to believe" (*They persuaded him that loyalty comes first*) or "cause to do" (*They persuaded him to leave*). The SAWE forms, then, are *convince that, convince of, persuade that,* and *persuade to.* **Caution:** Though *convince to* is widely used in both speech and writing, many readers object to it.

> NOT THIS:   They **convinced** him **to** leave.

> BUT THIS:   They **persuaded** him **to** leave.

**cool**   Both slang and vague as an expression of approval.

> NOT THIS:   a **cool** tape deck.

> BUT THIS:   a **fine** (or **high-fidelity**) tape deck.

**COORDINATING CONJUNCTIONS**  See **CONJUNCTIONS.**

**COORDINATION AND SUBORDINATION**  Words and phrases are coordinated if they are (or grammatically can be) connected by *and, or,* or *neither . . . nor: apples, [and] bananas, and pears; an apple, [or] a banana, or a pear; neither fish nor fowl; of the people, by the people, and for the people.* Clauses are coordinated if they are (or grammatically can be) connected by *and, but, for,* or *or: he was old but [he was] fit; John was nervous, for he trembled.*

Any modifier—an article, an adjective, an adverb, a prepositional phrase, or a clause—is subordinate to whatever it modifies: *a boy; the boy; white houses; he ran fast; the dog in the window; by dawn, he was on the road; when I was in Florida,* I met Dan.

**COORDINATOR**   One of the twelve functions that a part of speech—in this case, a coordinating conjunction—can perform in a clause. (See **FORMS AND FUNCTIONS.**)

A **coordinator** conjoins two expressions of equal grammatical rank: two nouns, for example (*boys and girls*), two adjectives (*fit but fat*), two relative clauses (*who are fit or who are fat*), or two independent clauses (*he is fit, for he exercises*).

**cope**   Avoid unless followed by a *with* prepositional phrase.

> NOT THIS:   I can't **cope.**
>
> BUT THIS:   I can't **cope with stress** (or **with my job, with life**).

**cop, policeman, police officer**   All three terms are objectionable for one reason or another. *Cop* is slang (see **SLANG.**) *Policeman* is sexist (see **SEXIST LANGUAGE**). Although *police officer* suggests an army in which there are all officers and no privates, the term is generally accepted.

**corespondent, correspondent**   Sometimes confused. A *corespondent* is someone accused of being the third party in a divorce action. A *correspondent* is simply someone who writes letters.

**corps, corpse** Sometimes confused. A *corps* is an organization, usually military: *the Marine Corps.* A *corpse* is a dead person (or, more generally, dead animal).

**CORRECTNESS** Correctness in writing is conformity to the grammatical rules of the language. If an essay, for example, or a story conforms to these rules, it is correct. If it does not, it is incorrect. (See **GRAMMATICAL RULES.**)

In the broad sense, grammatical rules include syntactic rules, governing word order (see **SYNTAX**); morphological rules, governing word formation (see **MORPHEMES AND PHONEMES**); phonetic and phonological rules, governing the pronunciation of words and sentences; orthographic rules, governing the spelling of words; mechanical rules, governing punctuation, capitalization, italicizing, and the like; and semantic rules, governing the meaning of words and sentences. Correctness, in short, has many dimensions.

But there are at least three difficulties in trying to conform to these rules.

First, English, like every other language, is not a monolith but a collection of varieties, or dialects, spoken or written. What is correct in one dialect may be incorrect in another. The focus of this book is Standard American English, in particular Standard American Written English (SAWE). But it briefly describes two other dialects: Black English (see **BLACK ENGLISH**) and WASP language (see **WASP LANGUAGE**). For example, use of multiple negatives—for instance, *I don't have no money in no bank*—is incorrect in SAWE and WASP language but correct, indeed required, in Black English (see **MULTIPLE NEGATIVES**).

Second, SAWE and WASP language, like every other dialect, are constantly, if slowly, changing. Seventy-five years ago, perhaps every speaker or writer of these dialects distinguished sharply between *shall* and *will*—using *shall* for simple futurity (*I shall die some day*) and *will* for determination (*I will not put up with that any longer*). But few such speakers or writers do so nowadays.

Third, the grammatical rules are not readily accessible to speakers and writers who are not sure what they are. Indeed, not all these rules have been formulated. Almost all the rules concerning words can be found in one or the other of the two great dictionaries: *Webster's Third New International Dictionary* and *The Oxford English Dictionary*. But there are no comparable compendiums of rules concerning sentences.

To praise someone for speaking or writing correctly is like praising a singer for singing in tune. Correctness is a minimum requirement. Someone may write correctly but also wordily (see **CONCISION**), ineffectively, or unpersuasively (see **READERS, COMMUNICATION, AND PERSUASION** and **ARGUMENT AND PERSUASION**).

**CORRELATIVE CONJUNCTIONS**  See **CONJUNCTIONS**.

**could care less**  A mistake for the cliché *couldn't care less,* meaning "am/is/are completely unconcerned."

NOT THIS:  Harry **could care less** about Jane's future.

BUT THIS:  Harry **couldn't care less** about Jane's future.

**council, counsel**  Sometimes confused. A *council* is an organization: *a tribal council. Counsel* is either advice or someone who gives advice—a lawyer, for example.

**COUNT AND MASS NOUNS** A **count noun** is a common noun naming things that can be counted: *birthday, boy, mother, hotel, pencil, store.* A **mass noun** is a common noun naming things that cannot be counted: *courage, haste, purity, sugar, water.* Some nouns are count in some contexts but mass in others: *density, difficulty, fish.*

A common noun is a count noun only if (1) you can use it in the plural number (*few coins, many coins, three coins,*) and (2) you can use it in the singular number with an indefinite article (*a coin*) or with *one* (*one coin*). Otherwise, a common noun is' mass: *money, little money, much money, the money.* (See **ARTICLES; COMMON AND PROPER NOUNS; NOUNS;** and **NUMBER.**)

**couple, couple of** A *couple* or *a couple of* are often used in conversation or informal writing to mean "two" or "a few." **Caution:** Some readers object to this use in any writing, formal or informal.

> NOT THIS:   **a couple** (or **a couple of**) friends.

> BUT THIS:   **two** (or **a few**) friends.

**couth** *Uncouth* is SAWE and useful. But, for some reason, *couth* is very rare and a bit comic.

**credible, creditable, credulous** Sometimes confused. *Credible* means "believable": *credible testimony. Creditable* means "worthy of credit or commendation": *a creditable performance. Credulous* means "willing to believe anything": *a credulous person.*

**criminally assaulted** (1) The term is wordy (see **CONCISION**), because all assaults are criminal (so-called *military assaults* may be an exception). (2) As a euphemism (see **EUPHEMISMS**) for *rape,* it should be avoided.

**criterion, criteria; phenomenon, phenomena**  Both *criterion* and *phenomenon* are singular: *this **criterion**, one **phenomenon***. Both *criteria* and *phenomena* are plural: *these **criteria**, two **phenomena***.

**criticism**  In academic discourse, *criticism* is analysis or evaluation: *literary criticism, musical criticism*. In general usage, *criticism* is unfavorable comment except in the phrase *favorable criticism*.

**criticize, criticism, critique**  To *criticize* is either to evaluate or find fault with. *Criticism* is either the act or the product of criticizing. *Critique* is another name for criticism as product. Because the verb *criticize* is ambiguous (meaning either "evaluate" or "find fault with"), *critique* has become SAWE as a verb meaning "evaluate," largely replacing *criticize* in that sense.

**curious**  *Curious* means either "eager to know" (*curious about the causes of civil unrest*) or "odd" or "peculiar" (*a **curious** habit*).

**currently, presently**  Both SAWE for *now*. (1) **Caution:** Some readers object to this use of *presently*, insisting that the word be used to mean "before long" only: ***Presently**, I will leave*.

NOT THIS:   The 1916 Overland is **presently** on display in the Antique Car Museum.

BUT THIS:   The 1916 Overland is **currently** (or **now**) on display in the Antique Car Museum.

(2) **Caution:** Use of *currently, now,* or *presently* is wordy when the verb it modifies is in the present tense.

NOT THIS:   Sue is **presently** working at CBS.

BUT THIS:   Sue is working at CBS.

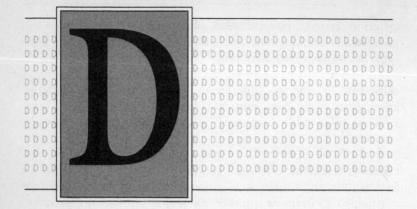

**damaged, injured** Synonyms except that *damaged* is said only of inanimate things (*a damaged car*); *injured* only of people or, more generally, animals (*no passengers were injured*).

**DASHES** Use a **dash** (typed as two hyphens [--]):

(1) To set off, more emphatically than commas would, a nonrestrictive modifier (appositive, phrase, relative clause) from the rest of the sentence:

The criminals--who were well known to the police--were not apprehended for months.

(2) To set off a phrase or a clause that breaks the continuity of a sentence:

The cabinet--the prime minister gave it no leadership--was in disarray.

(3) To introduce a summary following a series of words or phrases:

The president, the secretary, and the treasurer--these constitute the executive committee.

(4) To precede the source of a quotation:

"True wit is nature to advantage dress'd,
What oft was thought but n'er so well express'd"--Pope

**data** Now SAWE both as a singular noun (*This **data** was collected recently*) and as a plural noun (*These **data** were collected recently*). **Caution:** Some readers expect *data* to be plural in formal writing.

NOT THIS:   Much **data** is gathered hastily.

BUT THIS:   Many **data** are gathered hastily.

**Note:** When *data* is plural, the singular form is *datum: One **datum** was especially important.*

**dead body** Usually wordy (see **CONCISION.**)

NOT THIS:   **Dead bodies** were strewn over the site of the crash.

BUT THIS:   **Bodies** were strewn over the site of the crash.

**dearth, plethora** A *dearth* is a great undersupply of something (*a **dearth** of competent workers*); a *plethora*, a great oversupply (*a **plethora** of incompetent workers*).

**debut** Avoid as a verb.

NOT THIS:   Fernandez Blanco **debuts** tonight.

BUT THIS:   Fernandez Blanco makes his **debut** tonight.

**deceased, diseased** (1) Sometimes confused. *Deceased* means "dead"; *diseased* means "afflicted with a disease." (2) Prefer *dead* to *deceased*.

> NOT THIS:    My father is **deceased.**

> BUT THIS:    My father is **dead.**

**decimate** *Decimate* means "reduce to one-tenth of the original size": *The fifty-person work force was decimated* (that is, reduced to five). More generally, however, it means "reduce considerably." Avoid this more general usage because it is imprecise.

**deduce, deduct; deduction** *Deduce* always means—and *deduct* sometimes means—"infer": *From the broken lock, I deduced* (or, rarely, *deducted*) *that my apartment had been burglarized.* Deduct, however, usually means "subtract": *My employer deducted federal tax from my pay. Deduction* means either "inference" (*my deduction from the broken lock*) or "something subtracted" (*my employer's deduction from my pay*). (See also **INDUCTION AND DEDUCTION.**)

**DEEP STRUCTURE, SURFACE STRUCTURE, AND TRANSFORMATIONAL RULES** According to transformational grammars (for example, Noam Chomsky's), every sentence has both a deep structure and a surface structure. The **surface structure,** manifested in speech or writing, is caused by action of transformational grammatical rules upon the deep structure. A single **deep structure** (for example: *I like music*) may underlie a great variety of surface structures (for example: *I like music, Music I like, What I like is music, Do I like music?*), each surface structure being the result of the action of different **transformational rules.** What a transformational grammar claims to do is to make explicit native speakers' intuitions about relationships among different sentences (that is, different surface structures).

**definite, definitive** Sometimes confused. *Definite* means "well-defined, precise": *a definite goal, a definite period of time. Definitive* means "complete, authoritative": *the definitive catalog of the British Museum Library, the definitive edition of* The Canterbury Tales.

**DEFINITIONS** Statements of what a word or phrase is or was actually used to mean (lexical definitions: *In Shakespeare's time,* presently *meant "now"; today, it means "pretty soon"*) or of what a writer intends to use it to mean (stipulative definitions: *By* low-income family, *I will mean "family with a gross annual income of $30,000 or less"*). A third sort of definition—persuasive definition—is neither lexical nor stipulative but attempts through use of the word *true* before the word defined to persuade readers to think well of a group of people or things: *A true American supports his or her country right or wrong.*

**definition, sense** Sometimes confused. (1) The **definition** of a word or phrase is a statement of what it means, either in actual usage (a lexical definition—the kind found in dictionaries) or as stipulated in a certain context or for a certain purpose (a stipulative definition). An example of a lexical definition: Octogenarian *means "eighty-year-old person."* An example of a stipulative definition: *In this contract, the term* owner *refers to the person in whose name the vehicle is registered.*

(2) The **sense** of a word or phrase is not a statement of what it means but the meaning itself:

NOT THIS:   The bank uses the word *professional* in two **definitions.**

BUT THIS:   The bank uses the word *professional* in two **senses.**

(3) The term *persuasive definition* (coined by the philosopher Charles L. Stevenson) refers to a statement that is an exhortation disguised as a definition. It takes a word that is both honorific and vague—*scholar* is an example—and gives it a precise sense that suits

the writer's purpose. Its hallmark is the word *true: A true scholar (is a person who) is not influenced by changes in intellectual fashion.*

**DELETION OF WORDS**    Deletion of unnecessary words makes a sentence more concise.

> NOT THIS:    Alfonso is Spanish, Olaf is Norwegian, and Patrick is Irish.

> BUT THIS:    Alfonso is Spanish; Olaf, Norwegian; and Patrick, Irish.

The two deletions of *is* (together with some changes in punctuation) make the sentence both more concise and more forceful. (See **CONCISION**.)

**DEMONSTRATIVE PRONOUNS**    A **demonstrative pronoun** (DP) points out one or more people or things: *this, these; that, those; such.*

   When spoken, a demonstrative pronoun usually needs no antecedent. Something in the context—someone visible to both speaker and listener, for example—shows what it refers to:

DP
That is Amy sitting over there.

   When written, however, a demonstrative pronoun usually has an antecedent, often a whole clause or sentence:

ANTECEDENT                          DP
Inspiration and perspiration—these every writer needs.

ANTECEDENT CLAUSE            DP
Often executives are lazy. That is one cause of failure. [In other words, executives' being lazy is one cause of failure.]

**(See ANTECEDENTS and PRONOUNS.)**

**demur, demure**  Sometimes confused. *Demur* is a verb meaning "object": *He **demurred** to the proposal. Demure* is an adjective meaning "modest" or "coy": a ***demure manner.***

**DENOTATIONS AND CONNOTATIONS**  (1) The **denotations** (or meanings) of a word are the senses that a dictionary describes: the characteristics that a thing—a person, an animal, a plant, or an object; an action, an event, or a quality; a relationship—must have if, by the rules of the language, the word is properly to be applied to it. The noun *father,* for example, in one of its senses, means "male human who has at least one child."

(2) The **connotations** of a word are the things suggested by it or associated with the things to which it applies. These may vary from person to person, from place to place, or from time to time. *Father,* for instance, might have, among its connotations, authority, protectiveness, or sternness. But these connotations are not part of the meaning of *father.* A man may have no authority, protect no one, and be namby-pamby. He is, nevertheless, a father if the word *father,* in one of its senses, properly applies to him.

**depend on, depend upon**  Both are SAWE.

**deprecate, depreciate**  Sometimes confused. *Deprecate* means "criticize, belittle, disparage": *Republicans **deprecated** legislation proposed by Democrats. Depreciate* means "reduce in value, devalue": *The British government **depreciated** the pound sterling.*

**description**  Often a source of wordiness (see **CONCISION**).

NOT THIS:   The stolen car was a green 1992 Toyota Camry. A car of this **description** was found abandoned in a parking lot.

BUT THIS:   The stolen car, a green 1992 Toyota Camry, was found abandoned in a parking lot.

**DESCRIPTIVE AND EVALUATIVE WORDS** A **descriptive word**—often an adjective or an adverb—gives readers information about something: *tall, short; soft, hard; red, black; fragrant, odoriferous; salty, sweet; smooth, rough.* An **evaluative word** gives readers information about how the speaker or writer evaluates or feels about something: *good, bad; beautiful, ugly; superb, despicable.* What's more, an evaluative word, especially when evidence or a good argument supports it, can affect readers in the way the person or thing affects the writer. There can be a chain of cause and effect:

person or thing → writer → evaluative word → readers

The distinction between descriptive and evaluative words is not without complications. First of all, a given word may have both a descriptive and an evaluative component: *gloomy,* for example. *A gloomy day* gives readers information about the day (it is certainly not sunny and may well be rainy or cold) and also about how it affects the writer (it's depressing). Second, a given word may have a descriptive use in one context (*a sweet drink*) and an evaluative use in another (*a sweet person*). Third, as *a sweet person* suggests, a given evaluative use of a word may be a figure of speech as well: a sweet person, unlike a sweet drink, does not taste sweet. Fourth, a given descriptive word may be literal in one context (*a blistering burn*) and a figure of speech in another (*a blistering day, a blistering remark*): a blistering burn causes blisters; but a blistering day need not, and a blistering remark cannot.

**Caution:** Beware of evaluative words that began their lives as figures of speech. Figures of speech, like flashlight batteries, lose power with use and eventually die—that is, become literal. An evaluative word that is a dead figure of speech—*fabulous,* for instance, or *fantastic*—has no more power to affect readers than a literal evaluative word like *excellent.* Indeed, because it seems to strive for greater power, it may well have less. If you can think of a fresh figure of speech for evaluation, fine. If you cannot, use a literal evaluative word.

(See **ARGUMENT AND PERSUASION; CLICHÉS; CONTEXTS;** and **FIGURES OF SPEECH.**)

**despite**   See **in despite of.**

**despite the fact that**   Always wordy. (See **CONCISION.**)

NOT THIS:   **Despite the fact that** she is rich. . . .

BUT THIS:   Though she is rich. . . .

**device, devise**   Sometimes confused, because similar in meaning, sound, and spelling. *Device* is a noun; *devise,* a verb: *Shall we **devise** a **device**?*

**dialectal, dialectical**   Sometimes confused. *Dialectal* means "pertaining to a dialect or variety of a language, for example non-SAWE": '*cause is a **dialectal** pronunciation of* because. *Dialectical* means "pertaining to dialectic, the art of reasoning correctly": *Philosophers often study **dialectic.***

**DIALECTS**   Every language has several varieties, or **dialects,** differing from one another in, for example, vocabulary, grammar, or pronunciation. American English and British English, for instance, are dialects of English; and, within American English, one dialect is Black English. (See **BLACK ENGLISH.**)

**dialogue**   Avoid using as a verb.

NOT THIS:   Let's **dialogue** for a while.

BUT THIS:   Let's **talk** for a while.

**DICTIONARIES**   **A dictionary** is an alphabetical list of words with information about each—typically, about its spelling, its pronunciation, its part of speech, its etymology, and its meanings. The

most authoritative and comprehensive English language dictionaries are *The Oxford English Dictionary* (now in a two-volume
compact, but unabridged, edition) and *Webster's Third New International Dictionary of the English Language Unabridged*. But, for
most of your purposes as a writer, any one of the numerous
one-volume English desk dictionaries will do (including some
abridgements of the *Oxford* or the *Webster's*).

**different from, different than**    Both are SAWE. **Caution:** Some
readers object to the use of *different than*.

NOT THIS:    Milton's lifestyle is **different than** mine.

BUT THIS:    Milton's lifestyle is **different from** mine.

Usually, however, there is no objection to use of *different than*
before a clause when use of it makes the sentence less wordy.

WORDY:    People are **different from** what they used to be.

LESS WORDY:    People are **different than** they used to be.

**differential**    Prefer *difference*.

NOT THIS:    the **differential** between success and failure.

BUT THIS:    the **difference** between success and failure.

**differently abled**    A euphemism for *disabled* (see **EUPHE-
MISMS**). Many people who are disabled are weary of euphemisms, find them demeaning, and much prefer to be called
*disabled* or *handicapped*.

**differ from, differ with**    Sometimes    confused.    *Differ    from*
means "be unlike": *The sisters differ from each other in temperament. Differ with* means "disagree with": *The sisters differ with
each other about politics.*

**DIRECT OBJECTS**   One of the twelve functions that a part of speech—in this case, a noun, a pronoun, or a noun phrase—can perform in a clause.

The **direct object** (DO) of a clause is usually immediately to the right either of the verb (V) (always transitive) or of the indirect objective (IO) if there is one:

V      DO
kissed Ann

V      IO      DO
gave Ann a present

**disassemble, dissemble**   Sometimes confused. *Disassemble* means "take apart": *He disassembled the bicycle. Dissemble* means "conceal feelings, intentions, thoughts, or motives:" *Embarrassed by the revelation, he dissembled.*

**disassociate, dissociate**   Prefer the shorter, *dissociate.*

**discomfit, discomfort**   Sometimes confused. Though related in meaning, the two words are not synonymous. *Discomfit* means "distress, disturb, upset": *The pink slip with Harry's check discomfited him. Discomfort* means "make uncomfortable": *The broken armchair discomforted Harry.*

**DISCOURSE: DIRECT AND INDIRECT**   Direct discourse is quotation of what a speaker or writer said, the actual words in the actual order:

Sanderson asked, "Shall I go to Atlanta next week?"

**Indirect discourse** is paraphrase:

Sanderson asked whether he should go to Atlanta next week.

(See **PARAPHRASE** and **PARAPHRASE VS. QUOTATION.**)

**discover, invent** Sometimes confused. To *discover* is to find something that exists but has been unknown: *discover the Sandwich Islands, discover the cause of congestive heart failure.* To *invent* is to bring something into existence: *invent a laser death ray.*

**discreet, discrete** Sometimes confused, because identical in sound and similar in spelling. To be *discreet* is to be cautious and tactful and to know when to keep your mouth shut: *The ideal secretary is discreet.* To be *discrete* is to be separate or distinct: *Atoms, like gum balls, are discrete.*

**disinterested, uninterested** Both SAWE for either (a) *impartial* or (b) *indifferent* or *bored.*
 (1) **Caution:** Because both words are, therefore, extremely ambiguous, avoid them. Use *impartial* or *indifferent* or *bored* instead, depending upon what you mean.
 (2) **Caution:** Some readers strongly object to the use of *disinterested* for (b).

> NOT THIS:   Judge Horton is **disinterested,** always falling asleep in court.

> BUT THIS:   Judge Horton is **uninterested** (or, better, **indifferent** or **bored**), always falling asleep in court.

**disqualified, unqualified** Sometimes confused. To be *disqualified* is to lose one's eligibility, certificate, or license to perform a certain task, even though qualified to perform it: *disqualified from competition in the tournament.* To be *unqualified* is to lack the knowledge, talent, skill, or training necessary to perform a certain task: *unqualified to practice psychiatry.*

**disremember** Avoid. Though it has been well established for almost two centuries as a synonym for *forget,* some readers find it a bit comic, like a sprig of hay in one's hair.

NOT THIS:    I **disremembered** her birthday.

BUT THIS:    I **forgot** her birthday.

**dissimulate, simulate**  Not antonyms (see **ANTONYMS**). To *dissimulate* is to conceal one's feelings, thoughts, or condition: *Though almost at death's door, Ronald dissimulated.* To *simulate* is to feign or create the effect of: *Though bored, Mary simulated interest.*

**distinct, distinctive**  Sometimes confused. Something is *distinct* if it is already recognizable: *a distinct smell of garlic.* Something is *distinctive* if it has a style, manner, or quality that individualizes it among things of its kind: *Henry James's distinctive sentences; Picasso's distinctive use of blue.*

**dived, dove**  Both are SAWE. **Caution:** Some readers object to *dove.*

**divide up**  Wordy for *divide.* (See **CONCISION.**)

**dollars**  Except on signs, prefer *dollars* to *$*, and never use both.

NOT THIS:    $30,000 dollars.

OR THIS:    $30 thousand dollars.

BUT THIS:    thirty thousand dollars.

OR THIS:    $30,000.

**donate**  Prefer *give.*

NOT THIS:    He **donated** two-hundred dollars to the Community Chest.

BUT THIS:    He **gave** two-hundred dollars to the Community Chest.

**done**  NonSAWE either for *did* or as an adverb meaning "already."

NOT THIS:   At first, readers don't know who **done** it.

BUT THIS:   At first, readers don't know who **did** it.

NOT THIS:   He has **done** decided.

BUT THIS:   He has **already** decided.

**don't**  SAWE with a plural subject or with *you* as subject, non-SAWE with a singular.

NOT THIS:   It **don't** work.

BUT THIS:   It **doesn't** work.

## DOUBLE (or MULTIPLE) NEGATIVES

(1) A **double** (or **multiple**) **negative** consists of more than one negative (*neither, no, none, nohow, nowhere, nor, not, n't, hardly, scarcely, un-*) for a single negation: can't hardly (= can hardly), don't like nobody (= don't like anybody), have no money nohow (= have no money anyhow), scarcely none (= scarcely any). **Note:** The construction *neither . . . nor* is not a double negative, because it is for two negations.

(2) In some dialects (or varieties) of English, double negatives are not only permitted but required. (For an example, see **BLACK ENGLISH.**) SAWE, however, does not permit double negatives.

## DOUBLE SUBJECTS  A double subject—a noun phrase followed by a pronoun that has it as its antecedent—is not permitted in SAWE.

NOT THIS:   **Dr. Rupert, she** is an expert.

BUT THIS:   **Dr. Rupert** is an expert.

(See also **ANTECEDENTS; NOUN PHRASES;** and **PRO-NOUNS.**) **Note:** A double subject is different from a compound subject—*Dr. Rupert and her assistant,* for example—which is quite unobjectionable.

**downsize**  A fashionable term to mean "reduce the size or the scope of": *The commission decided to **downsize** the recreational program.*

**drag**  Both the past tense and the past perfect are *dragged,* never *drug: They **dragged** the lake (or have often **dragged** the lake) for bodies.*

**drama, dramatic**  Except in discussion of plays, avoid these words.

> NOT THIS:    a **dramatic** conclusion to the evening.

> BUT THIS:    a **striking** (or **alarming** or **spectacular** or **memorable**) conclusion to the evening.

**draw a conclusion**  Wordy for *conclude.* (See **CONCISION.**)

**due course**  Prefer a less vague expression (see **VAGUENESS**) such as *by the end of the month, in a few days,* or *within the week.*

**due to**  (1) Use of *due to* to introduce a subject complement is SAWE: *Her fever is **due to** mononucleosis.*
(2) Use of *due to* to introduce a verb or clause modifier is also SAWE. **Caution:** Some readers object to this use.

> NOT THIS:    **Due to** the weather, the meeting was cancelled.

> BUT THIS:    **Because of** the weather, the meeting was cancelled.

**dumb** SAWE only in the sense "unable to speak," not in the sense "ignorant" or "stupid."

**during the course of** Wordy for *during*. (See **CONCISION**.)

NOT THIS: **during the course of** the trial.

BUT THIS: **during** the trial.

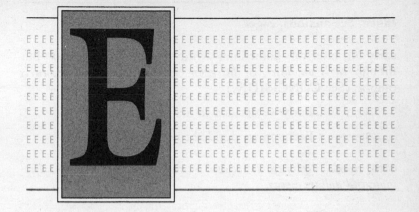

**each** The pronoun *each* is always singular and, when a subject, requires a singular verb: *Each of the dozens of survivors **was** taken care of.* Notice that the plurals between *each* and *was—dozens, survivors—*have no bearing on the number of the verb. (See **AGREEMENT: VERBS WITH SUBJECTS.**)

**each and every** Wordy for *each* or for *every.* (See **CONCISION.**)

NOT THIS: **Each and every** citizen is alarmed.

BUT THIS: **Each** (or **every**) citizen is alarmed.

**each and everyone** Wordy. Choose one: *each* or *everyone.* (See **CONCISION.**)

**each other, one another** Both are SAWE and synonymous.

---

**115**

**eager**  See **anxious, eager.**

**early on, later on**  Sometimes wordy for *early* and *later.* But though *early on, later,* or *later on* can begin a sentence, *early* cannot. (See **CONCISION.**)

> NOT THIS:   **Early** we decided to marry.

> BUT THIS:   **Early on** we decided to marry.

**earn, make**  Prefer *earn,* because more precise: *Wilson earns fifty-thousand dollars a year.*

**easy, easily**  With the exception of such sentences as *Easy does it* and *Take it easy, easy* is an adjective (*an easy task*); *easily,* an adverb (*winning easily*).

**economic, economical**  Sometimes confused. *Economic* means "pertaining to money, wealth, the economy, and so on": *economic conditions. Economical* means "thrifty, unwasteful, and so on": *an economical diet.*

**-ed, -d**  Most past-tense verbs and past participles end in the suffix *-ed* or *-d: asked, laughed, supposed, worried.* Perhaps in conversation you do not always pronounce this suffix. **Caution:** Whether you do or not, you should always spell it out in writing.

> NOT THIS:   Yesterday I ask Don to lunch.

> BUT THIS:   Yesterday I asked Don to lunch.

**EDITING**  The first words that pop into your head are often not the best ones to communicate your meaning. Reread your first draft several times: two or three times to see whether it is clear, forceful, and, if not elegant or graceful, at least fairly smooth; and at least once to check

> spelling and punctuation. How much time you should spend on editing depends upon the importance of what you are writing (a constitution deserves more care than a note on the refrigerator) and upon the time you have to give to it. In any case, the time will come when you must submit it to a teacher—or some other audience. (See **RE-VISION.**)

**edition, issue** Sometimes confused. An *edition* of a periodical is the form it takes for a particular region (*the city edition, the suburban edition*) or a particular audience (*the students' edition*). An *issue* is, for a given edition (when there is more than one), a publication for a certain date or period (*the June 1994 issue, the spring 1995 issue, the 6 April 1993 issue*).

**educationist, educator, teacher** To refer to a teacher, use *teacher. Educationist* and *educator* are vague terms (see **VAGUE-NESS**) used to refer to anyone (including administrators) somehow connected with education; and *educationist* is pejorative, suggesting a preference for form over substance.

**effect** See **affect, effect.**

**effeminate, female, feminine** Sometimes confused. *Effeminate* is used only to refer to males whose appearance or mannerisms resemble those of women. Used of humans, *female* and *feminine* are synonymous as adjectives.

**e.g., i.e.** Often confused. The abbreviation *e.g.* (for Latin *exempli gratia*) means "for example": *Several presidents (e.g., Carter) have been consumer advocates.* The abbreviation *i.e.* (for Latin *id est*) means "that is": *Mark Twain (i.e., Samuel Langhorne Clemens) was a satirist.* Like other Latin abbreviations, *e.g.* and *i.e.* are used chiefly in parenthetical explanations (as in the examples above) and in footnotes, bibliographies, and tables.

**egregious**  Always pejorative, meaning "flagrant" or "outstandingly or outrageously bad": *an egregious error.*

**either . . . nor, neither . . . or**  NonSAWE for *either . . . or* and *neither . . . nor.*

**either . . . or, neither . . . nor**  Two singular subjects joined by *either . . . or* or *neither . . . nor* take a singular verb: *Either adoption or foster care is acceptable.*

**ELEGANT VARIATION  Elegant variation** is variation of words without much variation in meaning or message.

In one kind of elegant variation, words vary, but meaning is more or less constant:

> An informal poll of 238 students showed that 87 percent **advocate** an intramural **fee,** 65 percent **favor** a union **assessment,** 63 percent **support** a parking **charge,** and 38 percent **approve of** a health-service **levy.**

In this context, the words *advocate, favor, support,* and *approve of* have practically the same meaning. And so do the words *fee, assessment, charge,* and *levy.*

In the other, rarer kind of elegant variation, words *and* meaning vary, but what the words refer to is constant:

> **Nebraska** beat **Missouri** Saturday. John O'Leary ran forty yards for a touchdown as **the third-ranked Cornhuskers** stormed to a victory over **the twelfth-ranked Tigers.**

*Nebraska* and *the third-ranked Cornhuskers* are different expressions with different meanings, but both refer to the same team.

The case is similar with *Missouri* and *the twelfth-ranked Tigers*. At best, elegant variation gives readers additional information—that the Nebraska team ranks third, for instance, and Missouri, twelfth. At worst, it suggests a distinction where there is none and therefore confuses readers:

> The test showed that 27 of the 119 men had **high blood pressure** and that 31 of the 123 women had **hypertension.**

Readers with little or no medical expertise may wrongly imagine that *high blood pressure* and *hypertension* refer to different diseases: different words, thus different things.

Between its best and its worst, elegant variation is merely pretentious variety that distracts or annoys many readers:

> Art sharks are surfacing everywhere, **plundering** churches in France, **looting** private collections in England, **ransacking** museums in Spain, **stripping** archaeological sites in Peru.

An often-given defense of elegant variation is avoidance of repetition. But a better—both less affected and less wordy—way of avoiding it is deletion. Choose one word, use it for the first phrase or clause, and then delete it:

> Art sharks are surfacing everywhere, **plundering** churches in France, private collections in England, museums in Spain, and archaeological sites in Peru.

**elicit, illicit**   Often confused. *Elicit* is a verb meaning "draw out" or "evoke": *His comic routine elicited applause. Illicit* is an adjective meaning "illegal": *Sale of beer on Sunday is illicit in some states.*

**ELLIPSES**   Use **ellipses** [ . . . ]:

(1) To indicate (by using three spaced dots) the deletion of one or more words from within a quotation:

He said, "Statistics show that the rate of failure . . . is high."

(2) To indicate (by using four spaced dots) the deletion of one or more sentences from within a quotation or one or more words at the end of a quoted sentence (the last dot represents the period):

"Reflective apologists for war at the present day all take it religiously. . . . Its 'horrors' are a cheap price to pay for rescue from the only alternative supposed. . . ."—William James.

(3) To indicate (by using a line of spaced dots) the deletion of one or more lines of verse:

They hadna been a week from her
. . . . . . . . . . .
 Whan word came to the carline wife
That her three sons were gane.
—"The Wife of Usher's Well"

**elude**   See **allude, elude.**

**emigrate from, immigrate to; emigrant, immigrant**   Often confused. *Emigrate from* means "leave (a country) for permanent residence in another": *Albert Einstein **emigrated from** Nazi Germany in 1934. Immigrate to* means "enter (a country of which one is not a native) for permanent residence": *Albert Einstein **immigrated to** the United States in 1934.* The nouns and adjectives derived from these two verbs are *emigrant* and *immigrant: Einstein was an **emigrant** from Germany and an **immigrant** to the United States.*

**eminent, immanent, imminent**   Often confused. *Eminent* means "outstanding" (*an **eminent** person*); *immanent,* "dwelling within" (*a power **immanent** in everyone*); *imminent,* "threateningly near" (*an **imminent** invasion*).

**empathy, sympathy** Both mean "sharing another's feelings, especially sadness." But *empathy* suggests identification with the other.

**end** Such phrases as *come to an end, end product,* and *end result* are wordy. Prefer *end, product,* and *result,* respectively. (See **CONCISION.**)

**energize, enervate** These antonyms are sometimes confused. *Energizing* gives energy; *enervating* takes it away: *energized by a long sleep; enervated by a long illness.* (See **ANTONYMS.**)

**enjoy** Avoid using without a direct object.

NOT THIS: Enjoy.

BUT THIS: Enjoy your trip.

**enthuse** Now SAWE as either a transitive verb (meaning "cause enthusiasm") or an intransitive verb (meaning "show enthusiasm"). **Caution:** Some readers object to this verb because it is a back-formation (from *enthusiasm*). (See **BACK-FORMATION.**)

NOT THIS: He **enthused** about the dinner.

BUT THIS: He **was enthusiastic** about the dinner.

**enviable, envious** Sometimes confused. *Enviable* means "worthy of envy" (*an **enviable** opportunity for doing good*); *envious* means "having envy" (***envious** of another's success*).

**epic** Avoid except in reference to such works as *The Iliad* and *The Faery Queen* and such events as landing a person on Mars and discovery of a cure for cancer.

NOT THIS: an **epic** football game.

BUT THIS: a **memorable** football game.

**epithet**   A description but usually an unfavorable one: *such epithets as* sponge *and* wastrel.

**equable, equitable**   Sometimes confused. *Equable* means "uniform" or "unvarying" (*an equable temperament*); *equitable*, "fair" (*an equitable distribution of favors*).

**equally as**   Wordy for *equally* or *as*.

> NOT THIS:   Torrential rains are bad, but drought is **equally as** bad.

> BUT THIS:   Torrential rains are bad, but drought is **equally** (or **as**) bad.

**equivocate, prevaricate**   To *prevaricate* is to lie. To *equivocate* is to skirt the truth by using ambiguities, evasions, and half-truths: *He **equivocated** by saying that he was merely affiliated with the Ku Klux Klan*. *Prevaricate* is often confused with *procrastinate* ("delay or put off action").

**erotic, erratic, exotic**   Sometimes confused. *Erotic* means "pertaining to sexual emotion or stimulation": *an **erotic** photograph*. *Erratic* means "irregular" or "unpredictable": *an **erratic** performance*. *Exotic* means "foreign": *an **exotic** perfume*.

**errata**   A list of errors found after a book was set in type. The word is plural in Latin (the singular is *erratum*), but usually construed as singular in English: *the **errata** is long*.

**err, error**   Sometimes confused. *Err* is a verb meaning "do wrong" or "make a mistake": *In calculating the total indebtedness, he **erred***. *Error* is a noun (never a verb) meaning "mistake": *an **error** in arithmetic*.

**especially, specially**   *Especially* means "more than anyone or anything else": *Clear thinking is especially necessary in a crisis.* *Specially* means "for a certain reason or in a certain way": *specially made for use by the handicapped.*

**essential, must**   Sentences such as *It is essential that care must be taken in storing gasoline* are wordy. Delete *must.*

**-ess, -ette, -trix**   (1) Whenever you can, avoid these feminine suffixes (*poetess, farmerette, aviatrix*) and other feminine designations (*lady doctor, postmistress*). Readers find them objectionable because of their sexist and even racist overtones (Why should there be *negress* but not *whitess* or *caucasianess? Jewess* but not *Christianess?*) In some words, however, these feminine suffixes are unavoidable: *actress, baroness.*
   (2) Also avoid neuter designations that are compounds with *-man.* (See **SEXIST LANGUAGE.**)

   NOT THIS:   chair**man,** sales**man.**

   BUT THIS:   chair**person** (or **chair**), sales**person** (or sales**clerk**).

**estimate, estimation**   Sometimes confused. An *estimate* is a prediction about the time or the expense a project will require: *The estimate is that repairs will take two weeks and cost about a thousand dollars.* An *estimation* is an opinion: *In my estimation, he's a good carpenter.*

**et al.**   An abbreviation of a Latin phrase meaning "and others." Used only in notes and bibliographies for works with more than three authors: *J. R. Twimbly et al.*

**etc.**   An abbreviation of *et cetera,* meaning "and other things of the same kind": *Swimming, running, etc., are good exercise.* **Caution:** Though widely used in informal writing, usually replaced by *and so on* or *and so forth* in formal writing. **Caution:** Wordy after *and* (*and* etc.), because *et* means "and." Also wordy after *like* or *such as*.

NOT THIS: People like Stalin, Hitler, **etc.**, are evil.

BUT THIS: People like Stalin and Hitler are evil.

**-ette** See **-ess, -ette, -trix.**

**EUPHEMISMS** A **euphemism** is a substitute for a taboo word or phrase—an expression designating a reality so disagreeable or so humble that use of the expression is discouraged or even forbidden. By replacing the taboo word, a euphemism tries to make that disagreeable or humble reality sound or look good (Greek *euphemos,* "sounding good").

President Marcos of the Philippines replaced *martial law* with *constitutional authoritarianism;* President Regan, *taxes* with *revenue enhancement* and *MX missile* with *Peacemaker.* The Pentagon won the 1977 Doublespeak Award of the National Council of Teachers of English by replacing *neutron bomb* with *radiation enhancement weapon.*

What's to be said for euphemisms? They are sometimes kind—*passed away* for *died,* for instance, in a letter of condolence. And few people can bring themselves to call a paraplegic a *cripple.*

On the whole, however, the purpose of euphemisms is to conceal, not reveal, meaning. In pretending that something is more agreeable or exalted than it is, they are pretentious. They succeed only so long as they conceal this disagreeable or humble reality. As soon as they cease to conceal it, they become taboo and are replaced by new euphemisms. There are no immortal euphemisms.

The word *undertaker,* for example, goes back to the late seventeenth century and was, perhaps, a euphemism then. By the early 1920s, it had become taboo in the United States and was gradually replaced by the euphemism *mortician.* Then *mortician* became taboo and was gradually replaced by the euphemism *funeral direc-*

*tor.* The words *janitor, custodian, superintendent,* and *building manager* have a similar, though briefer, history.

Among the many other euphemisms spawned in recent years are:

| | |
|---|---|
| aggressive merchandising | deceptive advertising |
| attendance teacher | truant officer |
| camisole restraint | straitjacket |
| chemical dependency | drug addiction |
| child-care worker | babysitter |
| controlled substance | drug |
| corrections facility | prison |
| euthanize *or* put to sleep (animals) | kill |
| express a concern | complain |
| extended-care facility | nursing home |
| family-life courses | sex education |
| golden age | old age |
| identifying originating line | tracing a telephone call |
| inaccurate claim | lie |
| incursion | invasion |
| internal-security situation | riot |
| liberate | invade and occupy |
| motion discomfort | nausea |
| nonreader | illiterate |
| personal-confinement facility | solitary-confinement cell |
| premature unauthorized partial disclosure | information leak |
| preowned | used |
| problem-resolution office | complaint department |
| redeployment of troops | retreat |
| reduction in force | layoff |
| revenue enhancement | tax |
| sanitation worker | garbage man |
| scrap-metal recycler | junk dealer |

senior citizen               elderly person
surreptitious entry          burglary
underprivileged              poor
undocumented worker          illegal alien
waste water                  sewage

**evacuate, excavate**  Sometimes confused. *Evacuate* means "empty" or "vacate": *evacuate the premises*. *Excavate* means "dig out": *excavate the ancient pottery*.

**ever so often, every so often**  Sometimes confused. *Ever so often* means "frequently": *Ever so often I go to the movies, almost every night in fact*. *Every so often* means "occasionally": *Every so often I go to the movies, perhaps two or three times a year*.

**every**  See **each and every** and **ever so often, every so often**.

**every one**  See **any one, anyone; every one, everyone; some one, someone**.

**everywheres**  NonSAWE for *everywhere*.

> NOT THIS:   She looked **everywheres**.

> BUT THIS:   She looked **everywhere**.

**evoke, invoke**  Sometimes confused. *Evoke* means "cause": *Her remark evoked laughter*. *Invoke* means "ask for" (*invoke divine guidance*) or "use" (*invoke the government's police powers*).

**exact same**  Wordy (see **CONCISION**) for *exact* or *same*.

> NOT THIS:   his **exact same** words.

> BUT THIS:   his **exact** (or **same**) words.

**EXAMPLES**  An **example** is any one of a class or collection of things—artifacts, events, or people, for instance—that share one or more qualities. To cite one or more examples in an article or essay serves one or both of two purposes. One is clarity (see **CLARITY**), to make clear just what you mean by using a certain expression: *An example of a war criminal is Adolf Hitler.* The other is to provide evidence to support an assertion or an inductive argument: *There are still many good jazz pianists: an example is Ralph Sutton.* (See **INDUCTION AND DEDUCTION.**)

**except**  See **accept, except.**

**exception**  Do not write, *The exception proves the rule.* It is a cliché (see **CLICHÉS**). Moreover, it makes sense only if *prove* is taken (as few take it) to mean "test."

**exceptional**  Originally, *exceptional* meant "unusual": later, "unusually good or well endowed." Now it is sometimes a euphemism for *handicapped* (see **EUPHEMISMS**).

**exceptional, exceptionable**  Sometimes confused. (See **exceptional.**) The meaning of *exceptionable*—"objectionable" ("worthy of being taken exception to")—is so little known that the word should be used with care.

**EXCLAMATION POINTS**  Use an **exclamation point** [!] following an exclamatory word, phrase, or sentence—but use it sparingly for maximum effect:

The audience recalled her—amazing!—for a fifth encore.

What a superb painting!

**exercise, exorcise**  Sometimes confused. To *exercise* is either to engage in vigorous bodily motion or to use (*exercise an option*). To *exorcise* is to get rid of (ghosts or spirits).

**exhausting, exhaustive** Sometimes confused. *Exhausting* means "debilitating": *an exhausting experience*. *Exhaustive* means "thorough" or "complete": *an exhaustive search*.

**exist, subsist** For a human or an animal to *exist* is simply to be alive. What one *subsists* on (or upon) is what one takes in to stay alive: *John subsists on cornflakes*.

**exit** Prefer *leave* to *exit* as a verb because less pretentious.

NOT THIS: Before **exiting** Europe, we go to Rome.

BUT THIS: Before **leaving** Europe, we go to Rome.

**expect** SAWE for *believe, presume, suppose,* or *think*. **Caution:** Some readers object to this use in formal writing.

NOT THIS: The President's word is, I **expect,** to be trusted.

BUT THIS: The President's word is, I **presume** (or **believe** or **suppose** or **think**), to be trusted.

**expedient, expeditious** Sometimes confused. *Expedient* means "motivated by self-interest"; *expeditious,* "acting quickly and efficiently."

NOT THIS: It was **expeditious** for the senator to vote for the bill.

BUT THIS: It was **expedient** for the senator to vote for the bill.

**explain** Avoid substituting for *say* or *feel*.

NOT THIS: Asked by the customs officer for my place of birth, I **explained** that I was born in Manhattan.

BUT THIS: . . . I *said*. . . .

**EXPLETIVE PRONOUNS** Unlike a typical pronoun, an **expletive pronoun** (EP) refers to nothing and therefore has no antecedent. Its sole use is to fill out a sentence or clause (Latin *expletus:* "filled out") by performing a function that the grammatical rules of English require—subject (S) or pseudosubject (PS):

EP = S

It    is raining.

EP = PS

There   are two sexes.

A pseudosubject (the only one is *there*) looks like a real subject, because it precedes the verb—usually some third-person form of *to be* (*is, are, was, were,* and so on). But it is not one. When a sentence or a clause has a pseudosubject, the real subject (*two sexes,* for instance) follows the verb. A pseudosubject is often necessary because the grammatical rules forbid sentences or clauses such as *Two sexes are.*

(See **ANTECEDENTS; FORMS AND FUNCTIONS; GRAMMATICAL RULES; PERSONS; PRONOUNS; SUBJECTS;** and **VERBS.**)

**explicit, implicit** Often confused. *Explicit* means "precisely developed or stated": *The threat was explicit: "Shape up or get out,"* *he said. Implicit* means "implied" or "unstated": *The threat was implicit in his frown.*

**expose oneself** Avoid unless you mean "flash" or "display one's genitals."

NOT THIS:   Cecil **exposed himself** to ridicule.

BUT THIS:   Cecil **subjected himself** to ridicule.

**express, expressed** Sometimes confused. *Express* means "clear" or "definite": *the express policy of the corporation. Expressed* means "stated": *the expressed wish of the deceased.*

**extra-**  Avoid to mean "unusually."

NOT THIS:    **extra**-smooth gin.

BUT THIS:    **unusually** smooth gin.

But use of *extra* to mean "additional" is unobjectionable: *extra care*.

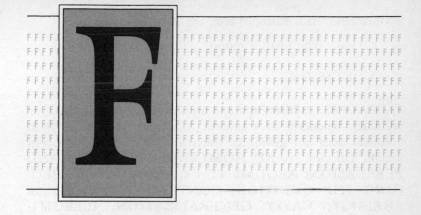

**fabulous** A superlative that, because of excessive use, has lost much of its force. (See **SUPERLATIVES.**)

**facetious, factious, factitious** Sometimes confused. *Facetious* means "not serious": *a facetious comment. Factious* means "divisive," "pertaining to factions": *a factious meeting. Factitious* means "artificial" or "contrived" or "not genuine": *a factitious compliment.*

**facility** Avoid, not only as a euphemism for *toilet,* but as a substitute for such specific terms as *cloakroom, hangar, library, locker room,* and *ramp.* (See **EUPHEMISMS.**)

**fact** Sometimes a source of wordiness.

NOT THIS: The **fact** of the matter is that Columbus discovered America.

BUT THIS: Columbus discovered America.

NOT THIS:   As a matter of **fact,** the Earth is round.

BUT THIS:   The Earth is round.

(See **CONCISION.**)

**FALLACIES** A **fallacy** is a bad argument (or an invalid way of arguing). Whenever an argument is a fallacy, the truth of its premises does not guarantee the truth of its conclusion. For specific fallacies, see **AD HOMINEM; ARGUMENT AND PERSUASION; ARGUMENT BY ASSOCIATION; BEGGING THE QUESTION; CONTRADICTIONS; FALSE ANALOGY; HASTY GENERALIZATION; ILLEGITIMATE AUTHORITY;** and **POST HOC ERGO PROPER HOC.**

**FALSE ANALOGY** An argument by **false analogy** is a fallacy. (See **FALLACIES.**) You commit this fallacy whenever you conclude that, if two things are alike in one way, they are alike in some other ways—*unless* what causes them to be alike in one way causes them to be alike in others. Being identical, for example, causes twins to be alike in a great many other ways—hair color, for instance, and susceptibility to certain diseases. The following is a false analogy:

PREMISES:   (1) Amelda and Mario are both Italian.
                    (2) Amelda is a very fine musician.

CONCLUSION:   Mario is a very fine musician.

This argument is fallacious because it assumes that being Italian causes people to be alike in other ways—in being very fine musicians, for example. Some Italians are very fine musicians, but many Italians are not musicians at all. Whether a certain Italian is a very fine musician depends, not upon being Italian, but upon talent, training, and practice.

**famous, notorious**  Both words mean "widely known." But *notorious,* unlike *famous,* strongly connotes "being unfavorably known."

NOT THIS:    Mother Teresa is **notorious.**

BUT THIS:    Mother Teresa is **famous.**

**farther, further**  Use of *farther* and *further* interchangeably is SAWE. **Exception:** Only *further* is used to mean "moreover": *Further, the market is rising.* **Caution:** Some readers insist that *farther* be used only to mean "more distant" or "at a greater distance" (*They drove three miles farther*) and that *further* be used for all other meanings (*The judge refused to consider the case further*).

**feel**  Avoid using to mean "believe." This use is SAWE, but some readers object to it.

**feel bad, feel badly**  The latter is a hypercorrection of the former, founded in the mistaken belief that the word following the verb *feel* must be an adverb (*badly*), not an adjective (*bad*). But *bad* modifies not the verb, but some noun clear from but not expressed in the context. To feel *bad* is to be in bad health or in a bad mood or to have a bad conscience. To feel *badly* would be to have some disorder of the sensory system—inability to feel hot or cold, for instance. (See **bad, badly** and **HYPERCORRECTION.**)

**female companion, girlfriend, lover, mistress**  Not interchangeable. The most cautious is *female companion,* not being libelous though usually a euphemism for *mistress,* an old-fashioned, rarely used word. *Lover,* applicable to men as well as women, implies a sexual relationship; but *girlfriend,* which is informal and rather sweet, need not. (See **EUPHEMISMS.**)

**fewer, less**    Use of either *fewer* or *less* is SAWE to mean (a) "consisting of a smaller number": *fewer (or less) books, fewer (or less) friends.* And so is use of *less* to mean (b) "more limited in amount": *less sugar, less trouble.* **Caution:** Some readers object to use of *less* to mean (a).

> NOT THIS:    A week after publication **less** than fifty copies of the book had been sold.

> BUT THIS:    A week after publication **fewer** than fifty copies had been sold.

(See also **amount, number.**)

**few in number**    Always wordy for *few.* (See **CONCISION.**)

**FICTION**    (1) Often you cannot tell whether a work is fiction or nonfiction solely by examining its text. The opening words of Daniel Defoe's *The Life and Adventures of Robinson Crusoe,* for example, could well be those of an autobiography: "I was born in the year 1632, in the City of York, of a good family. . . ." If the text does not tell you, you must look to the title page for help (*A Novel, A Play in Three Acts, The Collected Short Stories of . . ., A History of the Chartist Movement, An Essay in Philosophical Analysis, A Treatise on Philately*) or check to see whether proper names (of people and perhaps of places) refer to anything outside the text.

But sometimes the text does tell you. The phrase *once upon a time,* for example, is a sure mark of fiction. And only a work of fiction can be written from the point of view of an omniscient narrator. An example is Edith Wharton's *The House of Mirth:* "Selden paused in surprise. In the afternoon rush of the Grand Central Station his eyes had been refreshed by the sight of Miss Lily Bart." In life itself, Wharton could know what pleases only her own eyes. But in her fiction, she knew anything she wished to know about the mental life of her characters.

(2) Fiction must not be confused with lying or even with false-hood, for it makes no claim to truth. It is unabashedly make-believe: "the poet" as Sir Phillip Sidney put it, "he nothing affirms, and therefore never lieth" (*Apologie for Poetrie*, 1595).

**fictional, fictitious, fictive** Sometimes confused. *Fictional* and *fictive* mean "pertaining to fiction": *Tom Jones is a fictional (or fictive) character. Fictitious* means "nonexistent" (*a fictitious rich uncle*) or "false" (*a fictitious account of the invasion of Panama*). (See **FICTION.**)

**fiction, falsehood, lie** Sometimes confused. A *falsehood* is sim-ply a statement that is untrue, whether or not the speaker or writer knows that it is. A *lie* is a falsehood intended to deceive. (There-fore, the phrase *deliberate lie* is wordy for *lie:* see **CONCISION.**) *Fiction,* far from being false, makes no claim to be true. Fiction cannot lie, because it never refers to anything outside itself, except for an occasional reference to an historical place, event, or person. The opening paragraph of Jane Austen's novel *Emma,* for in-stance, describes its heroine:

> Emma Woodhouse, handsome, clever, and rich, with a comfortable home and happy disposition, seemed to unite some of the best blessings of existence; and had lived nearly twenty-one years in the world with very little to distress or vex her.

But, because Emma does not exist outside the pages of this novel, this description is neither true nor false. No Emma, no falsehoods or lies about her—and no truths either. (See **FICTION.**)

**field** Often a cause of wordiness.

NOT THIS: **the field of** computer programming.

BUT THIS: computer programming.

**figurative, figuratively; literal, literally** Sometimes confused. *Literal* (or *literally*) means "in accordance with the explicit meaning of a word or phrase"; *figurative* (or *figuratively*), "based on figures of speech—not literal." Take care not to use *literally* to mean "figuratively."

> NOT THIS:    Aunt Agatha **literally** killed me. (If true, you could not say it.)

> BUT THIS:    Aunt Agatha **figuratively** killed me.

(See **FIGURES OF SPEECH.**)

**FIGURES OF SPEECH** The traditional definition of **figures of speech** is rather vague: "unusual or nonstandard or ornamental uses of language."

Two sorts of figures are often distinguished: schemes and tropes. In schemes, what is unusual is the sound of the figure or its appearance on a page. Examples are alliteration and rhyme (see **ALLITERATION**). In tropes, what is unusual is the meaning of the figure. Hereafter in this entry, and elsewhere in this book, *figures of speech* refers to tropes.

Perhaps the best way to describe a figure of speech (or trope) is to say that it is a way of saying what you mean by not meaning what you say. (To say what you mean by meaning what you say is to speak or write *literally*.) (See also particular figures of speech: **ANALOGIES; HYPERBOLE; IRONY; METAPHORS AND SIMILES; METONYMY; OXYMORON; PERSONIFICATION; PUNS; RHETORICAL QUESTIONS; SYNECDOCHE; TRANSFERRED EPITHETS;** and **ZEUGMA.**) What you say, for instance, is "Food stamps only nibble at hunger." What you mean by this metaphor is quite different. You don't, of course, mean that food stamps nibble: only people and animals can. Nor do you mean that hunger is nibbled: only something material, like food or flesh, can be. What you mean is that combating hunger with food stamps is, in some ways, comparable to combating it by nibbling it. Like many other figures, a metaphor is a comparison, a statement that two things are alike in some ways. But which ways? Both the beauty and the danger of the metaphor is that it suggests many without specifying any: that, for example, neither the stamps nor the nibbling does much to relieve hunger. Guided by context and knowledge of food stamps, hunger, and nibbling, readers must choose for themselves, and different readers may choose differently. Some readers, moreover, may notice the comparison of hunger—strong desire for food—to food itself and wonder how to interpret it.

One danger, then, of a figure of speech, is that you have little control over how your readers interpret it. Another is that it may be a cliché—a trite, stale, hackneyed figure like *to cap the climax* or *couldn't get to first base*. (See **CLICHÉS**.) Still another danger is that it may be a mixed figure—one that combines unrelated images. A mixed metaphor, for instance, may amuse your readers in a way you don't intend: *Some delegates vainly tried to dilute the plank; We've come into the harbor safely, turned the corner, and seen the light at the end of the tunnel; The council's action fuels a credibility gap, leads to a dead end, and may scuttle the ship.* Indeed, a mixed metaphor can mix clichés as well: *The cat is out the bag in very large doses.*

If a figure of speech catches on, it ceases to be recognized as a figure of speech and thereby enriches the language. A recent example is the metaphor *computer virus,* now so well established in the language that new editions of dictionaries will include it.

**final analysis** The phrase *in the final analysis* is a wordy cliché for *finally, in the end,* and so on. (See **CLICHÉS** and **CONCISION.**)

NOT THIS: **In the final analysis,** we decided to go to Florida.

BUT THIS: **In the end,** we decided to go to Florida.

**finalize** SAWE. **Caution:** Some readers object to it (and many other verbs ending in *-ize:* see *-ize*).

NOT THIS: The company **finalized** plans for the conference.

BUT THIS: The company **completed** plans for the conference.

**fine** Informal and vague as an expression of approval.

NOT THIS: The car runs **fine** now.

BUT THIS: The car runs **well** (or **properly** or **satisfactorily** or **smoothly**) now.

**first and foremost** A wordy cliché for *first* or *foremost.* (See **CLICHÉS** and **CONCISION.**)

**firstly, secondly, and so on** Prefer the shorter adverbs *first, second,* and so on.

**fix** Prefer a more specific verb such as *adjust, mend, overhaul,* or *repair.*

**fixing to** A synonym for *getting set to* or *about to* and often used in conversation in some parts of the United States. **Caution:** Rarely used in writing, formal or informal.

NOT THIS: The concert was **fixing to** end.

BUT THIS: The concert was **about to** end.

**flair, flare** Sometimes confused. *Flair* means "aptitude" or "talent": *a flair for after-dinner speaking. Flare* means "burning light" or "torch": *The flare was visible for miles.*

**flammable, inflammable** Both words mean capable of being ignited easily. *Flammable* was coined to replace (and it has replaced) *inflammable* because some thought the latter to mean "not burnable."

**FLATTERY** If your readers are intelligent, be wary of flattering them. They will recognize it, and their response may well be quite the opposite of pleasure. And be especially wary of flattering people you don't know, as in a mass mailing:

Dear Friend,
    You are among a group of well-informed people to receive the enclosed AIDS PUBLIC PERCEPTION SURVEY.

Even a marginally intelligent reader may think: "You are no friend of mine. Indeed, I've never even heard of you. And you can have no reason to believe that I'm well informed."

**flaunt, flout** Use of either is now SAWF to mean (a) "treat with contempt": *flaunt (or flout) public opinion.* And so is use of *flaunt* to mean (b) "display ostentatiously": *flaunt his loud suits.* **Caution:** Some readers object to use of *flaunt* to mean (a).

NOT THIS:  By setting up smoking lounges, the school encouraged students to **flaunt** the law.

BUT THIS:  By setting up smoking lounges, the school encouraged students to **flout** the law.

**flay** Widely used to mean "strongly criticize," although many readers object to this figurative use of *flay,* which literally means "to skin."

**flounder, founder** Sometimes confused. To *flounder* is what a fish (the flounder, for example) does out of water (move clumsily); figuratively, to be active without accomplishing anything. To *founder* is to sink because full of water: figuratively, to fail (*The corporation foundered*). (See **FIGURES OF SPEECH.**)

**flunk** SAWE for *fail*. **Caution:** Not used in formal writing.

> NOT THIS:   Many good students **flunk** physics.
> BUT THIS:   Many good students **fail** physics.

**focus** The SAWE plural is either *foci* or *focuses*.

**folks** SAWE for *people generally* or for *parents* and often used in conversation and informal writing. **Caution:** Not used in formal writing.

> NOT THIS:   Some **folks** prefer Toyotas to Chevrolets.
> BUT THIS:   Some **people** prefer Toyotas to Chevrolets.
> NOT THIS:   My **folks** are Democrats.
> BUT THIS:   My **parents** are Democrats.

**foot, inch, mile, story** Precede by a numeral (however large) to form a compound adjective; each is plural.

> NOT THIS:   a ten-**miles** hike.
> BUT THIS:   a ten-**mile** hike.

(See **HYPHENS.**)

**for a limited time only** Because true of everything except eternity, a vacuous phrase. Be specific: *during March, throughout September, until Christmas.*

**for all intents and purposes** Wordy for *essentially* or *for most purposes.* The phrase is so nearly vacuous that it sometimes mistakenly appears as *for all intensive purposes*. (See **CONCI-SION**.)

**forced, forceful, forcible**  Sometimes confused. *Forced* means either "caused by something beyond one's control" (*a forced confession*) or "strained" (*a forced laugh*). *Forceful* means "effective" or "strong" (*a forceful plea for mercy*). *Forcible* means "done by physical force" (*a forcible deportation*).

**FOREIGN EXPRESSIONS**  Use a **foreign expression** only if no English expression seems quite right (*Weltschmertz* [roughly, weariness of life], for instance, seems to have no exact English equivalent) and if your readers almost certainly know what it means. Put a foreign word into italics or within double quotation marks unless English has fully taken it over (as it has *à la carte*, for example). Be sure to preserve any diacritics (`, ´, ~, and the like) that the word may have. (See **LATINISMS**.)

**FOREIGN EXPRESSIONS AND WORDINESS**  Use of a foreign expression may lead to wordiness (see **CONCISION**).

NOT THIS:  chile con carne with meat.

BUT THIS:  chile con carne. (In Spanish, *carne* means "meat.")

NOT THIS:  Rio Grande river.

BUT THIS:  Rio Grande. (In Spanish, *rio* means "river.")

**foreword, forward**  Sometimes confused. *Forward* is an antonym (see **ANTONYMS**) of backward: *looking forward, forward march*. A *foreword* is a part of the front matter of some books, much like a preface or an introduction.

**for free**  Wordy for *free*. (See **CONCISION**.)

NOT THIS:  The second serving was **for free**.

BUT THIS:  The second serving was **free**.

**former, latter**   In formal writing, *former* refers to the first of two things mentioned; *latter,* to the second: *Sir John Rhys believes that there were two King Arthurs, a mythical and a historic; but, though he says much about the **former**, he says little about the **latter**.* When three or more things have been mentioned, use *first* and *last,* not *former* and *latter: For spring break, I can go to Florida, go home, or stay at school and study. The **first** is too expensive; the **last**, too dreary.* (See also **later, latter.**)

**FORMS AND FUNCTIONS**   Much neglected, often blurred, rarely made explicit, the distinction between forms (or parts of speech) and functions is basic to grammar. What's the distinction? Forms or parts of speech are like *actors* in a play. But functions are like the *roles* that actors play.

One actor may perform several roles: the role of Hamlet in one play but the role of MacBeth in another. Similarly, one form or part of speech may perform several functions: the function of the subject in one sentence but the function of direct object in another.

And one role may be performed by several actors: the role of Hamlet performed by John Gielgud in one production but by Laurence Olivier in another. Similarly, one function may be performed by several forms or parts of speech: the function of subject performed by a noun in one sentence but by a pronoun in another.

Consider, for instance, the parts of speech noun and pronoun and the functions subject and direct object.

In sentence (1), the noun *Fido* performs the function of the subject; the pronoun *you,* the function of direct object:

|  |  |
|---|---|
| **Form: Noun** | **Form: Pronoun** |
| **Function: Subject** | **Function: Direct Object** |
| (1) Fido          bit | you. |

In sentence (2), however, the pronoun *you* performs the function of subject; the noun *Fido*, the function of direct object:

> **Form: Pronoun**    **Form: Noun**
> **Function: Subject**    **Function: Direct Object**
> (2) You            bit   Fido.

Difference in function, then, marks a vast difference in meaning. In sentences (1) and (2), it marks the difference between the biter (referred to by the subject) and the bitten (referred to by the direct object).

In English, there are eight traditional parts of speech: noun and pronoun (the chief nominals), verb, adjective, adverb, preposition, conjunction, and interjection. Parts of speech also include one nontraditional part of speech (pro-verb) and phrases and clauses of various kinds—adverb phrase, noun clause, for example.

Parts of speech perform twelve functions (though not every part of speech can perform every function): subject, predicate, verb (both a part of speech and a function), direct object, indirect object, subject complement, object complement, modifier, object of preposition, head, appositive, coordinator, and subordinator.

(See entries for individual parts of speech and for individual functions.)

**for the purpose of** Wordy for *due to* (*The delay was **due to** a tire-change*), *for* (*The stop was **for** lunch*), or *to* (*We stepped out **to** see the sunset*).

**for the reason that** Wordy for *because: We lay down **because** we were tired.*

**for . . . to**  Sentences such as *He asked for to go home* are non-SAWE. Delete *for: He asked to go home.*

**fortuitous, fortunate**  Sometimes confused. *Fortuitous* means "unexpected": *a fortuitous refund from the IRS. Fortunate* means "bringing good fortune": *a fortunate coincidence.*

**frankly**  Avoid. If used (as almost always it is) to introduce a derogatory statement, it is a source of wordiness.

NOT THIS:   **Frankly,** I distrust politicians.

BUT THIS:   I distrust politicians.

**free**  See **for free.**

**free gift**  Wordy for *gift.* All gifts are, by definition, free. (See **CONCISION.**)

**-ful**  The plural of words such as *cupful* and *spoonful* is *-fuls: cupfuls, spoonfuls.*

**fulsome**  Best avoided. Its usual current meaning is "disgusting" or "obnoxious" (*fulsome praise*); but it once also meant "abundant" or "very full" (*fulsome specifications*), and your readers may not know which meaning you intend.

**fun**  Prefer *enjoyable* or *entertaining* as an adjective, because some readers object to this use of *fun.*

NOT THIS:   a **fun** time.

BUT THIS:   an **enjoyable** time.

**FUNCTIONAL SHIFTS**  A **functional shift** is a shift of a word from one part of speech to another—from verb to noun (*run* to *a run*), for example, or from noun to verb (*blacklist* to *black-*

*lists*). Functional shift is a traditional, quite acceptable means of language change.

**funny** In the sense "odd" or "peculiar" SAWE but informal.

**further** See **farther, further.**

**future plans** Wordy. All plans are, by definition, for the future. (See **CONCISION.**)

**gambit** This metaphor, from chess, is a cliché in the sense "beginning" or "opening."

> NOT THIS:  His conversational **gambit** was, "Haven't we met before?"

> BUT THIS:  His conversational **opening** was, "Haven't we met before?

**-gate** On the model of *Watergate,* this has become an overworked suffix meaning "scandal": *Iran-Contra-gate.*

**gay** Now SAWE for "homosexual," especially "male homosexual": *gay rights.* A popular song from the thirties with the lyrics "I might act bold, / I might act gay, / it's just a pose, / I'm not that way" no longer carries quite the same meaning.

**gender**   A rather recent replacement for *sex* in the sense "male or female": *whatever the gender of the questioner*. Also an unrelated grammatical term: in Spanish, for example, *el* ("the") is masculine; *la* ("the"), feminine.

**generally always**   Prefer *almost always*, because this is a contradiction (see **CONTRADICTIONS**).

**general public**   Wordy for *public* (see **CONCISION**.)

**generate**   Except in technical concepts (*generate electricity*), prefer more familiar words like *make* and *create*.

> NOT THIS:   **generate** cars.
>
> BUT THIS:   **make** cars.
>
> NOT THIS:   **generate** ideas.
>
> BUT THIS:   **create** (or **think up**) ideas.

**GENRE CONVENTIONS**   A set of **genre conventions** defines a genre or kind of discourse—legal discourse, for example, or medical. Chiefly, it includes definitions of the specialized or technical terms of the genre: in legal discourse, for instance, *replevin* and *tort*; in medical, *lesion* and *elevated* (for *high*, as in *elevated blood pressure*). A set of genre conventions may also prescribe how to interpret works in the genre. The genre conventions of Elizabethan drama, for instance, prescribe that audiences or readers interpret a soliloquy (Hamlet's "To be or not to be . . .") not as a character's speaking to himself or herself, but as a device for economically revealing what the character cannot plausibly reveal to other characters: motives, intentions, and plans.

**genteel**   Often a word of praise. **Caution**: Another meaning is "affectedly well-bred" or "ostentatiously refined."

**GERUNDS**    A **gerund** is a verbal combining the characteristics of a verb with those of a noun. Like a verb in the progressive tense, it ends in *-ing*. Like a noun, it can perform any of the twelve noun functions. An example is *running*:

> **Running** [subject] is a pleasure.
> I like *running* [direct object].

(See **NOUNS; VERBS;** and **VERBALS**.)

**get, got, gotten**    (1) Both *got* and *gotten* are SAWE as past participles of *get* (though *got* is usually preferred): *I have* **got** (or **gotten**) a loan.

(2) **Caution:** Use of *get* for *has/have got* is nonSAWE.

> NOT THIS:    I **got** to work with these people.

> BUT THIS:    I **have got** (or **have**) to work with these people.

(3) **Caution:** Use of *has/have got* is often wordy.

> NOT THIS:    I have **got no** money.

> BUT THIS:    I **have** no money.

(4) **Caution:** In formal writing, avoid such informal or slang expressions as *get cracking, get lost, get there* ("be successful"), *gets to me* ("makes me upset"), and *get with it*. But many expressions using *get* are quite unobjectionable: *get after, get ahead, get away with*, and *get wind of*.

**gift**    Not a verb in SAWE.

> NOT THIS:    He **gifted** her a necklace.

> BUT THIS:    He **gave** her a necklace.

**gimmick**    SAWE but informal: *That shop comes up with a new gimmick every week.*

**girls**  See **boys, girls**.

**given**  SAWE to introduce an agreed-upon fact or plan: *Given that we mortgage the house.*

**GOBBLEDYGOOK  Gobbledygook** is wordy jargon often unintelligible even to experts in the relevant field. (See **CONCISION** and **EUPHEMISMS**.) Here is an example from sociology:

> In the emphasis on diversity, the notion of a hegemonic sexual discourse is deconstructed, even among those who claim to have one. . . . Exploration of sexuality within feminism is attentive to the postmodern concern with the multiplying mutations of self.

From literary criticism:

> The relationship between the otherless self and the selfless other is ineffable.

From government:

> The economic development goals assessment process impacts the entire community, both in terms of infrastructure and in terms of people, especially people living in poverty situations.

From education:

> Our school's cross-graded, multi-ethnic, individualized learning program is designed to enhance the concept of an open-ended learning program with emphasis on a continuum of multi-ethnic, academically enriched learning using the identified intellectually gifted child as agent or director of his own learning. Major emphasis is on cross-graded, multi-ethnic learning with the main objective being to learn respect for the uniqueness of a person.

**God**  SAWE generally follows the Bible in referring to God as male and capitalizes pronouns with *God* as antecedent (see **ANTECEDENTS**): *He, Him, His.*

**good**  *Good* to mean "very" is SAWE but informal in such expressions as *a good many exceptions* and *a good long time.*

**good and**  Not used in formal writing for *very.*

> NOT THIS:  Harriet was **good and** angry.

> BUT THIS:  Harriet was **very** (or **extremely**) angry.

**good and ready**  Wordy for *ready.* (See **CONCISION**.)

**good, well**  (1) Synonymous as adverbs, but almost all readers object to this use of *good*, especially in formal writing.

> NOT THIS:  You draw **good**.

> BUT THIS:  You draw **well**.

(2) *Well* is nonSAWE as an adjective meaning "good."

> NOT THIS:  Your new dress looks **well**.

> BUT THIS:  Your new dress looks **good**.

See also **bad, badly.**

**got**  See **get, got, gotten.**

**gotten**  See **get, got, gotten**

**graduated**  Prefer *graduated from* or *was graduated from* (*college, high school*) to *graduated* (*college, high school*).

**graffiti**   Always plural. (The singular, rarely used, is *graffito*.)

NOT THIS:   A **graffiti** on the wall.

BUT THIS:   Some **graffiti** (or **several graffiti**) on the wall.

**GRAMMAR**   See **GRAMMATICAL RULES**.

---

**GRAMMATICAL RULES**   Just as the rules of Monopoly guide your moves, and traffic rules guide your driving, **grammatical rules** guide your speaking, writing, and interpreting. In speaking or writing English, for example, you are guided by the grammatical rule that an attributive adjective (an adjective joined directly, without a pause or punctuation, to the noun it modifies) may come only before the noun. So guided, you say *the sad boy*, not *the boy sad*. This is a rule governing syntax (word order). (See **SYNTAX**.)

Like all other rules, grammatical rules are arbitrary: they are products of human decisions to behave in certain ways under certain circumstances—for instance, to put an adjective before a noun when it is attributive. Unlike the rules of most games, and unlike traffic rules, grammatical rules are almost always products of unconscious decisions, and who made them is unknown. (For some exceptions, see **SEXIST LANGUAGE**.) In the sixteenth century, for example, speakers of English—gradually, one by one, and doubtless unconsciously—decided to stop pronouncing *b* at the ends of certain words. They retained the *b* in spelling (*bomb, crumb, dumb, lamb, limb, thumb*) but not in pronunciation. In other words, they gradually and unconsciously created a new grammatical rule: the sound *b* may not end a word when the sound preceding it is *m*.

The great number of languages—in the thousands—and their great diversity testify to the arbitrariness of grammatical rules. The grammatical rule of English that causes speakers of English to say *the bad boy* is the product of one human decision. The corresponding grammatical rule of Spanish that causes speakers of Spanish to say *el muchacho triste* (the sad boy) is the product of a different human decision. The two rules are equally arbitrary: either could have been different from what it is.

Grammatical rules must not be confused with formulations of them—that is, sentences describing them. These rules are implicit in speaking and writing; they exist only in the minds of speakers and writers. But very few speakers and writers can formulate them. Indeed, only a fraction of this vast number of rules has even been written down by anyone.

Taken together, the grammatical rules of a language, like the rules of Monopoly, constitute a definition. If there were no rules of Monopoly, you could not play Monopoly. No rules, no game. Monopoly *is* its rules. Similarly, if there were no grammatical rules of English, you could not speak, write, or interpret English. English *is* its grammatical rules—in the broad sense of *grammatical* that includes not only rules for combining words into sentences but also (among many others) rules for pronouncing and spelling them.

Like other rules, grammatical rules can, as we have seen, change. The grammatical rules of English—and therefore the definition of English—changed when, about four-hundred years ago, speakers of English decided to stop pronouncing the sound *b* at the end of certain words. And they have begun to change again as many speakers prefer using *their* or *his or her* to *he, him,* or *his* as generic pronouns. Consequently, they no longer say *Every president has his cronies*; they say *Every president has their* [or *his or her*] cronies. (See **SEXIST LANGUAGE** [4].)

**grand, great** Unless something has grandeur (like the grand staircase at Blenheim) or greatness (Peter the Great), use a less enthusiastic (and more specific) adjective to describe it: *a memorable evening, a pleasant occasion.*

**grateful, gratuitous** Sometimes confused. *Grateful* means "feeling gratitude": *I am grateful for your patience. Gratuitous* means "free," "unwanted," or "unjustified": *a gratuitous insult.*

**grisly, grizzly, grizzled** Sometimes confused. *Grisly* means "gruesome" or "horrible": *a grisly experience in a dungeon. Grizzly* and *grizzled* mean "grayish": *grizzly* (or *grizzled*) *hair.*

**guess** SAWE but informal to mean "believe," "estimate," or "suppose."

**guesstimate** Avoid this blend of *guess* and *estimate.* Its day has come and gone.

**guts** SAWE but informal to mean "courage." Prefer *courage*—but never the humorous euphemism *intestinal fortitude* (see **EUPHEMISMS**).

**guy** Synonymous for *man* or *person* and often used this way in conversation. **Caution:** Rarely used this way in any writing, formal or informal.

NOT THIS:  These **guys** claimed to be inspectors.

BUT THIS:  These **men** claimed to be inspectors.

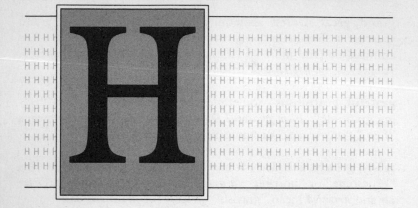

**had** (1) SAWE in such sentences as *I had my car stolen,* even though they may suggest that the speaker arranged for what happened.

(2) The expressions *had better* ("ought to"), *had rather* ("prefer"), and *would rather* ("prefer") are SAWE. (But see **had ought, hadn't ought.**)

**had have, had of** NonSAWE for *had.* (See also **of.**)

NOT THIS:   If only I **had have** (or **had of**) done that, she thought.

BUT THIS:   If I only **had** done that, she thought.

**had ought, hadn't ought** NonSAWE and wordy for *ought* and *ought not.*

NOT THIS:  You **had ought** to write more often.

BUT THIS:  You **ought** to write more often.

**haggle**  SAWE but informal to mean "bargain" or "negotiate (a price)."

**hail, hale**  Sometimes confused. *Hail* means "signal" (*hail a cab*) or (rather old-fashioned) "come" (*Where do you hail from?*). *Hale* means "well"—chiefly in the cliché (see **CLICHÉS**) *hale and hearty*.

**half**  Write either *a half* (*a half hour*) or *half a* (or *an*) (*half an hour*), but never *a half an* (or *a*) (*a half an hour*).

**hang**  In formal writing, avoid such informal or slang expressions as *hang one on*, *hang out*, *hangover*, and *hang-up*.

NOT THIS:  Morton **hangs out** at the YMCA.

BUT THIS:  Morton **lives** (or **spends much time at**) the YMCA.

But many expressions using *hang* are quite unobjectionable: *hang fire, hang on to, hang together*.

**hanged, hung**  *Hung* is nonSAWE for *suspended by the neck until dead*.

NOT THIS:  Those found guilty of high treason were condemned to be **hung**.

BUT THIS:  Those found guilty of high treason were condemned to be **hanged**.

**happen**  An expression such as *I happen to believe in capital punishment*, often used in conversation, is best avoided in writing.

It may suggest that you got the belief in the way you catch a cold—involuntarily. Write *I believe*. . . .

**hardly**   See **but, hardly, scarcely.**

**hard put to it**   SAWE in such sentences as *I am **hard put to it*** [that is, find it difficult] *to say what the cause is.*

**hardy, hearty**   Sometimes confused. *Hardy* means "long lasting," "able to endure adverse conditions": ***hardy** plants. Hearty* means "warm," "friendly": *a **hearty** handshake.*

**HASTY GENERALIZATION**   An argument by **hasty generalization** is a fallacy. (See **FALLACIES**.) You commit this fallacy whenever you hastily conclude that what is true of an *un*representative sample of a group of people or things is probably true of the whole group. To the extent that a sample falls short of being random, it is unrepresentative. A random sample is a sample selected purely by chance. Every person or thing in the group has as good a chance as any other of being in the sample:

PREMISES:   (1)  My guitar teacher is an alcoholic.
(2)  My cousin Milo's guitar teacher is an alcoholic.

CONCLUSION:   All (or most) guitar teachers are probably alcoholics.

It *could* be that all (or most) guitar teachers are alcoholics. But this argument gives no reason to think so. The sample is unrepresentative. It is too small (only two guitar teachers out of many thousands), and the only guitar teachers who had a chance of being in the sample are the two the arguer happened to know. Perhaps these two are the only alcoholic guitar teachers in the world.

**have**  Often pronounced like *of* after auxiliary verbs: *could*, *may*, *might*, *should*, *will*, *would*, and so on. **Caution:** *Of* is never an acceptable spelling of *have*.

NOT THIS:    He should **of** waited.

BUT THIS:    He should **have** waited.

**have done**  Though much used in Great Britain in response to did-you questions (*I might have done*), little used in SAWE, which prefers *have* alone.

**have reference to**  Usually wordy for *refer* (see **CONCISION**).

**HEAD**  One of the twelve functions that a part of speech—in this case, a noun—can perform in a clause. (See **FORMS AND FUNCTIONS**.)
 The **head** of a noun phrase is the noun modified, directly or indirectly, by all other words in the noun phrase; and, when the noun phrase is the subject of the clause, the head is the word with which the verb must agree in number:

| SUBJECT | PREDICATE |
|---|---|
| HEAD | VERB |
| The first of the three factors | is . . . |

**headquarter**  Prefer the verb phrase *has* (or *have*) *headquarters*.

NOT THIS:    The corporation **headquarters** in Miami.

BUT THIS:    The corporation **has headquarters** in Miami.

**head up**  Wordy for *head* in the sense that *head*, the noun, means "chief officer."

NOT THIS:    Dr. Smith **heads up** the committee.

BUT THIS:    Dr. Smith **heads** the committee.

**healthful, healthy**   Sometimes confused. *Healthful* means "good for one's health": *Carrots are healthful*. *Healthy* means "in good health": *a healthy woman*. *Healthy*, however, also means, in the appropriate context, "good for one's health": *a healthy respect for cobras*.

**heart-rendering**   Sometimes mistaken to mean "heart-rending." However, the human heart, unlike lard, cannot be rendered.

**HEDGES: SINGLE AND DOUBLE**   To **hedge** a statement is to indicate uncertainty about its truth: *Perhaps he is guilty; He may be guilty; He is, I think, guilty; I suspect that he is guilty*. To **double-hedge** is do this twice: *He may, I think, be guilty; I suspect that he might be guilty*. Some other hedging expressions are *apparently, conceivably, evidently, maybe, possibly, probably, in a sense, it is suggested that, it may be that, it seems that, there is reason to believe that*. Single hedges occur frequently and usually justifiably. If you are uncertain about the truth of a statement, it is only fair to your readers to say so. But double hedges—used with increasing frequency—are both wordy and namby-pamby. They suggest weak commitment to, and inspire little confidence in, your statements.

**help**   In the sense "avoid" (*I cannot help doing such and such*), prefer *avoid* or *refrain from* (*I cannot avoid doing such and such*).

**highfalutin**   SAWE but informal meaning "pretentious."

**highlight**   SAWE as both noun and verb.

**him, his; me, my; them, their; you, your**   An expression such as *him working* and one such as *his working* are both SAWE. **Caution**: Some readers object to the former on logical or semantic grounds: the reference is not to *him* (who happens to be working) but to (his) *working*. (See **CASES**.)

NOT THIS:     Father doesn't approve of **me living** alone.

BUT THIS:     Father doesn't approve of **my living** alone.

**hisself**   NonSAWE for *himself.*

**HISTORICAL PRESENT**   The present tense used to describe a past event: *Mondrian paints geometrically.* **Caution:** If you use the historical present, avoid unnecessary shifts between present and past tense. (See **SHIFTS**.)

NOT THIS:     Mondrian **paints** geometrically and **created** strong images.

BUT THIS:     Mondrian **paints** geometrically and **creates** strong images.

**historic, historical**   Both are SAWE to mean "pertaining to history." **Caution:** Some readers object to use of *historic* in this sense, preferring it to be used only to mean "famous in history."

NOT THIS:     The **historic** explanation is. . . .

BUT THIS:     The **historical** explanation is. . . .

**hokey**   SAWE but informal to mean "obviously contrived."

**home, house**   Use of *home* and *house* interchangeably is SAWE. **Caution:** Some readers object to the use of *home* for "building used as a residence."

NOT THIS:     Old **homes** are expensive to repair.

BUT THIS:     Old **houses** are expensive to repair.

**home in on, hone in on**   *Hone in on* is sometimes mistakenly used for *home in on*. To *home in on* is to move toward some source of radiating energy: *They **homed in on** the signal tower.* Though *hone* means something ("sharpen"), *hone in on* is meaningless.

**hooked, hooked on**    Slang when used to mean "entrapped" (*Once you've read the first page, you're **hooked***) or "addicted (to)."

> NOT THIS:    Joe is **hooked** on marijuana.

> BUT THIS:    Joe is **addicted to** marijuana.

**hopefully**    Use of *hopefully* is SAWE to mean either (a) "with hope" (*Harold waited **hopefully** for the telephone to ring*) or (b) "it is hoped" or "I hope" (***Hopefully**, Sarah will get the scholarship*). **Caution:** Some readers object to its use to mean (b).

> NOT THIS:    **Hopefully**, good times are coming.

> BUT THIS:    I **hope** (or **it is hoped**) that good times are coming.

**hot-water heater**    Wordy for *water heater*. That is what water heaters do: make water hot. (See **CONCISION**.)

**house**    See **home, house**

**how come**    Synonymous for *why* and often used in this way in conversation. **Caution:** Rarely used in writing, formal or informal.

> NOT THIS:    **How come** the governor pardoned that ax murderer?

> BUT THIS:    **Why** did the governor pardon that ax murderer?

**human**    SAWE as an adjective, but prefer *human being* as the noun, for some readers object to *human* as a noun.

**human, humane**    Sometimes confused. *Human* means "pertaining to human beings": *a very **human** failing.* *Humane* means "kind," "decent," "caring," and the like: *a humane immigration policy.*

**hung**  See **hanged, hung**.

**hurting**  Prefer *being hurt* in such sentences as *The auto industry is hurting.*

**hype**  SAWE but informal as a noun meaning "exaggerated promotional language": *The auto industry uses a great deal of hype to promote vans as family cars.*

**hyper-**  SAWE as a prefix meaning "extremely" or "over": *a hyperactive thyroid.*

**HYPERBOLE**  A figure of speech making an exaggerated statement: *I had a million telephone calls this morning.* (See **FIGURES OF SPEECH**.)

**HYPERCORRECTION**  **Hypercorrection** is unjustified correction of speech or writing. It is unjustified because it corrects it according to a grammatical rule that does not apply. Hypercorrection explains, for example, why some speakers and writers use such incorrect expressions as *between you and I, invited Helen and they, of we students,* and *favored two candidates, Larry and she.* Having been taught that, in formal speech and writing, the rule for subject complements is to use the subjective case (*I, we; he, she, they*), not the objective case (*me, us, him, her, them*), they correct *It is me/us/him/her/them* to *It is I/we/he/she/they.* Unfortunately, by a false analogy, they misapply this rule to objects of prepositions and to direct objects of verbs, correcting (or hypercorrecting) *me* to *I, us* to *we, him* to *he,* and *them* to *they* everywhere. They come to believe that the subjective case is everywhere correct or, at least, that it is more genteel or elegant or high class than the objective case. (For other examples of hypercorrection, see **were** and **who** [whoever], whom [whomever].)

**HYPHENS**    One use of the **hyphen** is to mark the division of a word at the end of a line. The most important use, however, is to separate the parts of some compound words (such as *quasi-historical*) and compound phrases (*old-print, print-dealer*). Because this use promotes clarity—often by eliminating ambiguity—it is reader-friendly. Notice that *an old print dealer* is ambiguous: it means both "a dealer in old prints" and "a print dealer who is old." But notice also how a hyphen can eliminate the ambiguity: *an old-print dealer* means only "a dealer in old prints"; *an old print-dealer* means only "a print dealer who is old." In *an old-print-dealer*, the hyphen shows that *old* modifies *print* and that *old-print* modifies *dealer*. In *an old print-dealer*, the hyphen shows that *print* modifies *dealer* and that *old* modifies *print-dealer*. (See **MODIFIERS AND MODIFICATION.**) Of course, many compound words (*baseball, candlestick*) and phrases (*flying saucer, used car*) require no hyphen.

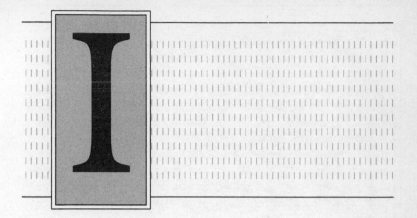

**-ics** (1)Names of academic disciplines, sciences, technologies, and so on ending in *-ics* (*acoustics*, *psychometrics*) are generally singular: *Acoustics is the science of sound.* (2) Other words ending in *-ics* are generally plural: *Plastics are in use all over the world.*

**IDEAL READERS** An **ideal reader** of a piece of writing knows everything necessary to understand it—notably, its language and its genre conventions (the conventions of legal or medical discourse, for example—see GENRE CONVENTIONS) and shares the factual beliefs (in evolution, for example) and the values (that charity is superior to greed, say) that it presupposes. In short, there are no barriers to an ideal reader's understanding and sympathetically considering what the writer has to say.

Perhaps the only ideal readers you will ever have are close friends to whom you write letters. If you write for publication, your readers are likely not only to be unideal but to be unideal in a variety of unpredictable ways. Exceptions are readers of specialized publications—technical, professional, or religious, for instance—whose knowledge and values are well known to you.

To the extent that you know that the readers you are about to address are not ideal, you can try to make them ideal by, for example, using only words you are sure they know or by replacing presuppositions with explicit statements.

**identical to, identical with**    Either preposition is SAWE: *His proposal is almost **identical to** (or **identical with**) mine.*

**identified with**    Prefer a less vague expression. (See **VAGUENESS**.)

NOT THIS:    Wilson is **identified with** the Bland Corporation.

BUT THIS:    Wilson is **employed by** (or is **counsel for** or **lobbies for**) the Bland Corporation.

**ideology**    Now SAWE to refer to any set of beliefs: *the **ideology** of basketball coaches.*

**IDIOMS**    An **idiom** is a phrase—such as *by and large, give up*, or *run short of*—whose meanings is not the sum of the meanings of its parts. The meaning of *by and large*, for example, is not the sum of the meaning of *by* plus the meaning of *and* plus the meaning of *large*. It is as though *by and large* were one word (*byandlarge*) meaning "generally." Some idioms began as figures of speech: *blaze a trail*, for instance ("innovate," "pioneer").

An idiom, then, is indivisible: you cannot divide its meaning into the meanings of its parts. Nor can you divide an idiom into parts and make substitutions. You cannot, say, substitute *or* for *and* in *by and large*: *by or large* is simply not English. Nor are *by and small*, *give down*, *run long of*, and *run short to*.

Ordinarily, idioms give writers little trouble. But, when the last part of an idiom is a preposition, you may not always be sure just what that preposition is. The phrase *compatible with*, for example, is idiomatic, but the phrase *compatible to* is not. Especially troublesome are idioms different from one another only in their prepositions:

agree *about* (Mary's problems)
agree *on/upon* (a strategy)
agree *to* (a suggestion)
agree *with* (Mary about John)

charge *for* (delivery)
charge *to* (an account)
charge *with* (a crime)

concur *in* (a verdict)
concur *with* (a judge)

consist *in* (sticking to your principles)
consist *of* (certain ingredients)

contend *for* (what you believe)
contend *with* (an enemy)

differ *about* or *over* (a method)
differ *from* (something in size)
differ *with* (a person about something)

fight *against* or *with* (a foe)
fight *alongside* or *with* (one's comrades)
fight *for* (a cause)

immune *against* (invasion)
immune *from* (taxation)
immune *to* (measles)

happy *about* or *with* (a possession or situation)
happy *at* (the thought of something)
happy *in* (a job)

impatient *at* (someone's behavior)
impatient *for* (a change)
impatient *of* (rules)
impatient *with* (someone)

occupied *by* (a tenant)
occupied *in* (prayer)
occupied *with* (a detective story)

part *from* (a person or place)
part *in* (the middle)
part *with* (an asset)

rewarded *by* (a general)
rewarded *for* (heroic conduct)
rewarded *with* (a medal)

wait *at* (a bus stop)
wait *for* (a bus or person)
wait *on* (a guest)
wait *out* (a war)

Some other idioms with prepositions:

according *to*
accuse *of*
acquiesce *in* or *to*
angry *with*
antipathy *to*
approach *to*
assent *to*
associate *with*
averse *to*
capable *of*
comparable *to*
complimentary *to*
comply *with*
conform *to* or *with*
criticism *of*
desirous *of*
die *of*
dissent *from*
enamored *of*
in accordance *with*
in consequence *of*
independent *of*
inferior *to*
jealous *of*
oblivious *to*
partake *of*
prior *to*

recipient *of*
reference *to*
rely *on* or *upon*
superior *to*
tolerant *of*

What can you do if you're not sure which preposition to use? If the idiom is not on either of the lists above, check your dictionary. If your dictionary doesn't say, ask a knowledgeable friend. If you're still not sure, don't use an idiom; find another way to express your idea.

   **Caution:** Though *idiomatic* sometimes means "conforming to a particular idiom or to idioms in general," it usually means "grammatical" or "conforming to the grammatical rules of language."

**i.e.**  See **e.g., i.e.**

**if and when**  Wordy for *if* or *when*. (See **CONCISION**.)

**if, if and only if**  The expression *if and only if* sounds a bit legalistic. Often the expression *if* is better, but not always. Consider this statement: *If its market value rises, I'll sell my house.* Your selling your house for some other reason—because you've decided to leave town, say—is quite compatible with this statement. But it is not compatible with *I'll sell my house if and only if its market value rises.*

**if that is true, is the case, and so on**  Wordy  for  *if so*. (See **CONCISION**.)

**if, whether**  Prefer *whether* in sentences such as *I don't know if (whether) she lives in New York.*

**illegal coup**   Wordy for *coup* or *coup d'état*. All coups are, by definition, illegal.

**illegal, illegitimate, illicit, unlawful**   All may mean "against the law," but *illegitimate* tends to be restricted to meaning "born out of wedlock" (*an illegitimate child*) or "unwarranted" (*an illegitimate use of authority*).

**illegible, unreadable**   Sometimes synonymous meaning "incapable of being read because the word cannot made out": *The text was so blurred as to be illegible* (or *unreadable*). More often, unreadable means "so badly composed that one is unwilling to read it": *an unreadable novel.*

**ILLEGITIMATE AUTHORITY**   An argument appealing to **illegitimate authority** is a fallacy. (See **FALLACIES**.) You commit this fallacy whenever you draw a conclusion about a subject from the premise that an illegitimate authority (an authority on some subject but not *that* one) says that the conclusion is true:

PREMISE:   Arnold Weisberg, who plays the lead in the television series *Intensive Care*, says that triple-bypass heart surgery is successful in nine cases out of ten.

CONCLUSION:   Triple-bypass heart surgery is successful in nine cases out of ten.

What Weisberg says about actors or acting might be a premise in a valid argument but not what he says about heart surgery.

**illicit**   See **elicit, illicit**.

**illiterate, unliterate**   Synonymous (though *unliterate* is old-fashioned) to mean either "unable to read or write" or, figuratively (see **FIGURES OF SPEECH**), "unable to write very well."

**ILLOGICAL COMPARISONS**    An **illogical comparison** is illogical because it compares something belonging to one category with something belonging to another:

> The average Bennington teacher makes about $30,000, 20 percent less than other small, prestigious liberal arts colleges. (Teachers and colleges belong to different categories. Write, ". . . 20 percent less than *teachers* at other small, prestigious liberal arts colleges.")

> The Texas death-penalty law differs from the thirty-seven other states that allow the execution of criminals. (Laws and states belong to different categories. Write, " . . . differs from *the laws of* the thirty-seven other states. . . .")

> The occasion [the inauguration of a governor] is a stark contrast to his flamboyant predecessor. (Occasions and governors belong to different categories. Write, ". . . to his flamboyant predecessor*'s inauguration*.")

Though illogical comparisons rarely, if ever, mislead readers, they do constitute sloppy writing.

**ill, sick**    Generally considered synonymous. But some writers think *ill* a bit genteel, while others restrict *sick* to mean "nauseated."

**illusion**    See **allusion, illusion.**

**I, me, my, mine, myself**    In contexts in which first-person pronouns are appropriate, avoid substituting *the author* or *the present writer* or using the passive voice. (See **VOICE**.)

**immanent**    See **eminent, immanent, imminent.**

**immigrant**    See **emigrate from, immigrate to; emigrant, immigrant.**

**immigrate to**  See **emigrate from, immigrate to; emigrant, immigrant.**

**imminent**  See **eminent, immanent, imminent.**

**impact**  The basic meaning of *impact* as a verb is "strike forcefully": *The billiard cue **impacted** the ball.* **Caution**: Avoid using it to mean "affect" or "influence."

> NOT THIS:  This legislation will **impact** the lives of many foster children.

> BUT THIS:  This legislation will **affect** (or **influence**) the lives of many foster children.

**implicit**  See **explicit, implicit.**

**imply, infer**  Both SAWE for *suggest* or *be a logical result of.* **Caution**: Some readers object to this use of *infer.*

> NOT THIS:  Do you mean to **infer** that Jack is a liar?

> BUT THIS:  Do you mean to **imply** that Jack is a liar?

> NOT THIS:  Democracy **infers** a free press.

> BUT THIS:  Democracy **implies** a free press.

No one, however, objects to *infer* to mean "conclude": *From his twitching, I **infer** that Bill is nervous.*

**important, importantly**  *Importantly* is sometimes a hypercorrection of *important.*

> NOT THIS:  More **importantly**, inflation is rampant.

> BUT THIS:  More **important**, inflation is rampant.

The adjective—*important*—is needed here, just as it is in the synonymous *That inflation is rampant is important*. (See **HYPERCORRECTION.**)

**impracticable, impractical**    Sometimes confused. *Impracticable* means "impossible": *It is **impracticable** to mix oil and water.* *Impractical* means "unwise": *an **impractical** business venture.*

**in**    SAWE but informal to mean "fashionable": *the layered look is in*.

**in any manner, way, shape, or form**    Always wordy. (See **CONCISION.**)

> NOT THIS:    Drugs are dangerous **in any manner, way, shape, or form**
>
> BUT THIS:    Drugs are dangerous.

**inappropriate**    Sometimes a euphemism for *illegal* or *immoral*. (See **EUPHEMISMS.**)

> NOT THIS:    Senator Smeech's use of government aircraft for personal travel was **inappropriate**.
>
> BUT THIS:    Senator Smeech's use of government aircraft for personal travel was **illegal**.

**inasmuch as**    Generally wordy for *because*. (See **CONCISION.**)

> NOT THIS:    **Inasmuch as** the price of the average share fell. . . .
>
> BUT THIS:    **Because** the price of the average share fell. . . .

**in back of**    Prefer *behind*.

> NOT THIS:    **in back of** the courthouse
>
> BUT THIS:    **behind** the courthouse

**INCOMPLETE COMPARISONS**  A comparison describes the similarities and differences between at least two things: *X is like Y in respect Z, unlike Y in respect W.* An **incomplete comparison** mentions only one thing: *X is more durable, X is whiter.* But more durable or whiter than what? **Note:** Avoid comparisons, complete or incomplete, that use only evaluative words. (See **DESCRIPTIVE AND EVALUATIVE WORDS.**)

NOT THIS:    X is better (or worse) than Y.

BUT THIS:    X is heavier (or lighter) than (or is twice as heavy as) Y.

**incredible, incredulous**  Often confused. *Incredible* means "unbelievable": *Bob's story about his weekend in Los Angeles is **incredible**. Incredulous* means "unwilling to believe (something)" or "skeptical": *When I heard Bob's story, I was **incredulous**.*

**indefinitely**  Prefer a specific adverb or adverbial phrase: *for a year, until Christmas, forever.*

**INDEFINITE PRONOUNS**  An **indefinite pronoun** (IP) names a number of persons or a number or quantity of things, often an indefinite number or quantity: *all, any, anyone, each, either, enough, everyone, few, many, most, nobody, none, one, several, some, someone,* and so on. An indefinite pronoun may have an antecedent, but usually it does not. (See **ANTECEDENTS** and **PRONOUNS.**)

**Caution:** In speech and in informal writing, *it, you,* and *they* are often used as indefinite pronouns. In formal writing, however, they are not:

INFORMAL WRITING:
IP                                    IP
It says in the instructions that you may use a pliers.

FORMAL WRITING:              IP
The instructions say that one may use a pliers.

INFORMAL WRITING:
  IP
They say that hard work never hurt anyone.

FORMAL WRITING:
  IP
Everyone says that hard work never hurt anyone.

**in despite of**   NonSAWE for *despite* or *in spite of*. Its origin is in
a confusion between *despite* and *in spite of*.

> NOT THIS:   **In despite of** storm warnings, Jim took out the
> canoe.

> BUT THIS:   **Despite** (or **in spite of**) storm warnings, Jim
> took out the canoe.

**Indian**   See **Native American**.

**INDIRECT OBJECTS**   See **DIRECT OBJECTS**.

**individual**   Use this noun only to emphasize that one person is
contrasted with many: *Generally, the crowd was orderly, but one
individual threw a rock.* Do not use *individual* as a synonym for
*person*.

> NOT THIS:   Several **individuals** called for a recount.

> BUT THIS:   Several **persons** (**people, members, delegates**)
> called for a recount.

**INDUCTION AND DEDUCTION**   **Induction** is inference
from the known to the unknown—from a sample (ideally, a random sample) of things or events of a certain kind to a more or less
probable conclusion about all (or a percentage) of things or events
of that kind. Induction is often called the scientific method. More
familiarly, it is simply learning from experience. (You have noticed
that, every time you have eaten at the Tip Top Cafe, the soup is

greasy. Your conclusion is that the soup there is probably always greasy.)

  **Deduction** is inference from one or more premises, by means of the rules of classical or symbolic logic, to a conclusion guaranteed to be true if the premises are true. For example:

PREMISES:   (1)  All men are mortal.
           (2)  Socrates is a man.

CONCLUSION:   Socrates is mortal.

**Caution**: Unfortunately, the term *deduction* is sometimes used to mean "induction" ("an elementary **deduction**, my dear Watson"). (See **ARGUMENT AND PERSUASION**.)

**ineffable**   If you say that something is ineffable ("incapable of being described"), then say no more about it. Someone has said, "Of the ineffable, one may not eff."

**inept, unapt**   Sometimes confused. *Inept* means "awkward": *an inept dancer. Unapt* means "unlikely" (**unapt** *to accept the challenge*) or "beside the point" (*an* **unapt** *comment*).

**inequity, iniquity**   Sometimes confused. *Inequity* means "inequality or unfairness in treatment": *the* **inequity** *of always awarding custody to the mothers. Iniquity* means "evil" or "evil state or deed": *the* **iniquity** *of genocide.*

**infer**   See **imply, infer.**

**inferior than**   NonSAWE for *inferior to.*

NOT THIS:   Gwen felt **inferior than** her sister.

BUT THIS:   Gwen felt **inferior to** her sister.

See also **superior than.**

**infinite**    Use to describe things that are boundless or without end: the number of numbers, for example (any number, however large, can be made longer by adding any other number to it). Use sparingly as hyperbole: *infinite love, infinite wisdom*. (See **HY-PERBOLE**.)

**INFINITIVE PHRASES**    An **infinitive phrase**—one consist-ing of *to* + verb + object (*to watch a parade*)—can occasionally betray you into saying something you don't mean.

>    NOT THIS:    He survived a long illness **to become the most vicious criminal in the nation.**

>    BUT THIS:    He survived a long illness **and became. . . .**

You don't mean that his purpose in surviving was to become a criminal, just that after the illness he did become one.

**INFINITIVES**    A verb form that functions as a noun and, in English, is usually introduced by *to* (the sign of the infinitive): *I like to eat; To eat is a pleasure.*
   A split infinitive is an infinitive split by an adverb: *to gladly teach.* Though split infinitives are, unless awkward, harmless, some read-ers object to them, and they are best avoided.

**informant, informer**    Almost but not quite synonymous. An *in-formant* is anyone who gives information, in a Gallup poll, for example. An *informer* is an informant who gives information to the police: a stool pigeon (slang).

**INFORMATION**    All nonfiction claims to give **information:** to make true statements. How much information you should give your readers depends upon what they know and don't know about your subject. If you tell them what they already know, you risk insulting them. If, on the other hand, you don't tell them what they don't know, you will certainly puzzle or frustrate them. The moral is that the more you know about what your readers know, the better you can decide what to tell them. If in doubt whether to tell your readers something, tell them—shielding yourself against their possible resentment with such expressions as *of course* and *as you may know*.

**ingenious, ingenuous**   Often confused. *Ingenious* means "inventive" or "clever": *Sarah is always **ingenious** in finding her way out of difficult situations; The MX is an **ingenious** missile. Ingenuous* means "artless," "candid," or "unable to hide one's feelings or thoughts": *The **ingenuous** manner of the witness inspired confidence.*

**in, into**   (1) Often confused. *In* designates either a location (*lying **in** bed*) or a state (*sitting **in** a trance*). *Into* designates either movement (*went from the hall **into** the room*) or change in state (*lapsed **into** unconsciousness*).

(2) **Caution:** In formal writing, avoid use of *into* to mean "involved in."

NOT THIS:   Bernie is **into** astrology.

BUT THIS:   Bernie is **involved in** (or **greatly interested in**) astrology.

**in my opinion, to me**   Usually a source of wordiness (see **CONCISION**). The expression *in my opinion* or *to me* is usually unnecessary. If you say, *Lying is wrong*, your reader need not be told that you are expressing your opinion of lying.

**in number**   *Few in number, two in number*, and the like are always wordy. Things cannot be few or two or three in any way other than in number. (See **CONCISION**.)

**innumerable, numerous** Sometimes confused. *Numerous* means "many": *numerous solicitations. Innumerable* means "too numerous to be counted": *innumerable microbes.*

**in place** This phrase has largely replaced *in effect* in some contexts: *The new computer program is in place.*

**inside of, outside of** Wordy for *inside* and *outside.*

NOT THIS:   He looked **inside of** the envelope.

BUT THIS:   He looked **inside** the envelope.

**insoluble, unsolvable** Synonymous for "not able to be solved," though perhaps *insoluble* is the more used.

**in spite of** See **in despite of.**

**instinctive, intuitive** Sometimes confused. *Instinctive* behavior is inborn: blinking and swallowing, for example. *Intuitive* behavior is unreasoned (though not necessarily unreasonable): suspecting that someone is untrustworthy, say, without being able to say why.

**intelligent, intellectual** Sometimes confused. An *intelligent* person is smart, has a high IQ. An *intellectual* person is interested, for instance, in the sciences; in literature, music, painting, and the other arts; and in the philosophies of art, language, mind, and science. A person may be both intelligent and intellectual, but some persons who are one are not necessarily the other.

**INTENSIVE PRONOUNS** An **intensive pronoun** (IP) is an appositive (AP) of its antecedent (ANT) and emphasizes it: *myself, yourself, himself* (not *hisself*), *herself, itself* (not *itsself*), *ourselves, yourselves, themselves* (not *theirselves*):

```
ANT    IP - AP
```
Richard himself told me.

(See **ANTECEDENTS; APPOSITIVES; and PRONOUNS.**)

**in terms of**   Almost always a cause of wordiness.

NOT THIS:   **In terms of** industry, Farmington has gone through several phases.

BUT THIS:   **Industrially,** Farmington has gone through several phases.

NOT THIS:   War is costly both **in terms of** blood and **in terms of** treasure.

BUT THIS:   War is costly both **in** blood and **in** treasure.

**interpersonal relationship**   Wordy for *relationship*. All relationships among people are interpersonal. (See **CONCISION.**)

**INTERROGATIVE PRONOUNS**   An **interrogative pronoun** (IP) introduces either a direct question or an indirect question and has no antecedent: *who* (*whoever, whosoever*), *whom* (*whomever, whomsoever*), *whose* (*whosever, whosesoever*), *what* (*whatever, whatsoever*), *which* (*whichever*):

```
                IP
DIRECT QUESTION:   Who is it?
```

```
                    IP
INDIRECT QUESTION:   Mary asked John which it is.
```

(See **ANTECEDENTS and PRONOUNS.**)

**in the final (or last) analysis**   Wordy for *finally*. (See **CONCISION.**)

**in the future, in the past**   Usually sources of wordiness. (See **CONCISION**.)

NOT THIS:   **In the future,** interest rates will rise.

BUT THIS:   Interest rates will rise.

**into**   Such expressions as *into drugs, into jogging,* and *into organic food* are SAWE but informal. (See also **in, into.**)

**invaluable, valuable**   *Invaluable* looks as though it might mean "not valuable." But the two words are synonymous meaning "having great value": *an invaluable* (or *valuable*) *gem.*

**INVERTED SENTENCES**   The normal order (or syntax) of the major elements of an English sentence is either subject + verb (*Susan sings*), subject + verb + direct object (*Susan loves Harry*), or subject + verb + predicate complement (*Susan is a nurse.*). (See **SYNTAX**.) An **inverted sentence** is any deviation from this normal order—notably, direct object + subject + verb (*Asparagus Susan detests.*) The effect of an inversion is to highlight or emphasize the displaced element (*asparagus*, for instance).

**invitation, invite**   For the noun, prefer *invitation*; use *invite* only as a verb.

**ironically**   Use sparingly to describe instances of nonverbal irony (see **IRONY**): *Ironically, while breaking the lock, the thief broke his thumb.*

**IRONY**   Irony is either a verbal or situational disparity or tension. Verbal irony is a disparity between what is said and what is meant (said: *he is a master of diplomacy*; meant: *he has no diplomacy*). Situational irony is a disparity, for example, between what is expected to happen and what happens, between what one deserves and what one gets, between policy and its execution, between light-hearted music and the grisly events (on stage or in life) that it accompanies.

**irregardless** NonSAWE for *regardless* (probably a blend of, or confusion between, *irrespective* and *regardless*).

NOT THIS:   I will write you **irregardless** of what happens.

BUT THIS:   I will write you **regardless** of what happens.

## IRREGULAR (STRONG) AND REGULAR (WEAK) VERBS

A regular verb (or, as it is traditionally known, weak) forms the past tense and the past participle by adding the suffix *-d*, *-ed*, or *-t*:

I once **loved** milk shakes.
I **bagged** groceries yesterday.
I **burnt** my finger on the iron.

An **irregular** (or strong) **verb** forms the past tense and the past participle, not by adding a suffix, but by an internal change or some other means. In most cases, the past tense and the past participle are identical but not in all:

I **bite** the bullet daily.
I **bit** the bullet yesterday.
I have often **bitten** the bullet.

I **sing** daily.
I **sang** yesterday.
I have often **sung**.

I **think** daily.
I **thought** yesterday.
I have often **thought** that. . . .

I **hit** the target daily.
I **hit** the target yesterday.
I have often **hit** the target.

(See **AUXILIARIES; PARTICIPLES;** and **VERBS.**)

**is composed of**  See **comprised of**.

**issue**  *Controversial issue* or *disputed issue* is wordy for *issue*. Issues are necessarily controversial or disputed. (See **CONCISION**.)

**is when, is where**  NonSAWE, though often used in informal definitions.

> NOT THIS:  Communism **is when** goods are owned in common and distributed to all as needed.

> BUT THIS:  Communism **is a system in which** goods are owned in common and distributed to all as needed.

> OR THIS:  *Communism* **means "a system in which** goods are. . . . "

**ITALICIZATION**  Use **italics** (or underlining) for: (1) A word, a phrase, a letter, or a numeral mentioned (that is, referred to as such) rather than used (see **USE AND MENTION**):

the word *great*      the letter *m*

> (2) The titles of a book, a movie, a musical work, a painting, a periodical, or a sculpture:

*The Last of the Mohicans*
*Chinatown*
*The New World Symphony*

*Guernica*

*Time*

(3) Foreign words:

*mutatis mutandis*  *Weltanschauung*  *joie de vivre*

(4) Names of ships and aircrafts:

the *U.S.S. Constitution*  *Enola Gay*

(5) Latin names of such things as genera and species:

*Sus scrofa* *Homo sapiens*

**its, it's** Often confused. *Its* is a personal pronoun in the possessive case: ***Its** cause is unknown.* *It's* is a contraction either of *it is* (***It's** a beautiful day*) or of *it has* (***It's** been a beautiful day*). You may confuse *its* with *it's* because a noun in the possessive case usually has the suffix *'s: The disease's cause is unknown.*

**-ize** A SAWE suffix added to a noun or an adjective to make a verb: *criticize, crystallize, hospitalize, idolize, mesmerize, plagiarize, rationalize, systemize, theorize.* **Caution:** Though no readers object to any *-ize* verbs in this list, many object to more recent *-ize* verbs such as *concretize* and (especially objectionable) *finalize* and *prioritize.*

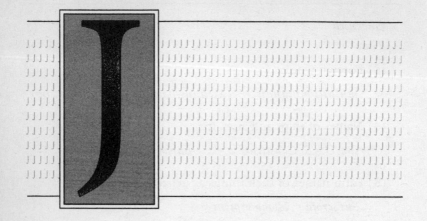

**JARGON** (1) The technical terminology used by the members of a clique, gang, occupation, profession, trade, or other special group. For example, the language of physicians: *bronchogenetic carcinoma* ("lung cancer"), *hyperingestion of ethanol* ("alcoholism"), *pneumoectomy* ("removal of a lung"). The language of criminals: *buttlegging* ("cigarette smuggling"), *pigeon* ("easily duped person"), *skin trade* ("prostitution" or "pornography").

(2) Confusing, hard-to-understand, or pretentious language. An example: *Computerwise, the bottom line in terms of utility is software.* (See **CLARITY; CONCISION;** and **GOBBLEDY-GOOK.**)

**job, position** Either word is SAWE, though *position* is perhaps a bit pretentious and suggests a grander status: *You have a job, I, a position.*

**joined together**  Wordy for *joined*. (See **CONCISION**.)

**judgment call**  Quite unnecessary. Every decision is based upon judgment.

> NOT THIS:  Her decision to cancel the meeting was a **judgment call**.

> BUT THIS:  She decided to cancel the meeting.

**judicial, judicious**  Sometimes confused. *Judicial* means "pertaining to courts": *judicial branch of government. Judicious* means "having and exercising good judgment": *a judicious administrator.*

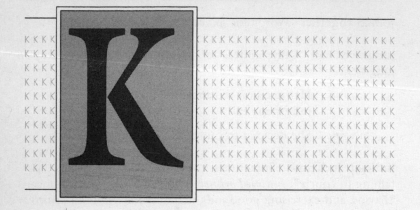

**kick** In formal writing, avoid such informal or slang expressions as *gets his kicks from*, *kicking about his small allowance*, *kicking around the north side*, *kicking in for the gift*, *kicking off* ("dying"), *kicked out of school*, and *on a new kick*.

NOT THIS:  Harry **gets his kicks from** tormenting his sister.

BUT THIS:  Harry **takes pleasure in** tormenting his sister.

**kind, sort, type** (1) Often a cause of wordiness.

NOT THIS:  Philip is an anxious **kind of** man.

BUT THIS:  Philip is an **anxious** man.

OR THIS:  Philip is **anxious**.

ACCEPTABLE:  This **kind of** transmission is more reliable than the old **kind**.

186

(2) **Caution:** *Kind, sort,* and *type* are followed by *of,* not by *of a.*

NOT THIS:    This sort **of a** snake is poisonous.

BUT THIS:    This sort **of** snake is poisonous.

(3) **Caution:** Use of *kind of* or *sort of* to mean "rather" or "in a way" is avoided in formal writing.

NOT THIS:    Louise is **kind of** worried.

BUT THIS:    Louise is **rather** worried.

(4) **Caution:** Because *kind, sort,* and *type* are singular, they are modified by singular pronouns.

NOT THIS:    **These type** of criminals are vicious.

BUT THIS:    **This type** of criminal is vicious.

OR THIS:    **These types** of criminals (or criminal) are vicious.

(5) **Caution:** Use of *kind, sort,* or *type* to modify a noun is avoided in formal writing.

NOT THIS:    that **type** leather.

BUT THIS:    that **type of** leather.

**know as**   Not SAWE as a substitute for *know that.*

NOT THIS:    I don't **know as** she believes that.

BUT THIS:    I don't **know that** she believes that.

**know-how**   One kind of knowledge: *knowing how* (to do something—operate a computer, say). The other kind is *knowing that*: knowing that something is the case (*that* George Washington was the first president of the United States, say). Because many readers object to the word *know-how*, at least in formal contexts, prefer *knowledge, ability,* or *skill* to refer to the first kind of knowledge.

**knowledge, facts, theories**  Knowledge is of two kinds: (1) knowing *that* something is the case: justified through belief; and (2) knowing *how* to do something: an ability or skill. The objects of (1) are facts and theories. You know, for example, that gold is malleable (a fact) if and only if you believe that it is, and it is. You know Newton's theory of gravitation if you know what it explains and predicts about the gravitational pull of one body upon another.

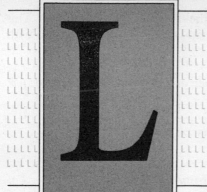

**lady, woman** Prefer *woman*. *Lady* is old-fashioned and, at times, excessive, except in the phrase *ladies and gentlemen*.

**LANGUAGE OF THOUGHT** Some, though not all, linguists and philosophers of language believe that, as part of the genetically given mental equipment of all human beings, there is a **language of thought** quite independent of any natural language, such as English or Mandarin, that they may learn. According to this belief, human beings understand a sentence of a natural language if and only if they can translate it into the language of thought. Second, when they translate a sentence of one language into another, they first translate it into the language of thought and then into the other language. Third, children who have not yet learned to speak think in the language of thought. Finally, the notions of synonymy and of saying the same thing in different ways—fundamental to the art or science of rhetoric—assume a language of thought in which "the same thing" is formulated. This belief, then, seems to explain many things human beings do with language.

**large number of, small number of**  Wordy for *many* and *few*. (See **CONCISION**.)

**last but not least**  Wordy for *last*. (See **CONCISION**.)

**last, latest**  For the sense "most recent," prefer *latest*, because *last* also can mean "final": *the latest issue of* Time.

**later, latter**  Once used interchangeably but now distinguished in formal writing. *Later* is the comparative of the adjective and adverb *late* and thus refers to time: *Joe was even later than Bill to the party. Latter* refers to the second of two things mentioned: *Ilse is fond of both peanut butter and caviar, but she can rarely afford the latter.* (See also **former, latter**.)

**later on**  Wordy for *later*. (See **CONCISION**.)

**LATINISMS**  English expressions obviously borrowed from Latin, especially ones pretty obviously borrowed: *ad hoc, alumnus, ex cathedra, homo sapiens, mutatis mutandis, obiter dictum, per capita, sine die, vox populi*. Perhaps the best advice is to use a Latinism only if it has no well-established English equivalent (an *ad hoc* committee) or a jargon requires it (the judge's *obiter dicta*). Your readers may find a Latinism pretentious or have to look it up, and you may have trouble getting its plural right (see **alumna, alumnae, alumni, alumnus**). Generally, for example, prefer *a* (or *an*) to *per*.

> NOT THIS:   once **per** week.
>
> BUT THIS:   once **a** week.

**lay (laid, laying), lie (lay, lying, lain)** Often confused because similar in sound. *Lay* has many meanings (chiefly, to "put," "place," or "produce"): *Mike lays bricks, laid some yesterday, is laying some now, and has laid them most of his life; The hen lays eggs; The government lays a tax on cigarettes;* and so on. *Lie* means "recline" or "rest": *The patient lies in bed, lay there yesterday, is lying there now, and has lain there for a week.* **Caution:** *Lay* for *lie* is nonSAWE.

NOT THIS:   **Lay** down, please.

BUT THIS:   **Lie** down, please.

But *lay for* (meaning "lie in wait for") is SAWE: *The murderers laid for him in the bushes. Lay,* in the senses noted, is a transitive verb, followed by a direct object. (DO):

DO
Merton **lays**   the blame   on his brother.

*Lie,* in the senses noted, is an intransitive verb, not followed by a direct object:

MODIFIER, NOT DO
The books **lie**   on the table   in disorder.

**layman** Originally meant only "someone not a clergyman." Now used also to refer to a person outside some other profession: *To the layman (or layperson), the machinations of accountants are mysterious.* (See **SEXIST LANGUAGE.**)

**lead, led** Sometimes confused because of identical pronunciation. *Lead* is the name of a metal: *heavy as lead. Led* is the past tense of the verb *lead: He led me into temptation.*

**learn, teach** Sometimes confused, because antonyms. *Learn* means "gain knowledge (of something)": *Juan learned photogra-*

*phy at summer school. Teach* means "cause (someone) to gain knowledge (of something)": *Professor Hawkins taught Juan photography.*

**leave**   NonSAWE for *let* (except before *alone: Leave* (or *let*) *me alone*).

> NOT THIS:   Dan won't **leave** me have my way.

> BUT THIS:   Dan won't **let** me have my way.

**leave me alone, let me alone**   In the sense "do not disturb me," prefer *let me alone,* because *leave me alone* also can mean "leave me by myself."

**lend**   See **borrow, lend.**

**lend, loan**   Both are SAWE as verbs. **Caution:** Some readers prefer that *loan* be used only as a noun.

> NOT THIS:   Jones **loaned** Smith money.

> BUT THIS:   Jones **lent** Smith money.

**less**   See **fewer, less.**

**let's go**   SAWE contraction of *let us go.* The opening lines of T. S. Eliot's "The Love Song of J. Alfred Prufrock"—

> Let us go then, you and I,
> When the evening is spread out against the sky . . .

are ungrammatical, because *you and I* is in apposition with *us* and therefore *I* should be in the same case, the objective case (*me*). (See **CASES** and **GRAMMATICAL RULES.**) Perhaps the justification is the *I-sky* rhyme.

**lexicographer, linguist, philologist, polyglot** Sometimes confused. A *lexicographer* writes or edits dictionaries (lexicons). A *linguist* is a student of linguistics, the science of language—especially morphology, philology, and syntax. (See **MORPHEMES AND PHONEMES** and **SYNTAX.**) A *philologist*—the word is little used nowadays—is a student of anything written or spoken, including literature, both modern and classical. A *polyglot* knows how to speak or write many languages.

**liable to, likely to** Sometimes confused. Both mean "probably going to," but *liable to*, unlike *likely to*, suggests unpleasant consequences: *John is **liable to** lose his job soon, but Sue is **likely to** get the scholarship.*

**libel, slander** Sometimes confused. Both are defamatory. But *libel* is written; *slander,* oral.

**lie, (lay, lying, lain)** See **lay (laid, laying), lie (lay, lying, lain).**

**like** See **as, like.**

**likely to** See **liable to, likely to.**

**line** See **case, line.**

**LINKING VERBS or COPULAS** Verbs that do not take objects: *George is (was, has been, will be) nice; Doris seems nice.*

**LISTS** Lists (of, for example, people, places, reasons, causes) are generally best set off by indention from the rest of the text, with listed items emphasized by such devices as *first, second, third; (1), (2), (3); (a), (b), (c);* or •, •, •.

**literature, advertising material, brochures** Use *literature* to refer to poems, short stories, and novels, but not to advertising material or brochures: *The novels of John Updike, not the catalog I was given today, are literature; In the mail today, I got a brochure about Eureka vacuum cleaners.*

**live audience** Wordy for *audience.* There are no dead audiences. (See **CONCISION.**)

**live, reside** *Reside,* in most contexts, is pretentious.

> NOT THIS: The Molloys **reside** at 248 Birch Street.

> BUT THIS: The Molloys **live** at 248 Birch Street.

**LOAN WORD** A word borrowed from another language. (See **née** for an example.)

**LOGIC** A fundamental discipline concerned with the rules of inference. Deductive logic includes mathematics. (See **INDUCTION AND DEDUCTION.**)

**logical, reason** Avoid expressions such as *It's only logical to believe that* . . . and *It stands to reason that.* . . . They are poor substitutes for argument and may alienate some readers.

**LOOSE AND PERIODIC SENTENCES** A sentence is periodic if it is not a sentence at all without its last word: *When he saw the cobra, he yelled.* Otherwise, a sentence is loose: *He smiled weakly, hesitantly.*

**loose, lose** Sometimes confused. *Loose* is both an adjective meaning "not tightly fastened or attached" (*a loose hinge*) and a verb meaning "untie" or "unfasten" (*She loosed the knot*). *Lose* is a verb meaning such things as "mislay" (*I lost my keychain*) and "fail to gain" (*Smithers lost the election*).

**lots of, many** Prefer *many: Many citizens voted for Roosevelt.*

**lousy**   Slang and vague as an expression of disapproval.

> NOT THIS:   I had a **lousy** experience at camp.
>
> BUT THIS:   I had a **painful** (or **unpleasant** or **humiliating**) experience at camp.

**loved one**   A euphemism for *relative*.

> NOT THIS:   Several of my **loved ones** live in the Bronx.
>
> BUT THIS:   Several of my **relatives** live in the Bronx.

(See **EUPHEMISMS.**)

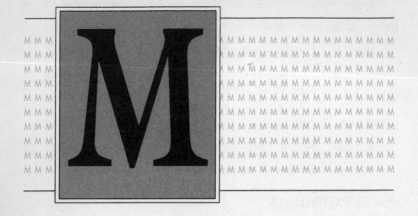

**MACARONICS**  Discourses mixing two languages. Common, even in print, in communities where many people are fluent in two languages—English and Spanish, for instance, in Southern California: *Tengo que make some dinero pronto* [= *I have to make some money quickly*].

**mad**  In SAWE, *mad* means both "psychotic" (*mad as a hatter*) and "angry" (*mad enough to scream*).

**magnitude, size**  Prefer *size: The size of the reception room is twenty-nine feet by forty.*

**MAIN CLAUSES**  See **CLAUSES.**

**majority of**  Use *majority of* to refer only to things that can be counted.

NOT THIS:    the **majority of** the business.

BUT THIS:    the **majority of** the members.

**majority, plurality** Sometimes confused. (1) As used of elections (and unless otherwise defined by law), *majority* means either "more than half the total votes cast" or "difference between half and the votes cast for the runner-up" (*won by a **majority** of only two votes*); *plurality* means either "largest number cast for any one of three or more candidates, but not more than half the votes cast (i.e., not a majority)" or "difference between the largest number and the next largest number" (*won by a **plurality** of only two votes*). (2) Do not use *majority to mean "most."*

NOT THIS:    the **majority** of my time.

BUT THIS:    **most** of my time.

**MALAPROPISMS** A **malapropism** is a word confused with another word similar in sound but different in meaning—*corroborated* ("support with evidence") confused with *collaborated* ("worked together"), for example:

Photographs found in the files indicated that the university police had **corroborated** with the army in gathering political information about students.

Malapropisms are so good for laughs that comic plays and novels are full of characters who use them: Shakespeare's Dogberry, confusing *odorous* with *odious* ("Comparisons are odorous"); Smollett's Winifred Jenkins, confusing *deception* with *conception* ("O Molly! you that live in the country have no deception of our doings in Bath"); and Sheridan's Mrs. Malaprop (who gave malapropisms their name), confusing *pineapple* with *pinnacle* ("He is the very pineapple of politeness").

Malapropisms can make a writer a comic character. How can you avoid them? Because they are usually long, unfamiliar words, the best way is to avoid such words unless no others can do the job. If you feel you must use a long, unfamiliar word, check your dictionary first. (See **DICTIONARIES**.)

You won't make a fool of yourself by confusing *institutionalized* ("put into an institution") with *instituted* ("begun"), for instance, if you use the shorter, more familiar *began*.

NOT THIS:   The district attorney **institutionalized** an investigation.—Newspaper story.

BUT THIS:   The district attorney **began** [or, if you must, **instituted**] an investigation.

Some other malapropisms captured alive in the wilderness of print:

| | |
|---|---|
| acquisition (accusation) | exult (exalt) |
| adopt (adapt) | exceed (accede) |
| admiral (admirable) | exonerating (extenuating) |
| affect (effect) | factitious (factual) |
| amiss (averse) | flag (flog) |
| anecdote (antidote) | foible (foil) |
| ascribe (subscribe) | harangue (harass) |
| attenuating (extenuating) | harass (harness) |
| bibliography (biography) | impugn (impute) |
| censor (censure) | inane (innate) |
| commiserate (communicate) | incredulous (incredible) |
| commitment (communication) | induced (seduced) |
| defer (refer) | interlocutor (intermediary) |
| delusion (illusion) | jingoistic (jingling) |
| demure (demur) | jurist (juror) |
| determinism (determination) | legend (legion) |
| distinct (extinct) | luxuriant (luxurious) |
| elicit (solicit) | mannerism (manner) |
| envious (enviable) | martial (marital) |

medal (mettle)
mitigate (militate)
mute (moot)
nauseous (nauseated)
offering (offing)
permeate (dominate)
personal (personnel)
perspective (prospective)
phase (faze)
phase (focus)
precipitant (precipitous)
predict (predicate)
prevaricate (procrastinate)
proffer (offer)
proscribe (prescribe)
prospective (perspective)

protégé (prodigy)
provoke (evoke)
qualms (quarrels)
ravage (rage)
regime (regimen)
renounce (denounce)
repute (repudiate)
resource (recourse)
respectful (respectable)
segregate (congregate)
subsume (assume)
supplant (supplement)
tenant (tenet)
tendentious (tangential)
virtuousity (virtue)
wrought (fraught)

**-man**    See **-ess, -ette, -trix.**

**mankind**    Still the generally used word to refer to people as a species. (See **SEXIST LANGUAGE.**)

**man or woman of letters**    A broader term than *author, poet, literary critic, scholar,* and so on. A *man or woman of letters* is an eminent person involved with literature in a variety of ways: author, editor, poet, founder of a literary movement, for instance. The late Malcolm Cowley is an example.

**may**    See **can, may.**

**may be, maybe**    Sometimes confused, because identical in sound and similar in meaning. *May be* is a verb meaning "is possibly": *Roy may be right. Maybe* is an adverb meaning "perhaps": *Maybe* Roy is right.

**maybe, perhaps**  Synonyms (see **SYNONYMS**). But *perhaps* is a little more formal or even literary.

**may, might**  (1) *May* has two senses, best made clear by examples. *You may go* means either (a) "You have permission to go" or (b) "It is possible that you will go."

(2) *Might* is the past tense of *may*. Nowadays, however, *may* and *might* are also synonyms (see **SYNONYMS**) in sense (b), though *may*, perhaps, suggests greater likelihood than *might: I may* (or *might*) *go.*

**mayn't**  Rare in SAWE. Prefer *may not.*

**me and**  NonSAWE as part of the subject of a sentence or clause.

NOT THIS:  **Me and** Barney went for a swim.

BUT THIS:  Barney **and I** went for a swim.

**MEANING AND REFERENCE  Meaning** and **reference** are sometimes thought of as being identical, but they are quite different.

The meaning of an expression (a word or a phrase) is the concept (the set of qualities or relations) that the grammatical rules of a language assign it (see **GRAMMATICAL RULES**). The grammatical rules of English, for example, assign the same concept to the word *black* that the grammatical rules of French assign to the word *noir,* and the same concept to the word *girl* that the grammatical rules of Spanish assign to the word *nina.*

Reference, on the other hand, is not a concept but a human act—a writer's or a speaker's act of using an expression to refer to (identify, name, point out) a person or a thing—using, for instance, *the black tower* or *la tour noir* to refer to a certain structure or of using the expression *the girl* or *la nina* to refer to a certain young female.

Clearly, using an expression to refer to someone or something presupposes knowledge of its meaning. (See **ASSUMPTIONS AND PROPOSITIONS.**)

**meaning, meaningful, meaningless** When used as vague expressions of approval (*meaning, meaningful*) or disapproval (*meaningless*), these words are clichés.

NOT THIS:    School has no **meaning** for me.

BUT THIS:    I **don't like** school.

NOT THIS:    a **meaningful** experience.

BUT THIS:    an **important** (or **interesting** or **valuable** or **worthwhile**) experience.

NOT THIS:    a **meaningless** relationship.

BUT THIS:    a **boring** (or **destructive** or **undesirable** or **uninteresting** or **unprofitable**) relationship.

**MEASUREMENT NOUNS AS MODIFIERS** Such words as *block, foot, mile; hour, minute, second, month, year;* and *ounce, pound, ton* are singular before the noun they modify but plural after it: *a three-block walk* (but *a walk of three blocks*), *a two-hour broadcast* (but *a broadcast of two hours*), *an eight-ounce tenderloin* (but *a tenderloin of eight ounces*).

**media** In Latin, *media* is plural (see **LATINISMS**). In English, however, it is often singular: *The **media** focuses upon the presidency.* The singular *medium* is little used. **Caution:** Some readers will object to the singular use of *media* in formal writing.

**mediocre** Avoid using *mediocre* (which means "average") to mean "bad" or "much below average."

NOT THIS:    His performance is **mediocre,** about as bad as it could get.

BUT THIS:    His performance is **mediocre**—middling.

**memorandum**  The SAWE plural is either *memoranda* or *memorandums*. (See **LATINISMS.**)

**meretricious, meritorious**  Sometimes confused. *Meretricious* is derived from a Latin word meaning "like a prostitute" and means "conspicuous in a vulgar or tawdry way." *Meritorious* means "having merit."

**METALANGUAGES AND OBJECT LANGUAGES**  Linguistics and the philosophy of language distinguish between metalanguages and object languages. A **metalanguage** is any language used to describe a language. An **object language** is any language described by a metalanguage. For example, the sentence "In French, the word *chien* means 'dog' " is part of a metalanguage (namely, English), and the language described is an object language (namely, French). Metalanguage and object language may be identical. For instance, in the sentence "In English, the word *if* is a preposition" is part of a metalanguage identical with the object language it describes (namely, English). Often some expressions in a metalanguage are mentioned rather than used. In the two sentences just cited (as in this sentence), the words *chien* and *if* are mentioned, but all the other words in these three sentences are used. (See **USE AND MENTION.**)

**METAPHORS AND SIMILES**  A **metaphor** is a figure of speech (see **FIGURES OF SPEECH**) in which one thing—person, place, object, action, event, idea—is, directly or indirectly, said to be another to suggest a resemblance between the two:

Ronald **is a sponge.**

The New World Order **is a chameleon.**

A **simile** is a metaphor containing *as, as though,* or *like:*

Ronald **is like a sponge.**
The New World Order **is like a chameleon.**

**METONYMY  Metonymy** is a figure of speech (see **FIGURES OF SPEECH**) referring to one thing by naming another, closely associated thing: *The White House* [= someone at the White House] *said . . . ; The nation* [= people in the nation] *is grateful; The state* [= the state legislature] *raised taxes; Here comes the law* [= a police officer].

Often metonymy is implicit in a phrase: *ailing health* [= a person], *cold temperatures* [= weather], *expensive prices* [= goods or services]. A famous example appears in *Hamlet: incestuous sheets.* It is not, of course, the sheets that are incestuous; it is the activity going on between them.

Metonymy is often just as clear as its literal alternative and much more effective. In many instances who knows or cares who at the White House was the spokesperson? And does not *incestuous sheets* conjure up a visual image that *incestuous activity* or even *incest* does not? (See **TRANSFERRED EPITHETS.**)

**middle-age, middle-aged; teenage, teenaged**  Prefer *-aged* to *-age: a teenaged boy.* (See **-ed, -d.**)

**mighty**  Informal for *very.*

NOT THIS:  a **mighty** nice person.

BUT THIS:  a **very** nice person.

**militate, mitigate**  Sometimes confused. *Militate* (an intransitive verb) means "have effect" or "have force as evidence"; *mitigate* (a transitive verb) means "alleviate," "extenuate," or "mollify."

NOT THIS:  Low grades **mitigated** against his admission.

BUT THIS:  Low grades **militated** against his admission.

**minus**    Avoid using to mean "without."

NOT THIS:    **Minus** his right arm, he could not play basketball.

BUT THIS:    **Without** his right arm, he could not play basketball.

**minutiae**    Meaning "small (or trivial) details" or "small-scale features" *minutiae* is rarely used in the singular: *minutia*. (See **LATINISMS**.)

**misremember**    See **disremember**.

**Miss, Mrs., Ms.**    *Miss* (plural: *Misses*) is a title of courtesy for an unmarried woman; *Mrs.* (plural: *Mmes.* or *Mesdames*), for a married woman. *Ms.* (plural: *Mses.* or *Mss.*) is a now much-used title of courtesy for a woman whose marital status is unknown or considered irrelevant. **Caution:** When in doubt, use *Ms.* (See **SEXIST LANGUAGE**.)

**MISSPELLING**    (1) **Misspellings** are the easiest errors to recognize and often count against you out of all proportion to their importance. There are, of course, a few rules that everyone knows (write *i* before *e* except after *c*). But most spellings you must memorize as you memorize telephone numbers. One neglected cause of misspelling is, however, worth mention: mispronunciation. You are unlikely to write *athelete,* for example, unless you mispronounce *athlete*. And be especially careful not to misspell people's names. Your misspelling someone's name suggests that you are not interested enough to pay attention to the name.

The following are some commonly misspelled words:

absence                          accidentally
accommodate                      achievement

acknowledgment
aggression
allege
all right
a lot
arctic
argument
athlete
balloon
besiege
bureau
bureaucracy
burglar
calendar
camouflage
cemetery
changeable
conscience
conscious
control
corroborate
counterfeit
deceive
defendant
definite
dependent
desirable
desperate
develop
dilemma
disastrous
dispensable
ecstasy
eighth

emanate
embarrass
equipped
exaggerate
exhilarate
exorbitant
fiery
foresee
forfeit
forty
fulfill
gauge
grammar
grievance
gruesome
guarantee
harass
heroes
idiosyncrasy
incidentally
incredible
indispensable
infinitely
inoculate
interrupt
irrelevant
irreplaceable
irresistible
jeopardy
judgment
knowledge
laboratory
legitimate
leisure

license
loneliness
maintenance
maneuver
mathematics
mischievous
missile
naive
necessary
noticeable
occasion
occurrence
omission
optimist
parallel
paralyze
pastime
perceive
permissible
phony
playwright
pleasurable
possess
prairie
privilege
psychology
receive
recommend
relevant
relieve
reminiscence
restaurant
rhythm

ridiculous
roommate
sacrilegious
schedule
seize
sheriff
siege
sophomore
sovereign
sponsor
subtlety
subtly
succumb
supersede
suppress
than
therefore
tranquillity
transferred
truly
unanimous
unconscious
unmistakable
unnecessary
unwieldy
vacillate
vengeance
villain
whether
wield
withhold
woeful

**Note:** Spelling of English words outside of the United States is not entirely in accord with spelling in the United States. In Canada, for instance, *color* is spelled *colour* and *recognize* is spelled *recognise*. These variations pose no barrier to communication; when you see these spellings in print, you are probably reading something published outside the United States.

**MISTAKES**  Mistakes in language use are violations of grammatical rules. (See **GRAMMATICAL RULES.**) The chief causes are

(1) ignorance of the relevant rule, usually by someone who is not a native speaker;
(2) confusion: "There is—I mean *are*—three things to bear in mind";
(3) hypercorrection, a misapplication of grammatical rules: "Show your pass to whomever is at the gate" (use of *whomever* is a misapplication of the rule that the object of a preposition [here: *to*] be in the objective case [e.g., *whomever*]; but the object here is the clause of which *whomever* [i.e., *whoever*] is the subject: "whoever is at the gate"). (See **HYPERCORRECTION.**)

**MODIFIERS AND MODIFICATION**  A **modifier** (MOD) is a word, a phrase, or a clause that limits or qualifies the meaning of another one. **Modification,** after naming and predication, is almost certainly the most basic process in any language. Even in the most ordinary sentence, the pattern of modification can be incredibly elaborate:

MOD      MOD MOD                    MOD
Luckily, the front door opened easily.

In this example, the adverb *luckily* modifies all the rest of the sentence; the article *the* modifies the phrase *front door;* the adjective *front* modifies the noun *door;* and the adverb *easily* modifies the verb *opened*.

Elaborate as this pattern is, every speaker of English can grasp it with no conscious thought. Knowing English is very largely the ability to recognize the meanings of English words and to recognize also how patterns of modification limit or qualify these meanings.

A modifier may confuse your readers, however, if you have either *misplaced* it or *dangled* it.

A modifier is *misplaced* if your readers take it to modify a word, a phrase, or a clause you do not intend it to modify or if they cannot tell for sure what you intend:

MISPLACED MODIFIER: Next year is our annual *48th* reunion. [Does the 48th reunion occur annually?]

WELL-PLACED: Next year is our 48th annual reunion.

MISPLACED MODIFIER: Two members of Hells Angels were sentenced to twelve years each for the sale of cocaine *by Judge Earl R. Larson.* [Did the judge sell the cocaine?]

WELL-PLACED: (if the members sold it): Two members of Hells Angels were sentenced to twelve years each by Judge Earl R. Larson for the sale of cocaine.

MISPLACED MODIFIER: All complaints are *not* justified. [Not all complaints are justified, or no complaints are justified?]

WELL-PLACED: (if the former is intended): Not all complaints are justified.

A modifier *dangles* if its implied subject is not the subject you intend it to have:

| | |
|---|---|
| DANGLING MODIFIER: | *Eating lunch,* the explosion made me jump. [The implied subject of the modifier is the actual subject of the main clause: *the explosion* ("the explosion was eating lunch"). Presumably, however, the intended subject is *I* ("I was eating lunch").] |
| NONDANGLING MODIFIER: | *While I was eating lunch,* the explosion made me jump. |
| DANGLING MODIFIER: | *An international financier,* his name was synonymous with riches. [The implied subject of the modifier is the actual subject of the main clause: *his name* ("his name was an international financier"). Presumably, however, the intended subject is he ("he was an international financier").] |
| NONDANGLING MODIFIER: | *Because he was an international financier,* his name was synonymous with riches. |
| DANGLING MODIFIER: | *While walking down the street,* the storm broke. [The implied subject of the modifier is the actual subject of the main clause: *the storm* ("the storm was walking down the street"). Presumably, however, the intended subject is *I* ("I was walking down the street").] |
| NONDANGLING MODIFIER: | *While I was walking down the street,* the storm broke. |

**MOOD**   The **moods** of a verb are the different forms or positions it takes in a clause or a sentence to indicate how the state or the action it expresses is to be taken: *indicative mood* (taken as a fact: You are good); *imperative mood* (taken as an order or a request: Be good); *subjunctive mood* (taken as a wish: Would you were good); *conditional mood* (taken as a condition: You would be good if you could).

**moonlight**    SAWE as a verb meaning "hold a second job": *Herman has been **moonlighting** for several years.*

**moot**    Use the adjective only to mean "unresolved," "open to question," "disputed," or "only of academic significance": *a **moot** issue, a **moot** question.*

> NOT THIS:    This project is too **moot** and unnecessary to justify discussion.

> BUT THIS:    The project is too **unimportant** and unnecessary to justify discussion.

**moral, morale**    Sometimes confused. *Moral* is both an adjective meaning "ethical" or "right" (*a **moral** decision, **moral** people*) and a noun meaning either "lesson" (*the **moral** of the parable*) or, in the plural, "code of behavior" (*the **morals** of gangsters*). *Morale* is a noun meaning "emotional or mental state": *The **morale** of the police force is low.*

**MORPHEMES AND PHONEMES  Morphemes**    are    the smallest elements of a language that are meaningful in themselves. In *ungirlish, un-* ("not"), *-girl-* ("young female human"), and *-ish* ("like") are morphemes; but *-ngi-* and *-li-*, because they are meaningless, are not morphemes. *Bound* morphemes must be parts of words: *un-* and *-ish,* for instance. *Unbound* morphemes can be words in themselves: *girl.* Some morphemes have two or more manifestations, called *allomorphs,* the choice depending upon context. The indefinite-article morpheme in English is an example: *a bank* but *an oyster.*

**Phonemes** are the smallest elements of a language that make differences in meaning. The evidence that two or more sounds (*not* letters) are different phonemes is the occurrence in the language of minimal pairs. A minimal pair is two words differing from one another in only one sound. In English, for instance, the numerous minimal pairs that can be formed from the words *pat,* *peat, pet, pit, pot, put,* and *putt* are evidence that sounds here represented by *a, ea, e, i, o, u* (as in *put*), and *u* (as in *putt*) are different phonemes. Some phonemes have two or more manifestations, called *allophones,* the choice depending upon context. The phoneme represented by *p* in English is an example. The initial *p* in *pump* is different from the final *p,* as you can determine by holding a finger in front of your mouth when pronouncing *pump.* With the initial *p,* but not the final *p,* you feel a puff of air. Every language has a different set of phonemes and allophones. Spanish, for example, has neither the phoneme represented by *i* in *Bill* and *Clinton* nor the phoneme represented by *o* in *Clinton.* That is why Spanish speakers are likely to say *Beal Cleantone.* In some Asian languages, the sounds represented in English by *l* and *r* are allophones of the same phoneme. That is why some Asians learning English pronounce *professor* as though it were spelled *plofessor.*

**mortician**   A euphemism for *undertaker.* (See **EUPHEMISMS.**)

**most**   SAWE for *almost* and often used this way in conversation and informal writing. **Caution:** Rarely used this way in formal writing.

NOT THIS:   **Most** anyone can learn to spell.

BUT THIS:   **Almost** anyone can learn to spell.

**most well**   Wordy for *best-.*

NOT THIS:   the **most well**-known comedian.

BUT THIS:   the **best**-known comedian.

**Mrs.**   See **Miss, Mrs., Ms.**

**Ms.**   See **Miss, Mrs., Ms.**

**much of anything**   A mistake for *much if anything*.

NOT THIS:   I don't know **much of anything** about
economics.

BUT THIS:   I don't know **much if anything** about economics.

**MULTIPLE NEGATIVES**   Though some dialects or varieties
of American English allow (or even require) **multiple negatives**
in a clause (*They didn't never get nothing nohow*), SAWE permits
only one negative per clause (*They don't ever get anything anyhow;*
or *They never get anything anyhow*).

**myself**   Use *myself* only as an intensive pronoun (I saw it *myself*)
or as a reflexive (*I hit myself*). (See **INTENSIVE PRONOUNS**
and **REFLEXIVE PRONOUNS**.)

NOT THIS:   Harriet and **myself** are members.

BUT THIS:   Harriet and **I** are members.

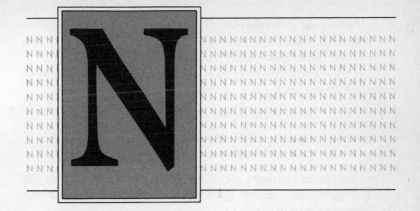

**nab** SAWE but informal to mean "apprehend": *I nabbed the thief.*

**namely** Always wordy. (See **CONCISION.**)

NOT THIS:  The professor of genetics—**namely,** Dr. Margaret Ashe—is well known.

BUT THIS:  The professor of genetics, Dr. Margaret Ashe, is well known.

**NAMES OF PERSONS** (1) When writing for publication, or in a business letter, use, for your first reference to a person, his or her full name, followed, perhaps, by an identifying phrase: *Louise A. Norton, president of the Lovell Foundation.* Use, for subsequent references, either (a) just the person's last name (Norton) or (b) the last name preceded by a title (*Ms. Norton, Dr. Norton, Presi-*

*dent Norton, the Reverend Ms.* or *Dr.* or *President Norton*). (See also **reverend.**) Note the difference in capitalization: *the president of the Lovell Foundation,* but *President Norton.*

(2) If the person you refer to is dead, use no title before his or her name except such a one as *President, Governor,* or *King.*

NOT THIS:    **Miss** Nightingale; **Mr.** Coolidge.

BUT THIS:    *Nightingale* or *Florence Nightingale; Coolidge, Calvin Coolidge,* or *President Coolidge.*

One exception (perhaps there are others) is a reference to the famous eighteenth-century English lexicographer: always either *Dr. Johnson* or *Samuel Johnson.*

**Native American**    Now the generally preferred expression for reference to American Indians. (See **POLITICAL CORRECTNESS.**)

**nature**    Often a cause of wordiness. (See **CONCISION.**)

NOT THIS:    The accident was of a fatal **nature.**

BUT THIS:    The accident was fatal.

**nauseated, nauseous**    *Nauseated* means "having nausea" (*so nauseated he vomited*); *nauseous,* "causing nausea" (*a nauseous odor*).

**naval, navel**    Sometimes confused. *Naval* means "pertaining to navies": *a naval officer. Navel* means either a "depression in the belly where the umbilical cord was attached" (*infection of the navel*) or "species of orange with a similar depression" (*navel oranges in the basket*).

**neat**    Both slang and vague as an expression of approval.

NOT THIS:    a **neat** car.

BUT THIS:    a **good-looking** (or **high-performance**) car.

**necessarily**  See **not necessarily.**

**necessary condition, sufficient condition**  Sometimes confused. A *necessary condition* is a condition without which a phenomenon of a certain kind cannot occur. Oxygen, for example, is a necessary condition of fire; fire occurs only if oxygen is present. A *sufficient condition* is a condition with which a phenomenon of a certain kind can occur. Rain, for instance, is a sufficient condition of ground-wetting; ground-wetting occurs if it rains. A condition may be both necessary and sufficient. Absence of air, for example, is both a necessary and a sufficient condition of smothering: smothering occurs if and only if air is absent.

**necessary requirement**  Wordy for *requirement.* That is what *requirement* means: something necessary. (See **CONCISION.**)

**née**  A loan word from French meaning "born" or "born as." It always takes the acute accent mark (′), even in English.

**need**  (1) Sentences such as *She **need** not go* (meaning "She does not need to go") and *Need she go?* ("Does she need to go?") are SAWE though a bit old-fashioned.
(2) The phrase *needs must* is both archaic and wordy for *must* (See **CONCISION.**)

NOT THIS:    Madison **needs must** go.

BUT THIS:    Madison **must** go.

**needless to say**  If really needless, don't say it. If needed, don't say *needless to say.*

**negative, positive**  Often pretentious for *unfavorable* and *favorable* or for *no* or *yes.*

NOT THIS:    Her response to my request was **positive.**

BUT THIS:    Her response to my request was **yes.**

**neglect, negligence**  Not quite synonymous. *Negligence* suggests carelessness or inattention. *Neglect* suggests more serious consequences than *negligence*, though not necessarily bad intentions.

**neither**  NonSAWE for *either* after a negative.

> NOT THIS:  Herman isn't smart **neither.**

> BUT THIS:  Herman isn't smart **either.**

**neither . . . or**  NonSAWE for *neither . . . nor.*

**NEOLOGISMS**  A **neologism** is simply a new word, a word someone has just created. Every language constantly changes, and the creation of neologisms is one of the chief agents of change. Writers and speakers create neologisms either because they are dissatisfied with an existing word or because they need to name a new thing or idea. Unfortunately, a neologism created because of dissatisfaction with an existing word is likely to be a euphemism (e.g., replacement of *disabled* with *differently abled* or of *prostitute* with *sex worker*), and euphemisms are best avoided. (See **EUPHEMISMS.**) But to discuss inventions or innovations requires, of course, that they be named. A new device for eliminating computer viruses, for instance, requires creation of a neologism—*compviruscide*, say.

**never, no, none, not, n't, nothing, nowhere**  Use of one or more of these negatives to emphasize another negative is nonSAWE; it makes a double (or multiple) negative.

> NOT THIS:  John doesn't have **no** chance of winning **nothing nowhere.**

> BUT THIS:  John doesn't have **any** chance of winning **anything anywhere.**

(See also **but, hardly, scarcely.**)

**new innovations**   Wordy. All innovations are, by definition, new. (See **CONCISION**.)

**news**   Shakespeare counted *news* as plural, but everyone nowadays counts it as singular: *The news is good*.

**nice**   Generally prefer a more specific word of praise: *considerate, decent, pleasant*. But use of *nice* to mean "subtle" or "precise" is quite unobjectionable: *a nice distinction*.

**'n', o'**   Avoid contractions like *'n'* and *o'* unless you wish to sound folksy.

NOT THIS:   doughnuts **'n'** coffee.

BUT THIS:   doughnuts **and** coffee.

NOT THIS:   a bucket **o'** chicken.

BUT THIS:   a bucket **of** chicken.

**no-account, no-count, no-good**   Not used in formal writing.

NOT THIS:   Horace is a **no-good** idler.

BUT THIS:   Horace is a **worthless** idler.

**nohow**   NonSAWE for *not at all* or *in no way*.

NOT THIS:   Harold is **nohow** qualified as an engineer.

BUT THIS:   Harold is **in no way** qualified as an engineer.

Also, NonSAWE for *anyhow* or *anyway*.

NOT THIS:   I'm not going there **nohow**.

BUT THIS:   I'm not going there **anyhow**.

**NOMINALIZATIONS**   A **nominalization** is the conversion of a nonnominal into a nominal, especially the conversion of an independent clause into a gerund phrase. (See **CLAUSES; GERUNDS;** and **NOMINALS.**) An example is the conversion of *the tornado ravaged the city* into *the tornado's ravaging the city*. A sentence with a gerund nominalization as subject and some form of *be* as verb is generally ineffective because it substitutes an abstract verb (in this case *was*) for a specific one (in this case *ravaged*).

NOT THIS:   The tornado's ravaging the city was unfortunate.

BUT THIS:   Unfortunately, the tornado ravaged the city.

**nominal, low**   Not synonymous. A *nominal* fee or amount is so low as to be merely symbolic or to satisfy a legal requirement—a one-dollar rental fee, say, for a million-dollar property.

**NOMINALS**   A **nominal** names one or more people, objects, places, or events. The chief nominals are nouns (*Betty, man, tennis*) and pronouns (*she, him, who, it*). But there are four other kinds: noun phrases (*the girl in the picture*), noun clauses (*whether he is home*), gerunds and gerund phrases (*keeping fit*), and infinitives and infinitive phrases (*to keep fit*).

Nominals are versatile. Most of them can perform different functions in sentences, clauses, and phrases: subject (S), subject complement (SC), direct object (DO), indirect object (IO), object complement (OC), object of preposition (OP), modifier (M), head (H), and address (A):

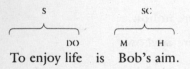

```
               S
        ┌───────┴───────┐
         OP              DO      OC
Members of the club   made    Harriet president.
```

```
                          DO
                 ┌────────┴────────┐
 S      A    S        IO   DO
You know, Helen, he gave Marie a job.
```

As you can see, one nominal may be part of another. In the first sentence above, for example, the nominal *life* (the direct object of the infinitive phrase *to enjoy life*) is part of the nominal *to enjoy life* (the subject of the sentence *To enjoy life is Bob's aim*).

(See **FORMS AND FUNCTIONS; GERUNDS; INFINI-TIVE PHRASES; INFINITIVES; NOUN CLAUSES; NOUN PHRASES; NOUNS;** and **PRONOUNS.**)

**non-** The prefix *non-* has always been used to mean (a) "not" or "absence of": *nonpolitical, nonresident, nontoxicity*. In recent years, *non-* has acquired two more meanings: (b) "unimportant" or "worthless" (*nonbook,* to refer to a coffee-table book—a large, expensive, lavishly bound book with many pictures and few words) and (c) "lacking the usual characteristics (of the thing specified)" (*noncandidate,* to refer to someone professing not to be, but regarded as being, a candidate). **Caution:** Some readers object to use of *non-* to mean (a) when the result is a euphemism: *nonacademic-minded* (for *stupid*), *noncitizen* (for *alien*), *nonobe-dient* (for *disobedient*), *nonsuccess* (for *failure*). And some readers object to use of *non-* to mean (b) when the result has become a cliché.

> Not this:   **non**event.

> But this:   **contrived** (or **staged**) event.

**none**  SAWE counts *none* as singular when it means "not one" (*none of the three articles is relevant*), but as plural when it means "not any" (*none were surprised*). (See also **never, no, none, not, n't, nothing, nowhere.**)

**NONSENSE**  Writers sometimes use the term *nonsense* to dismiss an opinion with which they disagree: *Your view of tariffs is nonsense.* More strictly, nonsense is of two kinds. One is the use of a sequence of sounds that appear to be words but are not. Famous examples abound in the verse of Lewis Carroll:

> 'Twas brillig, and the slithy toves
> Did gyre and gimble in the wabe. . . .

The other kind of nonsense consists of sentences that are perfectly grammatical English but that no one would ever seriously utter:

> Monday's regular meeting, generally held on Tuesday, can't be held on Wednesday because Thursday is a holiday.

**non sequitur**  Latin (meaning "it does not follow") for a statement said to follow, but not following from another: *Because she's a woman, she can't understand football.* (See **INDUCTION AND DEDUCTION** and **LOGIC.**)

**no other alternative**  Wordy for *no alternative*.

**nor**  Sometimes a source of a double negative. (See **DOUBLE (or MULTIPLE) NEGATIVES.**)

NOT THIS:    There are none in the state courts **nor** in the federal.

BUT THIS:    There are none in the state courts **or** in the federal.

**no such a/an**  Wordy and nonSAWE for *no such*.

> NOT THIS:   There is **no such an** animal as a unicorn.

> BUT THIS:   There is **no such** animal as a unicorn.

**not**  Take care where you place it in a sentence. *Not everyone is foolish* means "Some are and some are not foolish." *Everyone is not foolish* is ambiguous (see **VAGUENESS** and **AMBIGUITY**), because it means both "Some are and some are not foolish" and "No one is foolish." (See also **but, hardly, scarcely** and **never, no, none, not, n't, nothing, nowhere.**)

**notable, noticeable**  Sometimes confused. *Notable* means "worthy of notice": *a **notable** exception to the rule*. *Noticeable* means "easy to notice" or "likely to be noticed": *a **noticeable** crack in the vase*.

**not all that**  See **that (all that, not all that, not that).**

**not . . . but**  A sentence such as *I do **not** (or **don't**) own but one* is, unless it means "I own more than one," a double negative. If it means "I own only one," prefer *I own **but** (or **only**) one*. (See **DOUBLE (or MULTIPLE) NEGATIVES.**)

**nothing**  See **but, hardly, scarcely** and **never, no, none, not, n't, nothing, nowhere.**

**not necessarily**  (1) Often wordy.

> NOT THIS:   Denis is **not necessarily** in school.

> BUT THIS:   Denis is **not** in school.

(2) **Caution:** Often ambiguous.

> NOT THIS:   Shakespeare is **not necessarily** concerned with realism.

> BUT THIS:   Shakespeare is **not** concerned with realism.

OR THIS:   . . . **may not be** concerned with realism.

OR THIS:   . . . **is not always** concerned with realism.

OR THIS:   **It is not necessarily true that** Shakespeare is concerned with realism.

But, if this is all the statement means, there is little need to make it because the only statements necessarily true are tautologies, statements true by definition: *My father has at least one child; All mothers are women.*

**not only . . . but also**   Whatever follows *but also* must be identical grammatically with what follows *not only*. Both must be independent clauses, for example, or noun phrases, verbs, adjectives, or adverbs.

NOT THIS:   **Not only** do I like London **but also** Paris.

BUT THIS:   **Not only** do I like London **but also** I like Paris.

OR THIS:   I like **not only** London **but also** Paris.

**not that**   See **that (all that, not all that, not that).**

**not un-**   (1) Phrases such as *not unlike, not unfriendly,* and *not unwelcome* say less than they would with *not un-* deleted. A man who is not unfriendly, for instance, is not necessarily friendly. Indeed, he may be (as one might add) a bit stand-offish.

(2) *not un-* is not a double negative (see **DOUBLE (or MULTIPLE) NEGATIVES),** because the two negatives are not for one negation.

**NOUN CLAUSES**   A **noun clause** is a dependent, or subordinate, clause that begins with the subordinating conjunction *how, that, what, whatever, whether,* or *why* and that can function in some of the ways a noun can: subject, direct object, subject complement, object of preposition, appositive. (See **FORMS AND FUNCTIONS.**) Some examples: *That she is happy* [subject] *is obvious; I know how he feels* [direct object]; *The problem is that the time is not right* [subject complement]; *My explanation of why he does it* [object of preposition] *is simple; What he knows* [subject], *whatever he knows* [appositive], *is not clear.* (See **CLAUSES.**)

**NOUN PHRASES** A **noun phrase** (NP) is a nominal consisting of at least one noun (N). It may, in addition, contain other words. For example, an article (ART), an adjective (ADJ), or both may appear to the left of the noun; a prepositional phrase (PP) or a relative clause (RC), to the right of it:

NP = N
Harry

NP · PP

ART · ADJ · N · NP = N
the · smallest · town · in Michigan

NP

RC

ART · N · NP = N
a · town · that · people · like

Most noun phrases can perform the nine different functions that most nominals can perform: subject, subject complement, direct object, and so on. When a noun phrase consists of more than a noun, the noun performs the function of head (H):

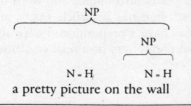

NP

NP

N = H · N = H
a pretty picture on the wall

As these examples show, one noun phrase may be part of another.

(See **ADJECTIVES; ARTICLES; FORMS AND FUNC-
TIONS; NOMINALS; PREPOSITIONAL PHRASES;** and
**RELATIVE CLAUSES.**)

**NOUN PILING** Avoid writing a long string of nouns, each
modifying the one following it.

> NOT THIS: The citizen committee leadership crisis
> controversy.

> BUT THIS: The controversy concerning the crisis in the
> leadership of the citizens' committee.

**Noun-pilings** are very difficult to read, because they must be
read, in effect, from right to left rather than from the customary
left to right.

**NOUNS** Like every other nominal, a **noun** names one or more
people (*girl*), objects (*motorcycle*), places (*garden*), or events
(*riot*). One way to tell whether a word is a noun is to see whether
it can take four forms or shapes varying with both case and
number:

(1) *a girl* (common case, singular number)
(2) *three girls* (common case, plural number)
(3) *one girl's room* (possessive case, singular number)
(4) *three girls' rooms* (possessive case, plural number)

Another way is to look at the words surrounding the word in
question. To its left, a noun (N) often has an article (ART), an
adjective (ADJ), or both; or it may have a preposition (P). To its
right, it often has a prepositional phrase (PP) or a relative clause
(RC):

```
            PP
        ┌────┴────┐
ART   ADJ   N   P   N
the  tallest girl in Boston
```

```
                    RC
        ┌───────────┴──────┐
ART   N                    N
 a    person who commands respect
```

A noun is always either a noun phrase in itself or part of a noun phrase. The noun *Boston* above is a noun phrase, as is the noun *respect*. The noun *girl* is part of the noun phrase *the tallest girl in Boston;* the noun *person,* part of the noun phrase *a person who commands respect.* (In this sense of *phrase,* a phrase may be either one word or several.)

Most nouns can perform any function that most nominals can perform: subject, subject complement, direct object, and so on. When a noun is not the only word in a noun phrase (NP), it performs the function of a head (H):

```
            NP
┌───────────┴──────────┐
         N = H
the tallest girl in Boston
```

For various kinds of nouns, see **COLLECTIVE NOUNS; COMMON AND PROPER NOUNS; CONCRETE AND ABSTRACT NOUNS;** and **COUNT AND MASS NOUNS.**

(See also **ADJECTIVES; ARTICLES; CASES; NOUN PHRASES; NUMBER; PREPOSITIONAL PHRASES; PREPOSITIONS;** and **RELATIVE CLAUSES.**)

**NOUNS VS. VERBS** Wherever you can, prefer verbs to nouns. Doing so will make your writing much clearer. (See **NOMINALI-ZATIONS.**)

NOT THIS: For maximization of contamination **reduction,** the installation of a water-**filtration** device is a priority.

BUT THIS: To **reduce** contamination best, **filter** the water.

**no way** Wordy and trendy for no. (See **CONCISION.**)

NOT THIS: Will you pay? **No way.**

BUT THIS: Will you pay? **No.**

**nowhere** See **never, no, none, not, n't, nothing, nowhere.**

**nowheres** NonSAWE for *nowhere.*

NOT THIS: Lynn could find her keys **nowheres.**

BUT THIS: Lynn could find her keys **nowhere.**

**n't** See **but, hardly, scarcely** and **never, no, none, not, n't, nothing, nowhere.**

**NUMBER** A grammatical category of pronouns, nouns, and verbs. English has two **numbers:** singular ("only one") and plural ("more than one"), illustrated in the table below:

| Part of Speech | Number | |
|---|---|---|
| | **Singular** | **Plural** |
| **Pronouns** | | |
| First Person | I, me | we, us |
| Second Person | you | you |
| Third Person | he, she, it | they, them |

| **Nouns** | art | arts |
|---|---|---|
| | ax | axes |
| | criterion | criterions, criteria |
| | octopus | octopuses, octopi |

| **Verbs** | | |
|---|---|---|
| First Person | am, was | are, were |
| Second Person | are, were | are, were |
| Third Person | is, was | are, were |

Some languages have—and English once had—yet another number: dual ("two"). (See **AGREEMENT: PRONOUNS WITH ANTECEDENTS** and **AGREEMENT: VERBS WITH SUBJECTS.**)

**number**  As a subject, *a number* is plural, but *the number* is singular: *A number of people are upset,* but *The number of people upset is small.*

**number of**  See **amount, number.**

# O

**OBJECT COMPLEMENTS**  One of the twelve functions that a part of speech—in this case, a noun or a noun phrase—can perform in a clause. (See **FORMS AND FUNCTIONS.**)

The **object complement** (OC) of a clause is usually immediately to the right of the direct object (see **DIRECT OBJECTS**).

   S           V       DO    OC
The president appointed  Smith  secretary.

**OBJECT OF A PREPOSITION**  One of the twelve functions that a part of speech—in this case, a pronoun, a noun, or a noun phrase—can perform in a clause. (See **FORMS AND FUNCTIONS.**)

The **object of a preposition** is usually immediately to the right of one preposition; and, taken together, they constitute a prepositional phrase: *of the people, by the people, for the people.*

**OBJECTS** See **DIRECT OBJECTS; OBJECT COMPLEMENTS;** and **OBJECT OF A PREPOSITION.**

**observance, observation**  Sometimes confused. *Observance* means either "complying with" (*observance of the law*) or "celebrating" (*observance of the holiday*). *Observation* means "seeing," "looking at," or "watching": *observation of the crime.*

**obsolescent, obsolete**  Sometimes confused. *Obsolete* means "no longer in use or favor": *an obsolete custom. Obsolescent* means "becoming obsolete": *an increasingly obsolescent custom.*

**of**  Often pronounced like *have* after auxiliary verbs: *could, may, might, should, will, would,* and so on. **Caution:** Never an acceptable spelling of *have.*

NOT THIS:    She could **of** gone.

BUT THIS:    She could **have** gone.

**of course**  Use sparingly. It may offend readers by suggesting that they don't know something that everyone is expected to know.

NOT THIS:    Gold, **of course,** is expensive.

BUT THIS:    Gold is expensive.

**official, officious**  Sometimes confused. *Official* means "pertaining to the duties of the authority of an office, typically a governmental office": *an official act. Officious* means "pertaining to volunteering services neither solicited nor needed": *an officious attendant.*

**off of**   Wordy for *off*.

> NOT THIS:   He dived **off of** the board.

> BUT THIS:   He dived **off** the board.

**OK, O.K., okay**   Three acceptable spellings of this SAWE but vague expression of approval. **Caution:** Not used in formal writing.

> NOT THIS:   This arrangement is OK.

> BUT THIS:   This arrangement is **all right** (or **agreeable** or **satisfactory**).

**old-fashioned**   Whether or not you pronounce it, always write the *-ed* at the end. (See **-ed, -d.**)

**on a regular basis**   Wordy for *regularly*. (See **CONCISION.**)

> NOT THIS:   We revise our forms **on a regular basis.**

> BUT THIS:   We revise our forms **regularly.**

**once and for all**   Prefer *finally* because shorter: *Finally, I won't withdraw my claim.*

**one and the same**   Wordy for *the same*. (See **CONCISION.**)

**one of the only people**   Prefer *one of the few people*.

**one of the things**   Often wordy for *one thing*. (See **CONCISION.**)

> NOT THIS:   **One of the things** I can't stand. . . .

> BUT THIS:   **One thing** I can't stand. . . .

**one of those who . . .**    The verb following *who* is plural, because the antecedent of *who* is plural (not *one* but *those*): *Smith is one of those who **are** [not *is*] likely to succeed.* (See **ANTECEDENTS.**)

**one, you**    (1) *One* is more formal than *you* as an impersonal pronoun: *One believes . . . ; You believe. . . .*

(2) If you are stating your own beliefs, say either *I believe that such and such is the case* or, better, *such and such is the case.* If you state something, you claim to believe it, even if you are lying or mistaken.

(3) When giving instructions, prefer a phrase such as *the cook* or *the trumpeter* to *one* or *you.*

NOT THIS:    **One** pushes (or **you** push) the first valve down.

BUT THIS:    **The trumpeter** pushes the first valve down.

**only**    In speech, whatever word, phrase, or clause it modifies, *only* almost always comes right before the verb: *He **only** knew that cocaine is dangerous.* Pronunciation clearly indicates what it modifies (in this example, *that cocaine is dangerous*). In writing, however, *only* should come right before what it modifies: *He knew **only** that cocaine is dangerous.* This difference between speech and writing is true also of such modifiers as *almost, even, exactly, hardly, just, merely, nearly, scarcely, simply.*

**on Saturday, on Sunday, etc.**    Wordy for *Saturday, Sunday,* etc. (See **CONCISION.**)

NOT THIS:    We leave **on** Sunday.

BUT THIS:    We leave **Sunday.**

**on, upon**    Prefer *on* to indicate a static condition: *the vase on the table.* Prefer *upon* to indicate motion: *he stood **upon** the chair.*

**opine**   Prefer *hold* (or *express*) *an opinion* because less stilted and pretentious.

**optimistic, pessimistic**   Prefer *favorable* or *unfavorable* unless referring to people.

NOT THIS:   The market forecast for February is **pessimistic.**

BUT THIS:   The market forecast for February is **unfavorable.**

**or**   The coordinating conjunction *or* (see **CONJUNCTIONS**) has two senses, the inclusive sense and the exclusive. The inclusive is illustrated by *In the evening, Hadley reads or watches TV.* (If, on some evening, Hadley both reads and watches TV, the writer's statement is accurate.) The exclusive sense is illustrated by *It's feast or famine.* (It can't be both feast and famine at the same time. One of the two is excluded.) If the context does not make clear which sense of *or* you intend, substitute *and/or* (an awkward expression to be used only as a last resort) for the inclusive *or* and *either . . . or* for the exclusive *or.*

**oral, verbal**   Often confused. *Oral* means "spoken"; *verbal* means "in words." For example, all verbal orders, whether spoken or written, are in words; but only oral orders are spoken.

NOT THIS:   The general gave **verbal** but not written orders for the retreat.

BUT THIS:   The general gave **oral** but not written orders for the retreat.

**ORGANIZATION**   Everything you write has some **organization:** it is simply the order in which you present your facts or ideas. A good organization—one that is easy for readers to follow and that focuses their attention upon what you wish to emphasize—is the result of two steps.

One is classification of your facts or ideas upon a carefully chosen basis. (See **CLASSIFICATION.**) The other is effectively ordering the resulting subclasses. Some often effective orders are the temporal (early to late, late to early), the spatial (near to far, far to near), the climactic (increasing importance or forcefulness), the familiar to the unfamiliar, the general to the specific, the specific to the general, question to answer, and problem to solution.

**orientate** A back formation from *orientation.* (See **BACK-FORMATIONS.**) Prefer the shorter *orient*.

> NOT THIS:    Freshmen must be **orientated.**

> BUT THIS:    Freshmen must be **oriented.**

**-oriented** Use sparingly, because often a source of wordiness. (See **CONCISION.**)

> NOT THIS:    a profit-**oriented** business.

> BUT THIS:    a business.

**ostensibly, ostentatiously** Sometimes    confused.    *Ostensibly* means "presumably": *an **ostensibly** disinterested witness. Ostentatiously* means "pretentiously": *an **ostentatiously** learned person.*

**other alternative** Wordy for *alternative*.

> NOT THIS:    no **other alternative** to X.

> BUT THIS:    no **alternative** to X.

**OUTLINES** An **outline** is a plan for organizing a paper (see **ORGANIZATION**), typically, a list of topics (groups or classes of facts or ideas) in the order you plan to present them. If your paper is to be saved from chaos or randomness, some sort of outline—however brief or sketchy, perhaps only in your head—is essential. An outline, of course, is not carved on Mount Rushmore, and you should alter it in any way you see fit as you write your paper.

**outside of**  Wordy for *outside*. (See **CONCISION**.)

NOT THIS:    She lives **outside of** the city.

BUT THIS:    She lives **outside** the city.

**outstanding**  Prefer a more specific word of praise: *clever, ingenious, learned, smart, wise.*

**over again**  Wordy for *again*. (See **CONCISION**.)

NOT THIS:    Play the disc **over again.**

BUT THIS:    Play the disc **again.**

**overall**  Sometimes a source of wordiness. (See **CONCISION**.)

NOT THIS:    the **overall** sum of his debts.

BUT THIS:    the sum of his debts.

**overexaggerated**  Wordy for *exaggerated*. (See **CONCISION**.)

**overlook, oversee**  Sometimes confused. To *overlook* is to neglect: *He **overlooked** one of his orders.* To *oversee* is to supervise: *He **oversees** the mail room.*

**over, overly**  Both are SAWE. **Caution:** But *over* is preferable because shorter.

NOT THIS:    **overly** eager or **overly** ingenious.

BUT THIS:    **over**eager or **over**ingenious.

**over time**    Avoid. It lacks precision.

NOT THIS:    **Over time,** she lost her fortune.

BUT THIS:    She gradually lost her fortune.

**over with**    Wordy for *over.* (See **CONCISION.**)

NOT THIS:    The concert is **over with.**

BUT THIS:    The concert is **over.**

**OXYMORON    Oxymoron** (plural: *oxymora* or *oxymorons*) is a figure of speech (see **FIGURES OF SPEECH**) combining two contradictory words: "darkness visible" (Milton), "faith unfaithful" (Tennyson), "loveless love" (popular song), "so musical a discord" (Shakespeare), "soundless noise" (D. H. Lawrence). A statement containing an oxymoron is, taken literally, a contradiction, usually an implicit one. Often the rhetorical effect of an oxymoron is to intensify the quality designated by the modified word. Darkness visible, for example, is extremely dark—so dark that it is (almost) visible. Phrases such as *chic YMCA* and *honest politicians* are the stuff of small jokes. (See **ANTONYMS** and **CONTRADICTIONS.**)

# P

**package** SAWE in the sense "group of related things offered as a whole." **Caution:** Some readers object to this use of the word.

> NOT THIS: The **package** included a car and a driver.

> BUT THIS: The **offer** included a car and a driver.

**pair** Both singular and plural in SAWE: *One pair of socks is dirty; three pair* (or *pairs*) *of socks are dirty.*

**paltry, petty** Sometimes confused. *Paltry* means "mean" or "meager": *a paltry contribution*. *Petty* also means "mean"; but typically it means "minor," "trifling," or "of little importance": *a petty offense*.

**PARAGRAPHS AND PARAGRAPHING**  A **paragraph** is a body of text designated by an indention. One function of any paragraph is visual or aesthetic: to make a page more attractive by breaking it up. But readers expect paragraphs to do more than that: they expect a paragraph to have a cognitive function as well, to signal some sort of turn or change in the discourse. If a paper is more than just a few paragraphs long, it generally contains four different sorts of paragraphs: an introductory paragraph, several development paragraphs, one or two transitional paragraphs, and a concluding paragraph.

An introductory paragraph, usually short, does something to interest readers in the paper and gives them some idea of what it is about. (See **BEGINNING A PAPER**.)

Developmental paragraphs are the heart of the paper: they develop the information or arguments that are the reason for the paper to be written.

Transitional paragraphs, always short, carry readers from a group of developmental paragraphs treating one aspect of the subject to a group treating a different aspect ("Turning, now, from the evidence for x to the evidence against it . . . ").

A concluding paragraph is usually a brief summary of the developmental paragraphs.

A developmental paragraph often begins with a topic sentence, either announcing the topic of the paragraph or stating the main point of the paragraph ("Two methods of doing x require explanation").

Be sure that a paragraph beginning with a topic sentence delivers neither more nor less than that sentence promises.

NOT THIS:    Two methods of doing x require explanation. The first method is. . . . The second method is. . . . A third method is. . . .

BUT THIS:   [Paragraph 1] Two methods of doing x require explanation. The first. . . . The second. . . . [Paragraph 2] A third method is. . . .

NOT THIS:   [Paragraph 1] Two methods of doing x require explanation. The first method is. . . . [Paragraph 2] The second method is. . . .

BUT THIS:   [Paragraph 1] Two methods of doing x require explanation. [Paragraph 2] The first method is. . . . [Paragraph 3] The second method is. . . .

OR THIS:   Two methods of doing x require explanation. The first method is. . . . The second method is. . . .

**Note:** The choice between these two alternatives should be determined by how much you have to say about each method. If you have a great deal to say, choose the first; if little, choose the second.

**PARALLELISM, CLIMAX, AND RHYTHM** About sixty years ago, the American labor leader John L. Lewis described Franklin Roosevelt's first vice-president, John Nance Garner, as "a poker-playing, whisky-drinking, labor-baiting, evil old man." Lewis's description is memorable and effective (so memorable, indeed, that it is about all that anyone remembers about Garner) not only because of his choice of words but also because of its **parallelism** (repetition of grammatically identical words or phrases), its **climax** (arrangement of words or phrases in an order from least forceful to most forceful), and its **rhythm** (repetition of sound patterns). **Parallelism:** Lewis's description is a noun phrase (see **NOUN PHRASES**) consisting of five premodifiers (see **MODI-**

FIERS AND MODIFICATION) of the noun *man*: *poker-playing, whisky-drinking, labor-baiting, evil,* and *old*. Moreover, each of the first three modifiers is a four-syllable participial phrase (see **PARTICIPLES** and **PARTICIPIAL PHRASES**). **Climax:** The first four modifiers constitute a climax—*poker-playing* the least forceful, *evil* the most. **Rhythm:** Lewis's description has a trochaic sound pattern (a stressed syllable followed by an unstressed syllable):

//pok/er//play/ing//whis/ky//drink/ing//and so on.

**parameter** Best avoided. It is a technical term in mathematics that few general readers understand. If what you mean is "boundary" or "perimeter," write *boundary* or *perimeter*.

**PARAPHRASE** A restatement of a text in different words and word-orders. Recently, paraphrase has acquired a second meaning: A quotation of a text with small alterations. To paraphrase Caesar: The cockroaches came, they saw, they conquered. (See **PARAPHRASE VS. QUOTATION.** See also **LANGUAGE OF THOUGHT.**)

**PARAPHRASE VS. QUOTATION** (1) Both a paraphrase and a quotation are reproductions of a text. A **quotation** reproduces a text exactly—word for word (even misspellings), punctuation mark for punctuation mark, and so on, indicating deletions by ellipses (see **ELLIPSES**) and additions by brackets (see **BRACKETS**):

According to the *Daily Courier,* "George Rundle's complaint is that his lawyer [Herbert Mester] failed to take proper steps to protect his rights . . . and to promote his interests."

A **paraphrase** preserves the meaning of a text while markedly changing the words and their order:

According to the *Daily Courier,* George Rundle has accused Herbert Mester, his lawyer, of not safeguarding his rights and advancing his interests.

(2) In general, prefer paraphrase to quotation unless the phrasing of the text is memorable.

(3) You may use both paraphrase and quotation to reproduce a given text, but only if you make clear which is which.

**PARENTHESES**  Use **parentheses** (  ):

(1) To set off, more emphatically than commas or even
   dashes, a nonrestrictive modifier (appositive, phrase,
   relative clause) from the rest of the sentence (see
   **RESTRICTIVE AND NONRESTRICTIVE**):

The senators (who were stunned by the revelations) fell to
bickering among themselves.

(2) To set off, even more emphatically than dashes, a phrase
   or clause that breaks the continuity of a sentence:

The first to be indicted (the mayor was beside himself) was
his secretary.

(3) To enclose an Arabic numeral repeating a spelled-out
   numeral:

They ordered ten-thousand (10,000) cases.

(4) To enclose numerals or letters in a series, as in this series.

**participating dealers**  A favorite of advertisers: *Now 25 percent
off at participating dealers.* About all this says is that an item is
now 25 percent off at those dealers where it is 25 percent off.

**PARTICIPIAL PHRASES**  A **participial phrase** consists of a
participle, present or past, preceded or followed by one or more
other words: *by running, running hard, eaten his spinach, brought
to justice.*

**PARTICIPLES** A **participle** is a verbal combining characteristics of a verb with those of an adjective (see **ADJECTIVES; VERBS;** and **VERBALS**). The present participle of any verb ends in *-ing: bringing, eating, singing, sinking, talking.* The past participle of a regular (or weak) verb is identified with the past tense, ending in *-ed: talked* (see **IRREGULAR (STRONG) AND REGULAR (WEAK) VERBS**). The past participle of some irregular (or strong) verbs is identical with the past tense: for example, *bring, brought.* But for most it is different:

| PRESENT | PAST | PAST PARTICIPLE |
| --- | --- | --- |
| begin | began | begun |
| blow | blew | blown |
| choose | chose | chosen |
| do | did | done |
| draw | drew | drawn |
| eat | ate | eaten |
| fly | flew | flown |
| know | knew | known |
| rise | rose | risen |
| sing | sang | sung |
| sink | sank | sunk |
| speak | spoke | spoken |
| steal | stole | stolen |
| swear | swore | sworn |
| swim | swam | swum |

**particular** Often a source of wordiness (see **CONCISION**).

NOT THIS: this **particular** place in Arizona.

BUT THIS: this place in Arizona

OR BETTER: Phoenix (for example).

**party**  Avoid using to mean "person." A *party* is a group of people.

> NOT THIS:    I called a certain **party** about arranging the conference.
>
> BUT THIS:    I called a certain **person**. . . .
>
> OR BETTER:    I called a **person**. . . .
>
> OR BETTER
> STILL:    I called Herbert Johnson (for example).

**passed, past**  Sometimes confused. *Passed* is the past tense and the past participle of the verb *pass: They* **passed** *the intersection. Past* is an adjective (*the* **past** *year*), an adverb (*ran* **past**), a noun (*in the* **past**), and a preposition (*ran* **past** *the doorman*).

**PASSIVE VOICE**  See **VOICE.**

**past history**  Wordy for *history.* All history is past. (See **CONCISION.**)

**PATHETIC FALLACY**  The attribution of human feelings to matter: *the cruel sea, the gentle breeze.* The phrase was coined by John Ruskin in *Modern Painters* (1850). (See **FALLACIES.**)

**pedal, peddle**  Sometimes confused. To *pedal* is to use a pedal (of a bicycle, for example, or a piano). To *peddle* is to go from place to place selling things: *peddle washing machines. Peddle* is often used figuratively (see **FIGURES OF SPEECH**): *Peddle your tiresome ideas somewhere else.*

**penniless, penurious**  Sometimes confused—probably because *penniless* means, and *penurious* once meant, "poverty stricken." *Penurious* now means "stingy": *a penurious stepfather.*

**per**   *Per* for *a* or *an* is much used in commercial or technical writing: *$5.00 per* (or *a*) *kilogram.* And *per* for *according to* is sometimes used in informal writing. (See **LATINISMS.**) Caution: *Per* is not used at all in noncommercial or nontechnical formal writing.

> NOT THIS:   **Per** your letter of 15 April, you will be in Phoenix later this month.

> BUT THIS:   **According to** your letter of 15 April, you will be in Phoenix later this month.

**perfect**   Has two senses: (1) "without blemish or fault" (*a perfect day*); (2) "almost without blemish or fault" (*a perfect spouse*). In (2), but not in (1), *perfect* may be qualified (as in the Constitution of the United States: "a **more** perfect union").

**PERIODS**   (See also **ELLIPSES.**) Use a **period** (.):

(1) To conclude a sentence or sentence fragment that is neither exclamatory or interrogative:

The die was cast.

(2) To conclude an abbreviation or a contraction:

a.m.  B.C.  cont.  etc.  Mr.  Mrs.

**persecute, prosecute**   Sometimes confused, perhaps because prosecution may be persecution as well. *Persecute* means "harass" or "oppress": *the Serbs are said to persecute the Croatians. Prosecute* means either "follow to the end" (*prosecute an inquiry*) or "take legal action against" (*prosecute an alleged murderer*).

**personal friend**   Wordy for *friend.*

> NOT THIS:   Orson Welles was a **personal friend.**

> BUT THIS:   Orson Welles was a **friend.**

**personality** Avoid use as a noun to mean "person" or "celebrity."

> NOT THIS: a television **personality.**

> BUT THIS: a television **celebrity.**

**personal, personally** Often a source of wordiness. (See **CONCISION.**) No opinion is *im*personal.

> NOT THIS: my **personal** opinion.

> BUT THIS: my opinion.

**PERSONAL PRONOUNS** A **personal pronoun** (PP) names one or more persons or things: *I* (*me, my, mine*), *you* (*your, yours*), *he* (*him, his*), *she* (*her, hers*), *it* (*its*), *we* (*us, our, ours*), *they* (*them, their, theirs*). Ordinarily, only a third-person personal pronoun (*he, she, it, they*) has an antecedent (ANT):

ANT                        PP
People are interesting because they are unpredictable.

(See **ANTECEDENTS** and **PRONOUNS.**)

**PERSONIFICATION** A figure of speech (see **FIGURES OF SPEECH**) in which something not a person is referred to as though it were a person: *Crime pities no one.*

**-person, person** Many advocate replacing *-man* or *man* with *-person* or *person* (*chairperson, garbage person, police person*), on the grounds that *-man* and *man* are sexist (see **SEXIST LANGUAGE**). The neologisms that result, however, are sometimes awkward. Prefer instead such expressions as *chairing the meeting, garbage collector,* and *police officer.*

**PERSONS** The **persons** of a pronoun, a noun, or a verb are grammatical categories corresponding to three things in any act of speaking or writing:

FIRST PERSON:  the person or persons speaking or writing.
**Pronouns:**  *I, we; me, us; my, mine; our, ours.*
**Nouns:**  none.
**Verbs** (examples):  *am, are.*

SECOND PERSON:  The person or persons spoken or written to.
**Pronouns:**  *you; your; yours.*
**Nouns:**  none.
**Verbs** (example):  *are.*

THIRD PERSON:  the person or persons, or the thing or things, spoken or written about.
**Pronouns:**  *he, she, it, they; him, her, them; his, her, hers; its, their, theirs.*
**Nouns** (examples):  *boy, boys, girl, girls; boy's, boys', girl's, girls'.*
**Verbs** (examples):  *is, are.*

**perspective, prospective** Sometimes confused. Apart from its technical meaning in the graphic arts and in architecture, *perspective* means "place or point from which a person mentally or physically views things": *his perspective on the economy. Prospective* means "in prospect," "lying in the future," or "expected": *a prospective bonus.*

**persuade** See **convince, persuade.**

**phenomenal** Use sparingly, only for things like the arrival of a spaceship in your garden.

**phenomenon** Has two senses: (1) "extraordinary person or thing" (plural: *phenomenons*); (2) "observable fact or event" (plural: *phenomena*). In sense (2), prefer *fact* or *event,* because less pretentious.

**phenomenon, phenomena** See **criterion, criteria; phenomenon, phenomena.**

**philosophy** Avoid using *philosophy* as a synonym for *policy.*

NOT THIS:   The **philosophy** of our store is to accept returns without question.

BUT THIS:   The **policy** of our store. . . .

**PHILOSOPHY OF LANGUAGE, LINGUISTICS, AND RHETORIC** Each of the other entries in this book—whether a topic entry (in capitals) or a word entry (in lower case)—is based upon research in one or more of these three disciplines, which are fundamental to the study of language. Though lines between them are not always easy to draw, here are descriptions of these disciplines:

The **philosophy of language** makes the most fundamental distinctions about language. (See **CLASSIFICATION; COMMUNICATION AND PERSUASION; MEANING AND REFERENCE; METALANGUAGES AND OBJECT LANGUAGES; ASSUMPTIONS AND PROPOSITIONS; PSEUDO-QUESTIONS;** and **USE AND MENTION.**)

**Linguistics** formulates (but does not create) the grammatical rules of languages (see **GRAMMATICAL RULES**): the rules of syntax, or word order (see **SYNTACTIC VARIATION**); the rules of morphology, or word formation (see **MORPHEMES AND PHONEMES**); the rules of phonology, or the sound system (see **MORPHEMES AND PHONEMES**); the rules of semantics or word and sentence meaning (see **ANTONYMS** and **SYNONYMS**); the rules of orthography, or spelling and pronun-

ciation; and the rules of pragmatics, or the uses of a language (see
**BACK-FORMATION; BLACK ENGLISH; and FIGURES
OF SPEECH**).

   **Rhetoric** is the study of the effective (and the ineffective) use
of language. (See **READERS, COMMUNICATION, AND
PERSUASION; ELEGANT VARIATION; EUPHEMISMS;
FALLACIES; PARALLELISM, CLIMAX, AND RHYTHM;
SEXIST LANGUAGE; SPECIFICITY; and SUPERLA-
TIVES.**)

**phony**   SAWE but informal to mean "not genuine."

**PLAGIARISM**   Passing off the words or the ideas of another as
one's own. **Plagiarism,** then, is dishonest; it is theft of intellectual
property. Whatever words or ideas you borrow from some other
writer, you must acknowledge, either informally or by means of a
citation.

**plans for the future or future plans**   Always   wordy:   all   plans
are, by definition, for the future.

   NOT THIS:   My **plans for the future**. . . .

   BUT THIS:   My plans. . . .

**playwright**   Sometimes misspelled *playwrite*. The morpheme (see
**MORPHEMES AND PHONEMES**) *-wright* (as in *wheel-
wright*) means "maker" and is unrelated to *write*.

**plenty**   SAWE and used in informal writing as an adverb meaning
"sufficiently" or "very" (*The driver was plenty drunk*) or as an
adjective meaning "quite sufficient" (*We have plenty of food for
everyone*). **Caution:** Avoid this use in formal writing.

   NOT THIS:   Jim is **plenty** skillful to operate that computer.

   BUT THIS:   Jim is **sufficiently** skillful to operate that computer.

**PLURALS** The rules for forming the **plural** of an English noun are:

(1) If the singular ends in *-ch, -s, -sh,* or *-z,* the plural is the singular plus *-es:*

churches      brushes
lasses         buzzes

(2) If the singular ends in *y,* the plural replaces *y* with *-ies:*

armies            ladies

(3) If the singular ends otherwise, the plural is the singular plus *-s:*

bins        calls

Some exceptions:
criterion         (criteria)
curriculum        (curricula, curriculums)
focus             (foci, focuses)
foot              (feet)
goose             (geese)
graffito          (graffiti)
libretto          (libretti, librettos)
ox                (oxen)
phenomenon        (phenomena, phenomenons)
woman             (women)

**plus** SAWE as a preposition meaning "in addition to": *A roll plus coffee is enough for breakfast.* **Caution:** Many readers object to the use of *plus* as an adverb, especially in formal writing.

NOT THIS:    Swanson is a deadbeat; **plus,** he beats his son.

BUT THIS:    Swanson is a deadbeat; **besides** (or **moreover**), he beats his son.

**p.m.**   See **a.m., p.m.**

**POINT OF VIEW**   The person, real (the writer or the reader) or fictional (one of the characters), through whose eyes and consciousness the reader views the action of a work of fiction. At least four **points of view** may be distinguished: (1) the omniscient author, who reports and evaluates the action, the setting, dialogues, and thoughts and feelings of the characters; (2) a character who tells the story; (3) a character who does not tell the story but whose thoughts and feelings the writer reports; and (4) the reader.

Similarly, a work of nonfiction, an article or essay, for example, may be written from the point of view either of the writer (reflecting his or her aims, goals, interests, or programs) or of the readers (reflecting theirs).

**point of view**   From my *point of view, such and such is the case* is wordy for *I believe that such and such is the case* or, simply, *Such and such is the case.* (See **CONCISION.**)

**police**   SAWE counts the noun *police* as plural: *The police are. . . .*

**policeman**   Prefer *police officer,* the commonly accepted term. (See **SEXIST LANGUAGE.**)

**POLITICAL CORRECTNESS**   A political and social movement (familiarly known as *PC*) on American college and university campuses (and in many public-school systems) whose adherents— students, faculty, and administrators—formulate and try to enforce codes of "politically correct" behavior, forbidding any behavior, especially speech or writing, that might offend minorities (notably, racial, ethnic, or sexual) or women. Prominent in these codes are lists of taboo expressions with corresponding PC expressions, many of which would ordinarily be regarded as euphemisms. *Homosexual,* for example, is taboo. The PC expression—the one most writers and speakers use anyway—is either *gay* or *lesbian.*

Indeed, partly because PC has counterparts in American society generally, many PC expressions are commonplace: *African-American* (for *black*), for instance, and *Native American* (for *Indian*). Many others, however, have not caught on: *differently abled* (for *disabled*), for example, and *sex worker* (for *prostitute*).

Should writers find out what these codes are and try to follow them? Not unless they have reason to believe that their readers do. Moreover, following these codes may well put off readers who do not. Such readers might, for instance, find *womyn* (for *women*) either offensively trendy or simply silly. Finally, like every other euphemism, today's PC expression can easily become tomorrow's taboo. (See **EUPHEMISMS.**)

**politician, statesman**   Very nearly synonymous, but with different connotations. (See **DENOTATIONS AND CONNOTATIONS.**) The connotations of *statesman* are impartiality and devotion to the public good; of *politician,* partisanship and devotion to his or her own interests and to those people and institutions that put, and keep, him or her in power.

**politics**   SAWE counts *politics* as plural when it refers to a set of beliefs (*Horton's politics are left wing*), but as singular when it refers to an art, an institution, a practice, or a science: *Politics is a dirty business.*

**poor, poorly**   To attribute poor health to a person, prefer *poor.*

NOT THIS:    Bentham has felt **poorly** for almost a week.

BUT THIS:    Bentham has felt **poor** for almost a week.

*Poor* is not an adverb describing what Bentham is doing (experiencing a malfunction in his sensory system) but an adjective describing his state of health. (See **HYPERCORRECTION.**)

**pore, pour**    Sometimes confused. *Pore* (usually followed by *over*) means "examine carefully": ***pore over a book***. *Pour* means "make a liquid run from a container": ***pour milk***.

**position**    Pretentious for *job*.

**positive**    Avoid using as a synonym for *favorable*.

NOT THIS:    a **positive** response.

BUT THIS:    a **favorable** response.

**POSSESSION**    SAWE usually indicates possession either by *'s* or *s'* (*Mary's brother, the twins' brother*) or by an *of*-phrase (*the brother of Mary, the brother of the twins*). Avoid using both the apostrophe and an *of*-phrase.

NOT THIS:    The brother **of Mary's.**

BUT THIS:    the brother **of Mary.**

OR THIS:    **Mary's** brother.

**POSSESSIVE PRONOUNS**    Pronouns in the possessive case. (See **CASE.**)

**possible, possibly**    Sometimes confused. *Possible* is an adjective meaning "capable of existing or being realized": *a **possible** reaction*. *Possibly* is an adverb meaning "conceivably": *He **possibly** stole the cash*.

NOT THIS:    a **possible** fatal crash.

BUT THIS:    a **possibly** fatal crash.

**POST HOC ERGO PROPTER HOC**    (Latin for "after which therefore because of which.") An argument that is **post hoc ergo propter hoc** is a fallacy. (See **FALLACIES.**) You commit this fallacy whenever you argue that, solely because one event followed another, it was caused by the other:

PREMISE:     The worst tornado in the history of the state came the very day after the legislature passed a bill forbidding discrimination against homosexuals in employment and housing.

CONCLUSION:  The tornado was caused by passage of this bill.

What may make a post-hoc argument seem persuasive is, of course, that an effect must come after its cause. But simply because one effect came after another is obviously not enough to establish a causal relationship between them. Think of the billions of other effects that this tornado followed: the Boston Tea Party and the death of President Garfield, for instance. And, perhaps, the day before the tornado the legislature also passed a bill giving tax breaks to the handicapped. Why pick the passage of the bill protecting the rights of homosexuals? Besides, like most other events, the tornado probably had a long chain of causes, the last link being the formation of a deep low-pressure area.

**practicable, practical**  Often confused, because similar in both sound and meaning. *Practicable* means "capable of being used" and therefore refers to a potential: *A nuclear-powered car is practicable. Practical* means either (a) "useful" and therefore refers to an actuality (*The jeep is a **practical** vehicle*) or (b) "sensible" or "concerned with practice, not theory" (*Mabel is a **practical** person*).

**pre-**  A prefix that is often a cause of wordiness.

NOT THIS:   a **preprepared** pie crust.

BUT THIS:   a **prepared** pie crust.

NOT THIS:   You're **preapproved** for a loan.

BUT THIS:   You're **approved** for a loan.

**precedence, precedents**  Sometimes confused. *Precedence* means "priority in importance or rank": *Safety takes **precedence** over convenience*. *Precedents* means "acts that sanction similar later acts": ***precedents** for refusing to pay taxes.*

**PREDICATES**  One of the twelve functions that a part of speech or a series of parts of speech can perform in a clause. (See **FORMS AND FUNCTIONS.**)

The **predicate** (PRED) of a clause is usually immediately to the right of the subject. It consists of everything in the clause other than the subject(s). It may be short and uncomplicated, consisting, at the minimum, of a verb (V):

PRED (V)
Zebras  exist.

It may be long and complicated and even interrupted by the subject:

PRED
If you can believe it, zebras exist.

(See **SUBJECTS** and also **INVERTED SENTENCES.**)

**predict**  Such phrases as *predict in advance* and *predict the future* are wordy. (See **CONCISION.**)

**premiere**  Avoid using as a verb.

NOT THIS:  The play **premieres** Friday.

BUT THIS:  The play **has its premiere** (or **opens**) Friday.

**premise, premises**  Sometimes confused. A *premise* is one of the two essential ingredients of an argument (see **ARGUMENT AND PERSUASION**). *Premises* are either (1) more than one premise or (2) a piece of land with structures on it ( *These premises are closed to the public*).

**preowned**   A euphemism for *used*. (See **EUPHEMISMS**.)

NOT THIS:   a superb **preowned** Mercedes.

BUT THIS:   a superb **used** Mercedes.

**prepared to**   Sometimes a source of wordiness. (See **CONCISION.**)

NOT THIS:   I am **prepared to** deny the charge.

BUT THIS:   I **deny** the charge.

**preplan**   Prefer *plan* (see **pre-**). All planning is pre- or in advance. You cannot plan for yesterday.

**PREPOSITIONAL PHRASES**   A **prepositional phrase** is a phrase consisting of a preposition followed by a noun or a noun phrase. (See **PREPOSITIONS.**)

**PREPOSITION AT END OF SENTENCE**   The belief that ending a sentence with a preposition is ungrammatical has no foundation in SAWE fact. Mocking this belief, Winston Churchill is said to have said, "A preposition is the worst thing to end a sentence with." (See **PREPOSITIONS.**)

**PREPOSITIONS**   Prepositions (P) are a part of speech that prefaces a noun phrase (NP) to form a prepositional phrase (PP), whose sole function is modification and which is the equivalent of an adjective or adverb. (See **FORMS AND FUNCTIONS; NOUN PHRASES; ADJECTIVES;** and **ADVERBS.**) Most prepositions are short ( *by, in, of*), but some are long ( *because of, in terms of* ), and not all short words or phrases are prepositions:

PP (= ADJECTIVE)          PP (= ADVERB)

P    NP          P    NP

The vase on the table shines in the sunlight.

**PREPOSITIONS: CASE OF OBJECTS** In SAWE, the case of the object of a preposition is the objective: *by her, for Harold and me* (see **CASES**). Because some speakers and writers seem to believe that the subjective case is somehow more refined or classy than the objective, they sometimes use the subjective case for objects of prepositions. The most notorious example is *between you and I.* (See **HYPERCORRECTION**.)

**PREPOSITIONS: LENGTHY** Prefer a short preposition (or other short expression) to a long one.

NOT THIS:   in the case of.

BUT THIS:   as to.

NOT THIS:   in regard to.

BUT THIS:   regarding.

**PREPOSITIONS: WITH VERBS** Often two or more verbs can precede one preposition: *He works [with] and cooperates with small groups.* But not always. (See **ZEUGMA**.)

NOT THIS:   He works and caters **to** small groups.

BUT THIS:   He works **with** and caters **to** small groups.

**PREPOSITIONS: WORDINESS** Avoid using a needless preposition. (See **CONCISION**.)

NOT THIS:   off **of** the wall.

BUT THIS:   off the wall.

NOT THIS:    opposite **to** the firehouse.

BUT THIS:    opposite the firehouse.

**present incumbent**  Wordy for *incumbent*. (See **CONCISION.**) *Incumbent* means "one presently in office."

**presently**  See **currently, presently.**

**present writer**  Wordy for *the writer.* (See **CONCISION.**) Unless the conventions of the genre in which you are writing (see **GENRE CONVENTIONS**) forbid the first person, prefer *I* to *the writer.* (See **I, me, my, mine, myself.**)

**pretense, pretext**  Sometimes confused. A *pretense* is a pretending: *a pretense to expertise.* A *pretext* is an excuse for doing something: *a pretext for not tipping the waiter.*

**PRETENTIOUS WORDS**  **Pretentious words** try to give ordinary matters an air of grandeur. They may impress your readers, but probably in the wrong way: unfavorably. Worse, pretentious words may conceal your meaning in a verbal fog:

> As McNerney found in Michigan, the rational relationship of personnel and facilities to optimize the provision of health services to maximize accessibility, to increase quality and to contain costs involved an organized system of relationships designed to create colleagueship interfaces in place of competitor relations.—Memorandum from the director of a public-health organization

**pretty**  SAWE but informal to mean "rather": *pretty competent.*

**previous to, prior to**  Pretentious and wordy for *before.* (See **CONCISION.**)

**principal, principle**   Often confused, because identical in sound. *Principal* is both an adjective meaning "most important" (*my principal objection*) and a noun with many meanings (*the principal of a high school, the principal plus interest*). *Principle* is a noun meaning "doctrine," "law," or "rule": *the principles of arithmetic.*

**prioritize**   See -ize.

**prior to**   Wordy and pretentious for *before.*

> NOT THIS:   **Prior to** graduation, I was optimistic about employment

> BUT THIS:   **Before** graduation. . . .

**problem area**   Wordy for *problem* (see **area, field** and **CONCISION.**)

**proceed**   Pretentious for *go.*

**process**   Often a cause of wordiness.

> NOT THIS:   **The process of campaigning** is hard work.

> BUT THIS:   **Campaigning** is hard work.

**procure**   Pretentious for *get.*

**PROFANITY**   Avoid except (sparingly) in quotation or, when appropriate, in fiction. Note that (putting aside taboos, the Lord's name in vain) what is profane is not copulation, defecation, urination, and the like or even the technical words just used for them. What is profane is the four-letter Anglo-Saxon words for them that are well known to every speaker of English. Note also that some words spoken, even in (fairly) polite conversation, may be out of the question in print.

**profession** Not long ago, the term *profession* was reserved for occupations requiring a degree beyond the bachelor's: law, medicine, and university teaching, for example. Because of the prestige of such occupations, the term is now often used by members of other occupations—barbering and insurance-selling, for instance.

**promise** Avoid using as a verb meaning "assure."

NOT THIS: I **promise** you that this is a good investment.

BUT THIS: I **assure** you that this is a good investment.

**PRONOUNS** (1) A typical **pronoun** is a substitute for, refers to, and gets most of its meaning from another expression, called its antecedent (see **ANTECEDENTS**). A pronoun agrees with its antecedent in number and, when singular, in gender:

| ANTECEDENT: PLURAL | ANTECEDENT: MASCULINE | PRONOUN: MASCULINE | PRONOUN: PLURAL |
|---|---|---|---|
| Employees | disliked Harvey | because he | exploited them. |

(2) For different kinds of pronouns, see **DEMONSTRATIVE PRONOUNS; EXPLETIVE PRONOUNS; INDEFINITE PRONOUNS; INTENSIVE PRONOUNS; INTERROGATIVE PRONOUNS; PERSONAL PRONOUNS; POSSESSIVE PRONOUNS; RECIPROCAL PRONOUNS; REFLEXIVE PRONOUNS;** and **RELATIVE PRONOUNS.**

(3) On avoiding sexist use of pronouns, see **SEXIST LANGUAGE.**

(4) On pronoun agreement, see **AGREEMENT; PRONOUNS WITH ANTECEDENTS.**

**PRONUNCIATION, PUNCTUATION, AND SPELLING**
Punctuation and spelling represent pronunciation, but only imperfectly. Not always, for instance, is there a one-to-one correspon-

dence between a certain spelling and a certain word or a certain pronunciation. The noun *record*, for example, is identical in spelling with the verb *record*. But they are different words with different pronunciations. The noun is stressed on the first syllable (*REcord*); the verb, on the second (*reCORD*). And every punctuation mark has more than one function. (See **COMMAS,** for instance. Also see **PUNCTUATION.**)

**proof positive**  Avoid. The best of proofs are only more or less probable.

> **PROOFREADING**  Either (1) comparing your final draft of an article or essay with a print (or proof) from, say, a typewriter, computer printer, or printing service or company, or (2) carefully reading and correcting the final draft itself for what it says as a whole and for such things as spelling, punctuation, and capitalization. (See **EDITING** and **REVISION.**)

**prophecy, prophesy**  Sometimes confused. *Prophecy* is a noun meaning "forecast" or "prediction": *a threatening prophecy. Prophesy* is a verb meaning "make a prophecy": *prophesy a glowing future.*

**proposal, proposition**  Synonymous in the sense "a plan or scheme." In one sense, however, a *proposition* is an indecent proposal (and in this sense *proposition* is a verb as well as a noun: *he propositioned her*). For a technical sense of *proposition,* see **ASSUMPTIONS AND PROPOSITIONS.** Avoid using *proposition* vaguely.

> NOT THIS:  Selling insurance is a hard **proposition.**

> BUT THIS:  Selling insurance is a hard **job** (or a hard **way to make a living**).

**protagonist** The main character—hero or heroine—of an epic, a play, a novel, or a short story. Also the main person in a social or political movement or controversy.

**PRO-VERBS** Perhaps because there are so few **pro-verbs**—*do, do it, do this, do that,* and *do so*—they are not traditionally recognized part of speech (see **FORMS AND FUNCTIONS**), but English has always had them. A pro-verb is pro- in precisely the way a pronoun is. It is a substitute for, refers to, and gets most of its meaning from another expression, called its antecedent (see **PRONOUNS** and **ANTECEDENTS**). The antecedent (ANT) of a pro-verb (PV) is either a verb (V) (see **VERBS**) or a verb phrase (VP) (verb + auxiliaries or objects or modifiers).

In themselves, the pro-verbs *do, do it,* and *do so* mean nothing more than something like "act" or "perform an action." But, taken with their antecedents, they mean whatever the antecedents mean:

> ANT: V               PV
> They treat   people as they do cockroaches.

> ANT: VP         PV
> If you won't call him I'll do it.

> PV      ANT: VP
> If you won't do it, I'll call him.

> ANT: VP
> To put up forever with his contemptible conduct is impossible.
> PV
> Certainly I won't do so.

**PSEUDO-QUESTIONS** A **pseudo-question** is a question that, in principle, no one can answer. One example is *Does the* *world have a purpose?* (No conceivable observation or experiment could answer it.) Another example is *What is the square root, of blue?* (Only a number has a square root, and blue is not a number.)

**punctilious, punctual** Sometimes confused. *Punctilious* means "meticulous" or "in full conformity with code or convention": *punctilious in carrying out her duties. Punctual* means "being on time": *punctual in keeping her appointments.*

**PUNCTUATION** One of the ways by which a written language represents a spoken one. Periods, question marks, and exclamation points, for instance, set off sentences; and commas represent certain pauses within sentences. See entries on particular marks of punctuation. Also see **PRONUNCIATION, PUNCTUATION, AND SPELLING.**

**PUNS** A figure of speech (see **FIGURES OF SPEECH**) in which homophones (words identical in sound but different in meaning and perhaps in spelling) are used humorously: *In a lie may lie the truth.*

**PURPOSE** Your purpose in writing an article or essay may be simply *expressive,* to express your attitude toward or feelings about a person, organization, event, or object—your distrust of bureaucracies or your enthusiasm for the singing of Liza Minelli, for example. Or it may be expository, to set down what you believe the facts of a matter are. Typically, however, your purpose is persuasive, to have an effect upon your readers or audience, to get them to believe something (that the federal government ought—or ought not—to raise the tax on cigarettes) or to do something (vote for a certain candidate for public office).

**purposefully, purposely** Sometimes confused. *Purposefully* means "with a strong purpose" or "with single-mindedness": *working purposefully from dawn to sunset. Purposely* means "intentionally": *She purposely upset the apple cart.*

**qua**  Latin meaning "as." Prefer *as*.

NOT THIS:   A man **qua** husband is not essential.

BUT THIS:   A man **as** husband is not essential.

**qualified expert**  Wordy for *expert*. All experts are, by definition, qualified. (See **CONCISION**.)

**QUANTIFYING MODIFIERS**  Note that, in such **quantifying modifiers** as *two-volume* and *five-story*, though the numeral is plural, the word following it is always singular. (See **MODIFIERS AND MODIFICATION**.)

NOT THIS:   a two-volumes work.

BUT THIS:   a two-volume work.

**queer** Regarded as derogatory in the sense "homosexual" and now largely replaced by *gay*.

**question as to whether** *He raised the question as to whether the project would succeed* is wordy for *He asked whether the project would succeed.* (See **CONCISION**.)

**QUESTION MARKS** Use a **question mark** (?):

(1) To conclude a direct question:

Is that Jack?

(2) To indicate ignorance or doubt:

The first (?) appearance was just before Christmas.

**Caution:** Do not use a question mark to conclude an indirect question.

NOT THIS:    He wonders whether that is fair?

BUT THIS:    He wonders whether that is fair.

**QUESTIONS, DIRECT AND INDIRECT** See **INTER-ROGATIVE PRONOUNS.**

**quick, quickly** Both SAWE as adverbs: *He responded **quick*** (or *quickly*).

**quid pro quo** Though Latin, a widely understood phrase and shorter than its English equivalent: something (given or received) for something (else).

**quite** Ambiguous, meaning either "completely" or "somewhat." Is a *quite favorable evaluation* completely favorable or just somewhat favorable? To avoid confusing your readers, write either *completely* or *somewhat* instead of *quite*.

**QUOTATION MARKS: DOUBLE**  Use **double quotation marks** (" "):

(1) To enclose a direct quotation:

"I won't," she said, "stand for that."

(2) Occasionally, to enclose a word or a phrase you believe misused or inappropriate or unjustified:

He's a so-called "patriot."

He's a self-styled "humanitarian."

(3) To enclose a word, a phrase, a letter, or a numeral mentioned (that is, referred to as such) rather than used (see **USE AND MENTION**):

the word "great"  the letter "m"

(4) To enclose a word or a phrase inappropriate to its context (use sparingly for maximum effect):

The secretary is a "whiz" at thinking up euphemisms.

(5) To enclose the title of a short story, a poem, a radio or television show, a chapter, a lecture, an article, a song or other short musical composition:

"Ozymandias"  "If I Were a Rich Man"

**Caution:** Do not use quotation marks for emphasis.

NOT THIS:  A "marvelous" book.

BUT THIS:  A *marvelous* book.

OR BETTER:  A marvelous book.

**Note:** Put a comma or a period inside a closing quotation mark; a semicolon or a colon outside; a dash, an exclamation point, or a question mark inside or outside, depending upon whether it applies to the quotation or the sentence of which it is a part.

**QUOTATION MARKS: SINGLE**    Use **single quotation marks** (' ') to enclose a direct quotation within a direct quotation: John said, "I heard Harvey say, 'I quit.' "

**QUOTATIONS, DIRECT AND INDIRECT**    A **direct quotation** reproduces within quotation marks (see **QUOTATION MARKS**) a writer's text (or a passage from it) exactly as it appears—word by word, punctuation mark by punctuation mark, capital letter by capital letter, and so on. The only exceptions are explanatory additions, enclosed in brackets (see **BRACKETS**), and deletions, marked by ellipses (see **ELLIPSES**). Neither additions nor deletions may distort the basic meaning of the text. The most often-used addition is "[sic]" to indicate what you believe to be a mistake—a misspelling, for instance, or a factual error.

An **indirect quotation**—or a paraphrase—reproduces not the text, but its meaning or sense, and without use of quotation marks. It represents the text in your words—above all, in your sentences—except, of course, for indispensable key terms.

To preserve one or two striking phrases from the text, you may insert some direct quotations into an indirect quotation: *Lindsay says that the board is incompetent, filled with both "non- and malfeasers."*

**quote**    SAWE for *quotation* (*a quote from Shakespeare*) or for *quotation mark* (*a word in quotes*) and often used these ways in conversation and informal writing. **Caution:** Rarely used these ways in formal writing.

**q.v.**    An abbreviation of Latin *quod vide,* meaning "which see." Prefer *see also* to *q.v.*

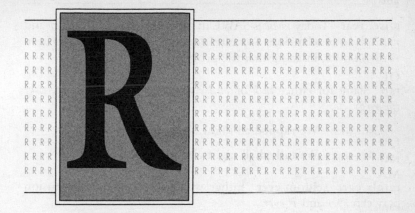

**raise (raised, raising), rise (rose, rising, risen)** Often confused, because similar in both sound and meaning. As a verb, the basic meaning of *raise* is "lift up"; of *rise*, "move up": *The mechanic raised the hood*, but *The hood rose*. *Raise*, in the sense noted, is a transitive verb, followed by a direct object (DO):

DO

The company **raised** my salary.

*Rise* is an intransitive verb, not followed by a direct object:

MODIFIER, NOT DO

My salary has **risen** twice in the last year.

**raise, rear**  Today *raise* is SAWE in phrases such as *raise sheep* and *raise children*. **Caution:** Some readers object to the use of *raise* in *raise children,* insisting that the proper word is *rear.*

**rap**  Slang for either *talk* or *bad consequences* (*beat the **rap**, take the **rap***).

NOT THIS:    We **rapped** all night about politics.

BUT THIS:    We **talked** all night about politics.

**rarely ever, seldom ever**  Either wordy for *ever* or a confusion between *ever* and *if ever.*

NOT THIS:    Grandfather **rarely ever** drives.

BUT THIS:    Grandfather **rarely** (or **rarely if ever** or **hardly ever**) drives.

**rather**  Always part of a hedge. *He is rather proficient* indicates some doubt about his proficiency. (See **HEDGES: SINGLE AND DOUBLE.**)

**rather than**  What comes after *rather than* must be grammatically equivalent to what comes before: *running **rather than** walking* (both present participles), *to respect **rather than** to despise* (both infinitives).

**rational, rationale**  Sometimes confused. *Rational* is an adjective meaning "governed by reason": *a **rational** action. Rationale* is a noun meaning "explanation or justification of a belief or an action": *the **rationale** for investing in junk bonds is suspect.*

**ravage, ravish**  Sometimes synonymous. *Ravage* means "destroy": *The army **ravaged** the city. Ravish* means "rape" or, figuratively, "ravage": *The army **ravished** the city.* (See **FIGURES OF SPEECH.**)

**READABILITY**  The quality of being easy to read. The **readability** of a given text is, of course, relative, varying with the age, the intelligence, and the education of the reader and with his or her knowledge of the subject. In general, a highly readable text has familiar words and uncomplicated syntax (see **SYNTAX**). The sort of syntax, for example, for which Henry James is famous is likely to rank low in readability for many readers.

**READERS, COMMUNICATION, AND PERSUASION**  All writers have two goals. One is **communication:** to write so correctly and clearly that their readers, or audience, will understand their assertions, questions, and requests. The other goal is **persuasion:** to write so convincingly that their readers will believe their assertions, answer their questions, and grant their requests (write checks, join clubs, boycott products, write their senators, vote for certain candidates). Successful communication and persuasion require writers to have a vast amount of knowledge—knowledge of their language and their subjects, of course, but also knowledge both of their readers and of rhetoric.

For successful communication, one thing writers must know is their readers' knowledge of language. What's the size and content of their vocabularies? No readers know every word in the English language. Some readers have larger vocabularies than others; some have more specialized vocabularies. All readers have *the, and, in, bright, woman,* and *look* in their vocabularies. But only architects are likely to have *entablature;* only jazz musicians, *gig;* only lawyers, *tort;* only linguists, *morpheme;* only physicists, *neutrino.* And only New Englanders are likely to have *bannock;* only westerners, *embarcadero;* only southerners, *goober.* Use a word readers don't know, and you jeopardize communication.

Another thing writers must know for successful communication is their readers' knowledge of the subject. If the subject is, say, Theodore Roosevelt, are the readers historians who know a great deal about him? Or are they, at the other extreme, people who have never heard of him? Knowledge is like money; it takes knowledge to get knowledge. Readers who know nothing about Roosevelt can understand essays about him only if writers begin, not by saying what they want to say about him, but by giving them the background knowledge they need to understand what the writers want to say. On the other hand, readers who already know a great deal about Roosevelt need no background knowledge. Indeed, if writers give it to them, they may well feel insulted. The rule is brief: Give readers as much background knowledge as, but no more than, they need.

For successful communication, writers need knowledge not only of their subject and of their readers but also of an indefinitely large number of rhetorical devices and strategies for writing clearly: how to be concise, for example, and how to use definitions, analogies, and examples. (See **CONCISION; DEFINITIONS; ANALOGIES;** and **EXAMPLES.**)

For successful persuasion, the most important thing writers need to know is how to argue well. (See the various entries on **ARGUMENT** and also **FALLACIES** and entries on particular fallacies.) Often, however, they need as well to know something about the values of their readers or audience—about their attitudes, commitments, allegiances, enthusiasms, politics, religion, what they think important, what they think unimportant. If writers are trying to persuade readers to vote for a Democrat, they need to know whether their readers are Democrats, Republicans, Socialists, anarchists, or an assortment. If they are trying to persuade their readers to work for (or against) abortion, they need to know whether they are Catholics, Jews, Protestants, free thinkers, or an assortment.

And, just as it takes knowledge to get knowledge, it takes shared values to persuade readers to take a certain stand on a heated issue. In writing his play *A Doll's House,* in 1878–89, Henrik Ibsen was trying to persuade an audience of in large part male chauvinists that the proper role of women in marriage is not just wife and mother but independent human being. To the extent that his persuasion was successful, it was not only because he was a master of the rhetoric of drama, but also because he and his audience shared certain values: notably, fairness and anticruelty. He could then show the audience that regarding women as having no role in marriage but wife and mother is both unfair and cruel.

**real**   (1) Avoid using as an adverb meaning "very."

NOT THIS:   a **real** provocative article.

BUT THIS:   a **really** (or **very**) provocative article.

(2) Often a source of wordiness (see **CONCISION**), as in *a real innovation.* Simply write *innovation.*

**reason**   Ambiguous, meaning either "cause" (*the reason for the delay was the weather*) or "motive" (*His reason was to avoid military service*). To avoid confusing your readers, prefer either *cause* or *motive.*

**reason is because**   See **because (2).**

**reason why**   Often wordy.

NOT THIS:   The **reason why** he wants it is obvious.

BUT THIS:   The **reason** he wants it is obvious.

OR THIS:   **Why** he wants it is obvious.

**rebut, refute; rebuttal, refutation**   *Rebut* is now SAWE as meaning either (a) "argue against" or (b) "successfully argue against." *Refute* is SAWE to mean (b). **Caution:** Some readers object to use of *rebut* to mean (b), wishing to preserve the distinction between a rebuttal and refutation (*a successful* rebuttal).

NOT THIS:   Senator Hansen won the debate because he **rebutted** Senator Woolbridge's arguments.

BUT THIS:   Senator Hansen won the debate because he **refuted** Senator Woolbridge's arguments.

**receive**   Often pretentious for *get*.

NOT THIS:   I **received** a promotion.

BUT THIS:   I **got** a promotion.

**RECIPROCAL PRONOUNS**   A **reciprocal pronoun** (RP)—either *each other* or *one another*—has the subject (S) of its sentence or clause as its antecedent (A). The antecedent refers to at least two persons or things. And the reciprocal pronoun indicates that each of these is related to the other or others in the way described by the verb (V):

  A + S         V   RP
Tina and Bill love each other.

   A + S        V    RP
Gangsters often shoot at one another.

(See **ANTECEDENTS; PRONOUNS; SUBJECTS;** and **VERBS.**)

**reckon**   NonSAWE for *suppose* or *think*.

NOT THIS:   I **reckon** that Smith will be elected.

BUT THIS:   I **think** (or **suppose**) that Smith will be elected.

**recommend**   In SAWE, followed by either (1) a noun or pronoun plus a prepositional phrase (*recommend you for the job*) or (2) a noun or pronoun plus a noun clause (*recommend that you do such and such*), never by a noun or pronoun plus an infinitive phrase.

NOT THIS:   We **recommend** Virginia to enroll in the class.

BUT THIS:   We **recommend** that Virginia enroll in the class.

**REDUNDANCY**   Use of more means than necessary to achieve an end; in language, of more sounds or marks on paper than necessary to represent a given meaning. *James is stingy in nature*, for example, is redundant because, without *in nature*, the sentence has the same meaning. (See **CONCISION**.)

**REFLEXIVE PRONOUNS** Reflexive pronouns (RP) are identical to intensive pronouns: *myself, yourself, himself,* (not *hisself*), *herself, itself* (not *itsself*), *ourselves, yourselves, themselves* (not *theirselves*). But their relationship to their antecedents is different. A reflexive pronoun has the subject (S) of its sentence or clause as its antecedent (A) but is not an appositive of the subject:

```
   A + S              RP
 Eleanor pinched herself.
```

(See **ANTECEDENTS; APPOSITIVES; PRONOUNS;** and **SUBJECTS**.)

**regardless**   See **irregardless**.

**regard, regards** Often confused. As a noun *regard* means (a) "respect" or "affection" or (b) "reference" and is singular; whereas *regards* means "friendly greeting" and is plural.

NOT THIS:    in **regards** to your promotion.

BUT THIS:    in **regard** to your promotion.

**Caution:** *in regard to* is often wordy. (See **CONCISION**.)

**relate to** NonSAWE in the sense "sympathize with" or "understand."

NOT THIS:    Jean **relates to** Zen.

BUT THIS:    Jean **sympathizes with** (or **understands**) Zen.

**RELATIVE CLAUSES** A **relative** (or adjectival) **clause** (RC) begins with a relative pronoun (RP) that has an antecedent (ANT), usually immediately before it:

RC

ANT    RP
the girl who loves me

RC

ANT    RP
the girl whom I love

RC

ANT    RP
the girl whose love I cherish

**Note:** If a relative pronoun (*whom* or *that*) is the direct object of a relative clause, it may be omitted:

RC
the girl  I love

(See **ANTECEDENTS; DIRECT OBJECTS;** and **RELATIVE PRONOUNS.**)

**relatively**  Often a source of wordiness. (See **CONCISION.**)

NOT THIS.   a **relatively** large number of voters.

BUT THIS:   a **large number** of voters.

OR BETTER:   **many** voters.

**RELATIVE PRONOUNS**  Relative pronouns are identical to interrogative pronouns (except for the relative pronoun *that*): *that, who* (*whoever, whosoever*), *whom* (*whomever, whomsoever*), *whose* (*whosever, whosesoever*), *what* (*whatever, whatsoever*), *which* (*whichever*). But relative pronouns have different uses from interrogative ones. A relative pronoun (RP) introduces either a relative clause (RC) or a noun clause (NC). It has an antecedent (ANT) only when it introduces a relative clause:

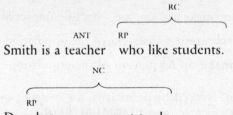

RC

ANT     RP
Smith is a teacher   who like students.

NC

RP
Do whatever you want to do.

(See **ANTECEDENTS; NOUN CLAUSES; PRONOUNS;** and **RELATIVE CLAUSES.**)

**religion, religiosity** Sometimes confused. A *religion* is a set of beliefs in the supernatural together with a set of rituals and, perhaps, a code of conduct. *Religiosity* is sentimentalized or pretentious religious observance.

**remainder** Prefer the shorter *rest*.

NOT THIS:   the **remainder** of the stock.

BUT THIS:   the **rest** of the stock.

**remediable, remedial** Sometimes confused. *Remediable* means "capable of being remedied or corrected": *a remediable problem*. *Remedial* means "designed to remedy or correct": *a remedial math class.*

**repeat again** Wordy for *repeat* (see **CONCISION**)—unless what is meant is "repeat for a second time."

**REPETITION** Though **repetition** is always wordy (see **CONCISION**), it is often effective: *"we cannot dedicate, we cannot consecrate, we cannot hallow this ground."*—Abraham Lincoln

**reply in the negative (or in the affirmative)** Pretentious   for *say no* (or *yes*).

**represent** Avoid to mean "make up" or "are," because imprecise.

NOT THIS:   The poor **represent** 65 percent of the population.

BUT THIS:   The poor **make up** 65 percent of the population.

**rescisions** A euphemism, favored by politicians, for *budget cuts*: *rescisions in the president's budget*. (See **EUPHEMISMS**.)

**respectfully, respectively** Often confused. *Respectfully* means "with esteem or respect": *He treats all religions respectfully. Re-*

*spectively* means "in the order given": *Paris and Rome are capitals of France and Italy,* **respectively.**

**restive**   Once meant "obstinate" but is now SAWE to mean "restless." **Caution:** Some readers may object to this use of the word.

NOT THIS:   a **restive** search.

BUT THIS:   a **restless** search.

**RESTRICTIVE AND NONRESTRICTIVE**   Unlike a nonrestrictive modifier, a restrictive modifier limits the reference of the word or phrase it modifies:

RESTRICTIVE:   My sister Helen is a chemist.

(The writer has more than one sister. The modifier *Helen* limits the reference of the word *sister* to only one—Helen.)

NON-
RESTRICTIVE:   My sister, Helen, is a chemist.

(The writer has only one sister. *Helen* does not limit the reference of *sister:* it gives the reader the name of that sister.)

RESTRICTIVE:   Smith's play *The Fatalist* is excellent.

(Smith wrote more than one play. The modifier *The Fatalist* limits the reference of the phrase *Smith's play* to only one—*The Fatalist.*)

NON-
RESTRICTIVE:   Smith's play, *The Fatalist,* is excellent.

(Smith wrote only one play. *The Fatalist* does not limit the reference of Smith's play: it gives the reader the name of that play.)

RESTRICTIVE:   People who are unpredictable are annoying.

(Not all people, the writer believes, are unpredictable. The modifier *who are unpredictable* limits the reference of the word *people* to those people who are unpredictable.)

NON-
RESTRICTIVE:   People, who are unpredictable, are annoying.

(All people, the writer believes, are unpredictable. The modifier *who are unpredictable* does not limit the reference of *people:* it gives the reader some information about all people.)

**Note:** In these examples, as in all others, absence of commas (or dashes or parentheses) marks a modifier as restrictive, and presence of commas marks it as nonrestrictive. A man who writes "My wife Mary is a teacher" either confesses to bigamy or is ignorant of how to punctuate nonrestrictive modifiers.
   (See **MODIFIERS AND MODIFICATION.**)

**return back**   Wordy for return. (See **CONCISION.**)

NOT THIS:   **return back** home.

BUT THIS:   **return** home.

**reverend**   Not synonymous with *clergyman, priest,* or *minister.*

NOT THIS:   **a reverend.**

BUT THIS:   **a clergyman** (or **priest** or **minister**).

Preceded by *the* and followed by a title or a full name.

NOT THIS:   **Reverend** Graham.

BUT THIS:   **the Reverend Billy** (or **Mr.** or **Dr.**) Graham.

**REVISION**  For an unambitious paper, your first draft may justifiably be your only one. But a long, carefully argued paper may require many drafts or revisions, and between drafts it is well to let the paper simmer for a day or two before you read it again. Some writers find that reading a draft aloud exposes problems they otherwise would not have noticed. A critical reading by a knowledgeable friend can be especially helpful.

Revision can, of course, be endless. Furthermore, excessive fussing with your writing may deprive it of all freshness and spontaneity. How much you do of it should be determined by the importance of the paper. (See **EDITING**.)

**revolt, revolution**  Sometimes confused. A *revolt* (or a rebellion) is an uprising against a government. A *revolution* is a successful revolt (an overthrow of a government).

**RHETORIC**  (1) **Rhetoric** is either the art or the study of the art of speaking or writing well. Most of the advice in this book is rhetorical. (See **CLARITY; CONCISION;** and **ARGUMENT AND PERSUASION,** for instance.)

(2) The word *rhetoric,* however, is often used to mean "pompous or bombastic language": *mere rhetoric.*

**RHETORICAL QUESTIONS**  A figure of speech (see **FIGURES OF SPEECH**) that in form is a question but in meaning is a negative answer to the question:

Are we going to put up with this outrageous treatment? =
We are not going to put up with this outrageous treatment.

**rich, wealthy**  These synonyms are both SAWE.

**riffle, rifle**  Often confused. The most common meaning of *riffle* is "leaf through," "shuffle," or "thumb"; of *rifle* (as a verb), "ransack" or "steal."

> NOT THIS:    He **rifled** the pages.

> BUT THIS:    He **riffled** the pages.

**right**  Avoid as an adverb meaning "very" because nonSAWE.

> NOT THIS:    a **right** good orthopedist.

> BUT THIS:    a **very** good orthopedist.

**rise (rose, rising, risen)**  See **raise (raised, raising), rise (rose, rising, risen)**.

**role, roll**  Sometimes confused. *Role* means "part in a play" or "function of a person in an activity": *a role in the Watergate thefts. Roll* means either (1) "turn over and over" (*rolled around on the floor*), (2) "list of names" (*called the roll*), or (3) "small piece of bread dough rolled and baked" (*rolls with jam*).

**row**  SAWE but informal as a noun meaning "minor dispute or quarrel": *a family row.*

**rudimentary, vestigial**  Sometimes confused, possibly because complementary in meaning. Something is *rudimentary* if it appears at the beginning of a process or an evolutionary development: *rudimentary fins.* It is *vestigial* if there is still a trace at the end: *a vestigial tail.*

**said** Not used for *previously mentioned* except in legal writing.

> NOT THIS: The **said** army was defeated.

> BUT THIS: **This** army was defeated.

**same** Not used as a pronoun without *the* except in legal or commercial writing.

> NOT THIS: It was either a diamond or a good imitation of **same.**

> BUT THIS: It was either a diamond or a good imitation of **one** (or **it** or **the same**).

**sanctimony, sanctity** Sometimes confused. *Sanctimony* means "pretended or hypocritical holiness"; *sanctity* means "holiness" or "inviolability."

NOT THIS:    the **sanctimony** of the lawyer-client relationship.

BUT THIS:    the **sanctity** of the lawyer-client relationship
(unless, of course, you mean "pretended or
hypocritical holiness").

**say**  (1) In general, use *say* to introduce a paraphrase or a quotation. And beware, in a series of paraphrases or quotations, of
elegantly varying *say* to, for instance, *assert, aver, claim, hold,* or
*state.* (See **ELEGANT VARIATION.**)
(2) SAWE as a synonym for *for example: Give me a little time—
say a week.*

**says**  When writing in the past tense do not use *says* for *said.*

NOT THIS:    The sheriff sat [past tense] silent for a moment
and then **says,** "Go."

BUT THIS:    The sheriff sat silent for a moment and then **said,**
"Go."

**say, state**  Prefer *say* because *state* is pretentious.

**scarcely**  See **but, hardly, scarcely.**

**science, scientism**  Sometimes confused. *Science* is either the sys-
tematic search for knowledge, especially of nature, or the knowledge itself. *Scientism* is the belief that the methods and the criteria
of the natural sciences should be used elsewhere, especially in the
humanities.

**science, technology**  Sometimes confused. *Science* is the search
for basic truths about the universe; *technology,* the search for
applications of them. Chemistry and physics are sciences; chemical
engineering and mechanical engineering, technologies.

**seat (seated, seating), set (set, setting), sit (sat, sitting)**    Often confused, because similar in sound. The basic meaning of *seat* is "give a seat to" (*Mary **seated** her guests on the porch*); of *set*, "place" (*Sue **set** a kettle on the stove*); of *sit*, "take or occupy a seat" (*She **sat** on a chair*). **Caution:** *Set* for *sit* is nonSAWE.

> NOT THIS:    He was **setting** on the couch for an hour.

> BUT THIS:    He was **sitting** on the couch for an hour.

Both *seat* and *set*, in the sense noted, are transitive verbs, followed by direct objects (DO):

DO                       DO<br>
He **seated** the mourners.    She **set**  the book   down.

*Sit*, in the sense noted, is an intransitive verb, not followed by a direct object:

MODIFIER, NOT A DO<br>
She **sat** down for a    moment.

**sectarian, secular**    Sometimes confused. *Sectarian* means "pertaining to sects or religious groups": *a **sectarian** appeal*. *Secular* means "not sacred" or "worldly": *a **secular** charity*.

**seeing as**    Prefer *because*.

> NOT THIS:    **Seeing as** the weather is warm, I'll dress light tonight.

> BUT THIS:    **Because** the weather is warm, I'll dress light tonight.

**see where**    Prefer *see that: I see **that** the tide is low.*

**seldom ever**    See **rarely ever, seldom ever.**

**-self, selves**  Pronouns ending in *-self* or *-selves* are always either intensive (*Jack himself raised the question*) or reflexive (*Helen pulled herself together*). (See **INTENSIVE PRONOUNS** and **REFLEXIVE PRONOUNS**.)

> NOT THIS:   Barbara called Harriet and **myself.**

> BUT THIS:   Barbara called Harriet and **me.**

**semi-**  See **bi-, semi-.**

**SEMICOLONS**  Use a semicolon (;):

(1) To separate independent clauses not joined by *and, but, either . . . or, for, neither . . . nor,* or *or:*

The main events were soon over; the others were an anticlimax.

(2) To separate independent clauses joined by *and, but, either . . . or, for, neither . . . nor,* or *or* if some of them have considerable punctuation within them:

The main events—some, but by no means all, of them, very entertaining, were soon over; and the others were an anticlimax.

(3) To separate independent clauses joined by conjunctive adverbs (see **CONJUNCTIVE ADVERBS**):

He argued; however, the rest of the committee did not.

**seminal**  Once a useful word meaning "creative" or "original." Perhaps now best avoided because it has pretty much come to mean "pertaining to semen."

**senior citizen**  A euphemism (see **EUPHEMISMS**) for elderly person but SAWE.

**sensuous**   Best avoided because it has pretty much lost its original meaning ("relating or devoted to the pleasures of the senses") and now is usually taken to mean "relating or devoted to sexual pleasure."

**SENTENCE EXTRA**   A word or phrase that has no function in its sentence (see **FORMS AND FUNCTIONS**). An example is the second *that* in the following sentence: *I know that, whenever I invest money hastily, that I lose.* The first *that* is a subordinating conjunction with the function of introducing the noun clause *that, whenever I invest money hastily, I lose.* The second *that* has no function: the intervening adverbial clause (*whenever I invest money hastily*) caused the writer to forget the first *that*. A sentence containing a sentence extra is ungrammatical. (See **GRAMMATI-CAL RULES.**)

**SENTENCE FRAGMENTS**   A **sentence fragment** is a string of words that is not a sentence. It lacks a subject or a predicate or both: *Sometimes working in the garden. Books, pens, paper, and computers, for example. Ran to the store.*

**SENTENCES**   The **sentence,** not the word, is the fundamental unit of any language. Native speakers of a language vary enormously in the size of their vocabularies. But what they all seem to know is whether a given string of words, even unfamiliar words, is a sentence.

A sentence is either declarative (*Tom is careful*), interrogative (*Is Tom careful?*), or imperative (*Tom, be careful*).

A declarative sentence is either analytic (true by virtue of its form or of its meaning: *Every mother either is or is not blonde; Every mother is female*), contradictory (false by virtue of its form or of its meaning: *No mother either is or is not a blonde; No mother is female*), or synthetic (true or false by virtue of the facts: *Every mother is a vegetarian*).

A sentence is either periodic (if shortened it is not a sentence:

*Harriet is thin*) or cumulative or loose (if shortened, it is still a sentence: *Harriet is thin now*).

**sentimentality**    Excessive or inappropriate expression of sentiment. But there are no objective, universally accepted criteria for excess or inappropriateness. What is sentimental for one person may well be entirely justified for another.

**separate**    Often a source of wordiness. (See **CONCISION**.)

> Not this:    four **separate** residences.

> But this:    four residences.

**SEQUENCING VERBS**    If a sentence or a passage contains a sequence of two or more verbs, the tense of each verb is determined by its place in the sequence, as the following sentences illustrate:

> After I **have finished** [present perfect] his letter, I **will answer** [future] it.

> After I **finish** [present] his letter, I **will answer** [future] it.

> After I **had finished** [past perfect] his letter, I **answered** [past] it.

> Before I **answer** [present] his letter, I **will have had** [future perfect] it a week.

> I **have bought** [present perfect] a new speaker, which I now **connect** [present] to my receiver.

> I often **read** [present] before I **go** [present] to sleep.

**Note:** As the first two sentences show, more than one sequence is acceptable.

set (set, setting)   See **seated (seated, seating), set (set, setting)
sit, (sat, sitting).**

**SEXIST LANGUAGE**  The recent drive for equality of the
sexes has dramatically changed the way many speak and write
English. About thirty years ago, many people of both sexes began
to believe that some language is sexist—that it both reflects and
promotes sexual inequality. Some of these people made well-pub-
licized proposals for eliminating sexist language; and, gradually
and often quite self-consciously, society accepted and acted upon
them. Unlike most changes in language, then, these were, to some
extent, the product of conscious decisions about how to speak and
write. (See **GRAMMATICAL RULES.**) There are four major
changes:

(1) Introduction of a new word: *Ms.* Until recent years, the
    courtesy title for a married woman was *Mrs.* (plural:
    *Mesdames*); for an unmarried woman, *Miss* (plural:
    *Misses*). Now the courtesy title for virtually any woman
    not in holy orders, especially a woman whose marital
    status is either unknown or considered irrelevant, is *Ms.*
    (plural: *Mses.* or *Mss.*). Some other courtesy titles are, of
    course, still used for any qualified person of either sex:
    *Doctor (Dr.), Lieutenant (Lt.), Professor (Prof.)*, and
    *Reverend (Rev.)*, for example. **Caution:** When in doubt,
    use *Ms.*, even though some women object to it.
(2) Virtual elimination of feminine suffixes: *-ess, -ette*, and
    *-trix*. Words like *poetess, usherette*, and *aviatrix*—and
    other feminine designations like *lady doctor* and
    *postmistress*—are often thought sexist or even racist. Why
    *Negress* but not *whitess* or *Caucasianess?* (Some feminine
    suffixes and other feminine designations, however, seem
    unavoidable: *duchess, mother superior,* the courtesy title
    *Sister.*)

(3) Virtual elimination of the suffix *-man: Chairman* has been replaced by *chairperson* or *chair, salesman* by *salesperson, policeman* by *police officer.*

(4) Virtual elimination of masculine pronouns with generic antecedents. Traditionally, masculine pronouns (*he, him, his, himself*) had two uses. One was to refer to a masculine antecedent: *John has his problems.* The other was to refer to a generic, human antecedent—either a singular indefinite pronoun (*anyone, each, everyone, someone,* and so on) or a singular generic, human phrase (*a person, the average American, every student*): *Every student has his problems.*

In recent years, nearly all speakers and writers have eliminated this second usage, considering it to be sexist. They believe that it suggests, for example, that either every student or the only student who counts is male. They have found at least four satisfactory substitutions for this sexist language:

(a) Use of *he or she, him or her,* etc. *Every student has his or her problems.* An advantage of (a) is that it is the most widely accepted substitute. **Caution:** A disadvantage of (a) is that, repeated, it is wordy and can be awkward: *Every student has his or her problems, which worry him or her a great deal.*

(b) Use of a plural pronoun with a singular generic antecedent: *Every student has their problems.* An advantage of (b) is that it is now standard in both speech and informal writing. (See **they, them, their, theirs.**) **Caution:** A disadvantage is that some readers object to it in any writing, formal or informal, because it constitutes a grammatical error (pronoun and antecedent do not agree in number).

(c) Making antecedents and pronouns plural whenever possible: *All students have their problems.* **Caution:** A disadvantage of (c) is ambiguous reference when more than one possible plural antecedent is present: *In choosing friends, people consider their tastes. (Whose tastes—their own or their potential friends?)*

(d) Eliminating pronouns whenever possible: *Every student has problems.*

Four other substitutes that have been tried are unsatisfactory:

(e) Use of *he/she, him/her,* etc.: *Every student has his/her problems.* (Note that such expressions are virtually unpronounceable.)

(f) Use of *she, her,* and so on: *Every student has her problems.* (Note that this usage may cause readers to think that the antecedent is feminine, not generic. Does *every student* refer only to female students?)

(g) Alternating between *he, him,* and so on, and *she, her,* and so on: *Every student has his problems, which worry her a great deal.* (Note that this usage may confuse readers even more than the one described in [f].)

(h) Coining a new pronoun, *s/he: Every student has problems, which s/he takes seriously.* (Note that, besides being virtually unpronounceable, [h] can replace only *he or she,* not *her or him, hers or his,* or *herself or himself.*

**shall, will**   Perhaps a half-century ago, some educated Americans tried, with only modest success, to distinguish between *shall* and *will* as follows:

(1) In the first person, to express a prediction or an intention about their conduct, they used *shall: I* (or *we*) *shall be at the seaside most of the summer.* To express a determination or a promise to do something, they used *will: I* (or *we*) *will pay all our bills by the first of the month.*

(2) In all other persons, they reversed this procedure. For prediction or intention, they used *will: He* (or *she* or *they* or *you*) *will*

*be at the seaside most of the summer.* For determination or promise, they used *shall: He* (or *she* or *they* or *you*) *shall pay all his bills by the first of the month.*

Nowadays, maybe only a few retired professors of English try to speak or write in conformity with (1) or (2). Other speakers or writers prefer *will* in most cases and use *shall* only in such questions as *Shall I pour you another martini?*

**share**  Avoid using this verb when what is shared is not material.

NOT THIS:  Let me **share** with you a spiritual experience I had.

BUT THIS:  Let me **tell** you about a spiritual experience I had.

**SHIFTS**  A shift in a composition is any change in the way you are writing it that is not required by a change in what you are writing (like a change of topic). Any shift may confuse your readers, endangering clarity (see **CLARITY**): a shift in grammatical structure (tense, mood, voice, person, number, or discourse); a shift in style, tone, or level of formality; or a shift in point of view.

NOT THIS (SHIFT FROM PAST
TO PRESENT TENSE):  I warned him not to be late, and he **gets** angry.

BUT THIS:  I warned him not to be late, and he **got** angry.

**(See VERBS and HISTORICAL PRESENT.)**

NOT THIS (SHIFT FROM
INDICATIVE TO
SUBJUNCTIVE MOOD):  Sanderson will run again if the party **were to ask** him.

BUT THIS:  Sanderson will run again if the party **asks** him.

**(See MOOD.)**

NOT THIS (SHIFT FROM
ACTIVE TO PASSIVE VOICE): First, you should turn on the power; then, the channel should **be selected.**

BUT THIS: First, you should turn on the power; then you should **select** the channel.

(See **VOICE.**)

NOT THIS (SHIFT FROM
THIRD TO SECOND PERSON): A **person** should always drive carefully, but **you** should take extra care on icy roads.

BUT THIS: A **person** should always drive carefully but take extra care on icy roads.

(See **PERSON.**)

NOT THIS (SHIFT FROM
PLURAL TO SINGULAR): Overdoses are dangerous but **an overdose** need not be fatal.

BUT THIS: Overdoses are dangerous but need not be fatal.

(See **NUMBER.**)

NOT THIS (SHIFT FROM
INDIRECT TO DIRECT
DISCOURSE): Smith asked whether the competition was closed and **"Can I get in?"**

BUT THIS: Smith asked whether the competition was closed and **whether he could get in.**

(See **DISCOURSE.**)

NOT THIS (SHIFT FROM PLAIN STYLE TO PSEUDO-POETIC): Our bird-watching society is creating **a sanctuary for our feathered friends.**

BUT THIS: Our bird-watching society is creating a **bird sanctuary.**

(See **STYLE.**)

NOT THIS (SHIFT IN POINT OF VIEW FROM OUTSIDE TO INSIDE): The great Victorian tower loomed against the evening sky. Looking out the circular window at the very top of the tower, Mario could see the glow of the city.

BUT THIS: The great Victorian tower loomed against the evening sky. In the circular window at the very top of the tower, Mario could be seen looking out at the glow of the city.

(See **POINT OF VIEW.**)

**shop**   Now SAWE not only as a noun (*the shop on the corner*) and an intransitive verb (*We shop in the mall*), but as a transitive verb (*We shop discount stores*).

**shortly**   Means "curtly" in SAWE but not "briefly."

NOT THIS: He spoke **shortly,** about ten minutes.

BUT THIS: He spoke **briefly,** about ten minutes.

**should, would**   *Should* and *would* are the past tenses of *shall* and *will,* respectively. At one time, some educated Americans tried to distinguish between them somewhat in the way they tried to distinguish between *shall* and *will* (see **shall, will**).

(1) In the first person, to express a polite preference, they used *should: I* (or *we*) ***should like to go to the party***. To express a strong preference, they used *would: I* (or *we*) ***would like to go to the party***.

(2) In all other persons, they used *would: He* (or *she* or *they* or *you*) ***would like to go to the party***.

Nowadays, few try to speak or write in conformity with (1) and (2). Speakers and writers generally use *should* only to express an obligation: *I **should** work harder; **Should** I work harder?*

**showcase**  Avoid using as a verb meaning "exhibit" or "publicize" because nonSAWE.

NOT THIS:   The network **showcased** the new series.

BUT THIS:   The network **publicized** the new series.

**show up**  (1) SAWE to mean "appear": *The guest of honor didn't **show up** until almost seven.*

(2) Although SAWE, informal for *expose* or *come*.

NOT THIS:   His answer **showed up** his ignorance.

BUT THIS:   His answer **exposed** (or **revealed**) his ignorance.

NOT THIS:   He didn't **show up** until late.

BUT THIS:   He didn't **come** until late.

**sic**  Enclosed in brackets, italicized (or underlined), and inserted into a quotation, *sic* (Latin for *thus*) indicates both that the quotation appears exactly as the quoter found it (thus) and that the quoter is aware that something about its form (spelling, grammar) or its content (truth) is questionable: " . . . in Paris, the capitol [*sic*] of France . . . "; "Signed in 1775 [*sic*], the Declaration of Independence. . . . "

**significant other**  A euphemism for *lover.* A gender-neutral replacement also for such words as *boyfriend, girlfriend,* and *mistress* (not to mention *concubine* and *sugar-daddy.*) (See **EUPHE-MISMS.**)

**SIGNS**  A **sign** is something that an observer can interpret— make inferences from—by means of relevant knowledge. A natural sign is not intentionally created by a human: dark clouds, a daisy, a mouse, tears, a clammy handshake. To interpret a natural sign, an observer must know a physical law or regularity: dark clouds mean rain, tears are a sign of sorrow. A conventional sign is intentionally created by a human to communicate: a text, a roadside sign. To interpret a conventional sign, an observer must know a set of conventions or rules: the English language, a diplomatic code.

**similar to**  Usually wordy for *like.* (See **CONCISION.**)

NOT THIS:    Ale is **similar to** beer.

BUT THIS:    Ale is **like** beer.

**simple, simplistic**  Sometimes confused. *Simple* means "uncomplicated": *a simple procedure. Simplistic* means "excessively or unrealistically simplified": *a simplistic program for reform.*

**SINGULAR-PLURAL WORDS**  Such words as *committee, council, public,* and *senate* can be either singular or plural, depending upon whether what is meant is the group as a unit (*The committee is in session*) or the group as a collection of individuals (*The committee are in disagreement*).

**sit (sat, sitting)**  See **seat (seated, seating), set (set, setting), sit (sat, sitting).**

**SLANG**  Informal language often highly figurative or consisting of neologisms (see **NEOLOGISMS**), rarely written and, when written, not SAWE; for example, *sauce* to mean "liquor."

**slay**  A verb best avoided. It survives only in newspaper headlines and in the conversational *You slay me* ("You amuse me greatly").

**sleeper**  SAWE but informal to mean "unpredicted success": *This TV show was a sleeper.*

**slow, slowly**  Both SAWE as adverbs.

**snooty**  SAWE but informal to mean "haughty" or "disdainful": *a snooty critic.*

**so**  SAWE but informal for *very.*

NOT THIS:  I was **so** excited.

BUT THIS:  I was **very** excited.

But *so* followed by a *that* clause is quite unobjectionable: *I was so excited that I nearly collapsed.*

**so as**  Wordy when followed by an infinitive.

NOT THIS:  I worked hard **so as** to save money.

BUT THIS:  I worked hard to save money.

**so-called**  The commonest meaning of *so-called* is "wrongly called": *His so-called supporters betrayed him.* **Caution:** Avoid using *so-called* when you don't mean this.

NOT THIS:  the **so-called** massacre at My Lai.

BUT THIS:  the **massacre** at My Lai.

**sociable, social**  Sometimes confused, though sometimes synonymous. In some contexts, both adjectives mean "friendly," "affable," "fond of people," even "gregarious": *a sociable* (or *social*) *choirmaster*. But *social* also means "pertaining to society or relationships among people": *the social contract, social diseases*.

**some**  SAWE as an adverb meaning "about": *Some twenty officers were indicted*. But not as an adverb meaning "somewhat."

NOT THIS:   The weather is **some** better today.

BUT THIS:   The weather is **somewhat** better today.

**some one**  See **any one, anyone; every one, everyone; some one, someone.**

**somewheres**  NonSAWE for *somewhere*.

NOT THIS:   There must be an answer **somewheres.**

BUT THIS:   There must be an answer **somewhere.**

**sooner**  SAWE as an adverb meaning "rather": *I would sooner starve than eat tuna fish.*

**sore**  SAWE but informal to mean "angry": *He is sore about his demotion.*

**sort**  See **kind, sort, type.**

**sound out**  SAWE to mean "seek someone's opinion": *We sounded out the architect about the remodeling plans.*

**spark**  SAWE as a verb meaning "is the immediate or precipitating cause of": *His speech sparked a debate.*

**spearhead**   A cliché meaning "act as the chief force behind." (See
**CLICHÉS.**)

NOT THIS:    Jones **spearheaded** the drive for lower taxes.

BUT THIS:    Jones **led** the drive for lower taxes.

**special**   Avoid using as a vague word of praise.

NOT THIS:    a **special** person.

BUT THIS:    a **charming** (or **kind** or **talented** or **remarkable**)
person.

**SPECIFICITY**   A word or phrase is specific or general only by
comparison with another. *Stroll,* for example, is more specific than
*walk, walk* more than *move. Meadowlark* is more specific than *lark,
lark* more than *bird,* and *bird* more than *animal.* All meadowlarks
are larks, but not all larks are meadowlarks. And so with larks and
birds and with birds and animals. "Be specific" is often good advice:

> In August 1945, I was a freshman at Nagasaki Medical
> College. The ninth of August was a clear, hot, beautiful
> summer day. I left my lodging house, which was one and a
> half miles from the hypocenter, at eight in the morning, as
> usual, to catch a tram car. When I got to the tram stop I
> found that it had been derailed in an accident. I decided to
> return home. I was lucky. I never made it to school that day.
>     At 11 a.m., I was sitting in my room with a fellow student
> when I heard the sound of a B-29 passing overhead. A few
> minutes later, the air flashed a brilliant yellow and there was a
> huge blast of wind.—Michito Ichimaru

Notice how the effectiveness of Ichimaru's narrative depends
upon specificity—not *late summer* but *August;* not *a student* but
*a freshman;* not *a medical school* but *Nagasaki Medical College;* not
*early August* but *the ninth;* not *a summer day* but *a clear, hot,*

*beautiful summer day;* not *a short distance* but *one and a half miles;* not *late in the morning* but *11 a.m.;* not *an airplane* or even *a bomber* but *a B-29;* not *yellow* but *a brilliant yellow.*

But "Be specific" is not always good advice. Because specificity calls attention to itself, save it for what you want to emphasize. Don't bore your readers with irrelevant specificity:

> A funny thing happened to me at 9:18 a.m. on Friday, January 20, 1994. I was sauntering along the north side of Clark Street between Tenth and Eleventh Avenues when. . . .

Does the exact time of day matter? The exact day and date? Does it matter that you were sauntering? That the street was Clark? The north side of it? Between Tenth and Eleventh Avenues? If not, be general. Save your specificity for describing the funny thing that happened to you. (See **VAGUENESS** and **AMBIGUITY**.)

**SPELLING** One of the ways—punctuation is another—by which a written language represents a spoken one. But **spelling** represents pronunciation only imperfectly. Not always, for instance, is there a one-to-one correspondence between a certain spelling and a certain word or a certain pronunciation. The noun *invalid,* for example, is identical with the adjective *invalid.* But they are different words with different pronunciations. The noun is stressed on the first syllable (*INvalid*); the adjective, on the second (*inVALID*).

Perhaps misspelling is the least important mistake a writer can make, for it rarely interferes with communication. Yet it is also the most easily detected, and many readers weigh it heavily against a writer. (See **MISSPELLING.**)

**spend time** Phrases such as *spend time worrying about* . . . are wordy for *worrying about* . . . (see **CONCISION**).

**stance** SAWE to mean "intellectual position": *my stance on free trade.*

**stanza, verse**   Sometimes confused. A *verse* is a single line of a poem. A *stanza* is a group of lines usually unified by sense and often by a rhyme scheme as well. *Verse* also means "writing in meter or rhyme": *verse is an older literary form than prose.*

**state of the art**   SAWE to mean "most advanced current stage of development (of some science or technology)": *This computer is* ***state of the art.*** The adjective is hyphenated: *the* ***state-of-the-art*** *computer technology.*

**stationary, stationery**   Often confused, because identical in sound. *Stationary* is an adjective meaning "fixed" or "not moving": *a* ***stationary heater.*** *Stationery* is a noun meaning "writing paper and envelopes" (*light blue* ***stationery***), "writing materials," or "store selling writing materials" (*the discount* ***stationery*** *in the shopping center*).

**statuesque**   Means "resembling a statue," not "tall" or "massive."

**statue, statute**   Sometimes confused. A *statue* is a form or likeness of an animal or human in cement, metal, stone, or wood. A *statute* is a law or an ordinance: *the* ***statute*** *of limitations.*

**stay, stop**   Prefer *stay at a hotel* to *stop at a hotel,* because the latter is ambiguous, meaning either "occupy a room or suite at a hotel" or "halt at a hotel."

**stewardess**   To refer to a person who waits on you in an airplane, prefer *flight attendant.* (See **SEXIST LANGUAGE**.)

**stick up for**   SAWE but informal to mean "side with": ***stick up for*** *one's country.*

**still**   Often a source of wordiness. (See **CONCISION**.)

NOT THIS:   The controversy **still** goes on.

BUT THIS:   The controversy goes on.

**stonewall**   SAWE but informal since Watergate to mean "pretend to know nothing about any wrongdoing": *Asked about a slush fund, the press secretary stonewalled.*

**straddle**   SAWE but informal to mean "seem to favor both sides (in a controversy)": *Senator Mitchum straddles the abortion issue.*

**strata**   Both *strata* and *stratums* are SAWE plurals of the rarely used *stratum,* meaning "layer": *three strata of rock.*

**STRESS**   The degree of loudness of a syllable relative to the other or others in a word. Two-syllable words have one degree of stress. *Tumult,* for example, has stress on the first syllable: **tu**-mult. Words of more than one syllable generally have two degrees of stress. *Composition,* for example, has primary stress on its next to the last syllable and secondary on its first: com-po-**si**-tion. Ordinarily, stress is not represented when a word is written.

> **STYLE**   A style is a way of doing something: walking, dressing, furnishing a room, making pizza, playing soccer, painting landscapes. A style of writing, then, is a way of writing.
>
> Style in writing can focus on two quite different concerns. One concern includes such things as punctuation, italics, capitalization, and the form of a piece of writing (in a letter, for example, the inside address, salutation, and complimentary close). This concern is the subject of such guides as *The Chicago Manual of Style.* The other concern includes uses of words and sentence patterns.

In this second sense, a style is often named for the writer who created it or uses it: the style of John Stuart Mill, of Jane Austen, of Henry James, of Elizabeth Bowen, of James Baldwin, of Gore Vidal, of Joan Didion. Or a style can be named for the sort of person who uses it: the bureaucratic style, the official style, the Internal Revenue style, the philosophical style. Or by the purposes to which it is put: the formal (or high) style (for sermons, charters, dedications, manifestos, inaugurations); the informal (or low) style (for recipes, letters to friends). Or by characteristics of the choice of words or sentence structure: the simple (or plain) style; a poetic style.

Some writers cultivate a style or styles. For others, their style or styles are like their blood pressure or their fingerprints, beneath their knowledge and beyond their control. They have no idea what their styles are or whether they serve their purposes. But no writer can escape having a style, and every style has effects upon readers, whether or not they are conscious of the effects.

One of the two chief ways to describe a style is by its preference for words of a certain kind: familiar (*woman, chair, house*) or unfamiliar (*concatenation, quantitation*); monosyllabic (*soon, try*) or polysyllabic (*kaleidoscope, reunification*); Native American (*tepee,* from Dakota), Anglo-Saxon or Scandinavian (*bag*), Greek (*sponge*), Latin (*opus*), and so on.

The other chief way of describing a style is by its preference for certain sentence patterns or structures. At one extreme is the simple style of such writers as Ernest Hemingway: short sentences; few inversions; few dependent clauses, very few of them embedded within other dependent clauses; few parenthetical clauses—"There was nothing to be gained by leaving them alone" (*For Whom the Bell*

*Tolls*). At the other extreme is the complicated style of Henry James—

> If the skin on Moddle's face had to Maisie the air of being unduly, almost painfully, stretched, it never presented that appearance so much as when she uttered, as she often had occasion to utter, such word (*What Maisie Knew*).

Every writer does well to cultivate several styles, each appropriate to a different sort of intention or purpose. For most purposes—letters to friends, instructions for operating an appliance, anecdotes—a plain or simple style is best, closer to that of Hemingway than that of James. For a subtle, closely reasoned argument, a more complicated style is appropriate.

**subject** Used to refer to a person only in police reports (*The subject was apprehended*) and in reports of psychological experiments (*The responses of the randomly selected subjects showed . . .* ).

**SUBJECT COMPLEMENTS** One of the twelve functions that a part of speech—in this case, a noun, a pronoun, a noun phrase, or an adjective—can perform in a clause. (See **FORMS AND FUNCTIONS.**)

The subject complement (SC) of a clause is usually immediately to the right of the verb (V) (always a linking verb—for example: *be, become, feel, seem*) and either modifies the subject (S) or refers to whatever the subject refers to:

| S | V | SC |
|------|--------|------|
|  | is |  |
|  | became |  |
| Jack | feels | fat. |
|  | seems |  |

a fatty.

Jack                is            the fatty.

the fat one.

**subject matter** Wordy for *subject*. (See **CONCISION**.)

NOT THIS: The **subject matter** of the discussion. . . .

BUT THIS: The **subject** of the discussion. . . .

**SUBJECTS** One of the twelve functions that a part of speech—in this case, a noun, a pronoun, or a noun phrase—can perform in a clause. (See **FORMS AND FUNCTIONS; NOUNS;** and **NOUN PHRASES**.)

The **subject** (S) of a clause is usually immediately to the left of the verb (V) (but see **INVERTED SENTENCES**). It may be short:

S  V

It is here.

Or long:

S                                        V

The man in the blue suit who tried to sell us insurance is here.

**SUBJECTS INCLUDING PREPOSITIONAL PHRASES**
Nothing in a prepositional phrase contained in a subject affects the number of the following verb.

NOT THIS: Parker, **as well as** thousands of other anthropologists, **rely** on the testimony of the natives.

BUT THIS: Parker, **as well as** thousands of other anthropologists, **relies** on the testimony of the natives.

**SUBORDINATE CLAUSES** See **CLAUSES**.

**SUBORDINATE CONJUNCTIONS** See **CONJUNCTIONS**.

**SUBORDINATION**   One of the twelve functions that a part of speech—in this case, a subordinating conjunction—can perform in a clause. (See **FORMS AND FUNCTIONS.**)

A **subordinator** introduces a subordinate clause (adjective clause, adverb clause, noun clause) without performing any function within that clause:

> **although** she is nice
> **because** she is nice
> **inasmuch** as she is nice
> **that** she is nice

**Note:** The first word of a subordinate clause is not necessarily a subordinating conjunction: often it performs a function in the clause—subject, for instance, or direct object:

> **that** faces the courthouse [*that* is the subject of the clause]
> **whenever** I go [*whenever* is an adverb modifying *go*]
> **which** is the best [*which* is the subject of the clause]
> **who** loves me [*who* is the subject of the clause]
> **whom** I love [*whom* is the direct object of the clause]

**subsequent to**   Wordy for *after.* (See **CONCISION.**)

> NOT THIS:   I went to Hawaii **subsequent to** graduation.

> BUT THIS:   I went to Hawaii **after** graduation.

**suffer, sustain**   Both are SAWE to mean "experience": *suffer* (or *sustain*) *a loss.*

**sufficient amount (or number) of**   Wordy for *enough.* (See **CONCISION.**)

> NOT THIS:   a **sufficient number of** coupons.

> BUT THIS:   **enough** coupons.

**sufficiently**  SAWE followed either by an adjective and an infinitive (*sufficiently cold to freeze*) or by an adjective and *for* (*sufficiently rigid for safety*).

**suggest**  Prefer to *assert, affirm, believe, declare, hold,* or *insist* for a weaker commitment to a statement: *I suggest that ten dollars will suffice.*

**super**  Avoid as a word of praise because vague.

NOT THIS:    This production of *Othello* is **super.**

BUT THIS:    The production of *Othello* is **convincing** (or **moving** or **splendid**).

**superior than**  NonSAWE for *superior to.*

NOT THIS:    Cotton is **superior than** polyester.

BUT THIS:    Cotton is **superior to** polyester.

(See also **inferior than.**)

**SUPERLATIVES**  A **superlative** is an evaluative word (see **DESCRIPTIVE AND EVALUATIVE WORDS**) intended to express high approval: *colossal, fabulous, fantastic, great, incredible, terrific.* But many superlatives are used so much that they have lost their force. Perhaps the best way to express high approval is to prefer a modest evaluative word like *good* or *admirable* accompanied by descriptive words accounting for your approval.

NOT THIS:    Cresswell is a **terrific** person.

BUT THIS:    Cresswell is an **admirable** person, **generous and considerate.**

(See also **COMPARISONS OF ADJECTIVES AND ADVERBS.**)

**supposed to**   SAWE to mean "expected to."

**suppose to**   See -ed, -d.

**sure, surely**   For the adverb, prefer *surely: The mayor is surely aware of the problem.*

**SYNECDOCHE** A figure of speech (see **FIGURES OF SPEECH**) referring to a whole by naming a part, to a part by naming a whole, to a species by naming a genus, or to a genus by naming a species:

> Here comes **big mouth** [ = a person]
> Here comes **the Marine Corps** [ = a Marine] .
> Here comes a **cutthroat** [ = a crook]
> I love **the republic** [ = the United States]

**SYNONYMS** (1) **Synonyms** are words that have the same meaning—for example, *chiropodist, foot-doctor,* and *podiatrist.* In use, however, synonyms do not necessarily have the same force or the same associations.

(2) When choosing among synonyms to express a certain meaning, prefer the familiar (*foot-doctor*) to the less familiar (*chiropodist*) and the shorter to the longer (*arbiter* to *arbitrator, interpretive* to *interpretative, preventive* to *preventative*).

**SYNTACTIC VARIATION** (1) Given a certain message or meaning, and given also a certain set of words to express it, the grammatical rules (see **GRAMMATICAL RULES**) permit a considerable variety of synonymous sentences:

> To Harriet, the consequences of their action were, it seemed, predictable.

> It seemed to Harriet the consequences of their action were predictable.

The consequences of their action were, it seemed to Harriet, predictable.

The consequences of their action, it seemed to Harriet, were predictable

The consequences of their action were predictable it seemed to Harriet.

(2) That these five sentences are synonymous guarantees nothing else about them. One sentence may be easier to read than another, say, or more effective in some other way.

(3) Though the grammatical rules permit a considerable variety of synonymous sentences using a certain set of words, they forbid many sentences—for example:

Harriet to, consequences the their of action seemed were it predictable.

**SYNTAX**   The **syntax** of a sentence is the order of its words. For example, subject + verb + direct object. (*Stanley despises spinach*); direct object + subject + verb (*Spinach Stanley despises*). As a linguistic discipline, syntax is the study of word order.

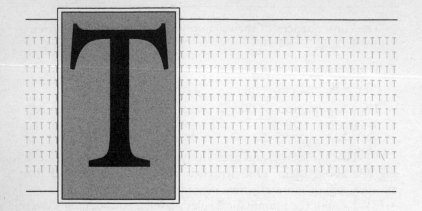

**tacky**  SAWE but informal to mean either "shabby" or "seedy" (*a tacky overcoat*) or "gaudy" or "in bad taste" (*a tacky reception*).

**take**  See **bring, take.**

**take in**  SAWE but informal to mean "attend": *take in a movie.*

**take on**  SAWE to mean either "hire" (*take on another clerk*) or "oppose in competition" (*take on the first-place team*).

**take something for granite**  A mistake for the cliché *take something for granted.*

>     NOT THIS:  Pedro **took Kate's friendship for granite.**
>     BUT THIS:  Pedro **took Kate's friendship for granted.**
>     OR BETTER:  Pedro **valued Kate's friendship too lightly.**

**target date**   SAWE to mean "date set as agreed upon": *the target date for the opening.*

**task environment**   Euphemism for *workplace.* (See **EUPHE-MISMS.**)

> NOT THIS:   Home is her usual **task environment.**
>
> BUT THIS:   Home is her usual **workplace.**

**task with**   NonSAWE to mean "assigned."

> NOT THIS:   **tasked with** responsibility for hiring.
>
> BUT THIS:   **assigned** responsibility for hiring.

**taunt, taut**   Sometimes confused. *Taunt,* a transitive verb, means "deride," "jeer at," or "mock": *He **taunted** his opponent. Taut,* an adjective, means either "tightly drawn" (*a **taut** rope*) or "very nervous" (***taut** after a difficult day*).

**teach**   See **learn, teach.**

**TELLING AND SHOWING   Telling** is describing a person, thing, or situation in relatively general or abstract terms: *a terrified girl, a noble person, a moving scene, a hilarious situation.* **Showing** is describing the particulars that justify the telling: *Turning pale, Harriet screamed, "That face again at the window!"*

Readers find telling much less interesting than showing; and, not surprisingly, good novelists do less telling than showing. (See **ARGUMENT AND PERSUASION.**)

**tell it like it is**   Wordy to mean "be candid" or "be truthful." (See **CONCISION.**)

> NOT THIS:   Masterson always **tells it like it is.**
>
> BUT THIS:   Masterson is always **candid.**

**temperature: cold, hot, and so on**   A *temperature* has no temperature: it is neither cold, hot, nor something in between. It is high, low, or in between. Only the weather, animals, plants, and artifacts have temperatures.

**temporal, temporary**   Sometimes confused. *Temporal* means "secular" or "pertaining to the world": *a temporal guide*. *Temporary* means "not permanent": *a temporary employee*.

**tend to**   SAWE but informal for *attend to: tend to business.*

**TENSES**   See **VERBS.**

**term as**   Wordy for *term*. (See **CONCISION.**)

> NOT THIS:   **termed as** a charlatan.

> BUT THIS:   **termed** (or, better, **called**) a charlatan.

**terminate**   Pretentious for *end* or *dismiss.*

> NOT THIS:   They **terminated** his employment

> BUT THIS:   They **dismissed** (or **fired**) him.

**terrible, terribly**   Prefer *bad* or *very* unless what you mean has something to do with terror.

> NOT THIS:   a **terribly** nice person.

> BUT THIS:   a **very** nice person.

**than**   (1) Abbreviated (or shortened) sentences containing *than* are often ambiguous.

> NOT THIS
> (AMBIGUOUS):   I like Betty better **than** Harry.

BUT THIS
(UNAMBIGUOUS):    I like Betty better **than** I like Harry.

OR THIS:    I like Betty better **than** Harry likes her.

(2) SAWE counts *than* as either a conjunction (see **CON-JUNCTIONS**) or a preposition (see **PREPOSITIONS**). Either (a) or (b) is SAWE:

(a) She works harder **than** [conjunction] I [i.e., than I work hard].
(b) She works harder **than** [preposition] me.

And (a) and (b) are synonymous.

**than any**    In a sentence such as *Rita is smarter than anyone in her office, else* is necessary after *anyone.* Otherwise the sentence is a contradiction (see **CONTRADICTIONS**), because it tacitly says that Rita is smarter than (among others) herself (who is one of the people in her office).

**than I/we/he/she/they; than me/us/him/her/them**    SAWE construes *than* as either (1) a conjunction introducing an elliptical clause (*Tim is taller than I [am tall]*) or (2) a preposition with an object (*Tim is taller than me*).

**than, then**    Sometimes confused, because similar in sound. *Than* is a conjunction used to introduce a comparison: *Susan is smarter than I. Then* is an adverb meaning "at the time indicated": *The delivery came in the afternoon. Susan was at school then.* (See also **than.**)

**than what**    Wordy for *than.* (See **CONCISION.**)

NOT THIS:    It is hotter **than what** I expected.

BUT THIS:    It is hotter **than** I expected.

**than whom**  A hypercorrection of *than who*. (See **HYPERCOR-RECTION.**)

NOT THIS:   a woman **than whom** there is no more gifted painter.

BUT THIS:   a woman **than who** there is no more gifted painter.

(That is, there is no painter better than who [is better].)

**that**  (1) Ordinarily a noun clause need not be introduced by *that* (see **SUBORDINATION**). Either (a) or (b) is SAWE: (a) *I know that he is guilty.* (b) *I know he is guilty.*

(2) But *that* is sometimes needed to prevent ambiguity.

NOT THIS:   He remarked on Saturday he would withdraw his offer.

BUT THIS:   He remarked **that** on Saturday he would withdraw his offer.

OR THIS:   He remarked on Saturday **that** he would withdraw his offer.

**that (all that, not all that, not that)**  Use of *that* as an adverb is SAWE to mean either "very" or "sufficiently to justify (doing something implied but not stated)": *Percy wore spats until he discovered they are not all that popular in Peoria* (that is, not sufficiently popular in Peoria to justify wearing them there). **Caution:** Some readers object to this use of *that* in writing, formal or informal.

NOT THIS:   Instead of going to the movies, Laura should have done her homework, but she doesn't take it **that seriously.**

BUT THIS:   Laura should have done her homework, but she doesn't take it **seriously enough to pass up the movies for it.**

**that of**  Necessary in some comparisons.

> NOT THIS:  The red of the chair is brighter than the sofa.

> BUT THIS:  The red of the chair is brighter than **that of** the sofa.

**that there**  See **this/these here, that there.**

**that, which**  (1) The relative pronoun *that* may have either an inanimate or an animate antecedent (an antecedent is the word or phrase for which a pronoun substitutes and to which it refers):

> INANIMATE
> THIS:  the town ← that I work in

> ANIMATE
> OR THIS:  the girl ← that I love

**Caution:** Some readers object to use of *that* to refer to people.

(2) The relative pronoun *which,* however, must have an inanimate antecedent:

> INANIMATE
> THIS:  the town  in which I work

> ANIMATE
> NOT THIS:  the girl ← which I love

(3) *That* is used only in restrictive relative clauses (see **RESTRICTIVE AND NONRESTRICTIVE**):

> RESTRICTIVE
> THIS:  the girl that I love

> NONRESTRICTIVE
> NOT THIS:  Helen,  that I love,

(4) *Which* is used in both restrictive and nonrestrictive relative clauses:

RESTRICTIVE

THIS:  the town  in which I work

NONRESTRICTIVE

OR THIS:  Albany,  in which I work,

**Caution:** Some readers object to use of *which* to begin a restrictive relative clause:

RESTRICTIVE

NOT THIS:  the town which I work in

RESTRICTIVE

BUT THIS:  the town in which I work

RESTRICTIVE

OR THIS:  the town that I work in

**the**  If two or more conjoined nouns refer to different people or things, each noun should have its own *the*.

NOT THIS:  **The** secretary and treasurer are elected.

BUT THIS:  **The** secretary and **the** treasurer are elected.

If, however, the nouns refer to the same person or thing, a single *the* is correct: *The secretary and treasurer is elected.*

**the fact that**  Almost always a cause of wordiness. (See **CONCISION**.)

NOT THIS:  Because of **the fact that** I was ill, I missed class.

BUT THIS:  Because I was ill (*or* because of my illness), I missed class.

OR THIS:  My illness caused me to miss class.

**theirs**  Note that, though a possessive like *Mary's,* it has no apostrophe.

**theirself, theirselves**   NonSAWE for *themselves*.

**their, there, they're**   Often confused, because identical in sound. *Their* is a possessive pronoun (*their friends*). *There* is either an expletive pronoun (*There are three of us*) or an adverb (*John is there*). *They're* is a contraction of *they are* (*They're here*).

**them**   NonSAWE for *these* or *those* used as a modifier.

> NOT THIS:   **them** people.

> BUT THIS:   **these** (or **those**) people.

**then**   See **than, then.**

**there**   See **their, there, they're.**

**there is ('s), are ('re), was, were, etc.**   (1) *There* is never the real subject of a sentence or clause but the pseudosubject. The real subject always comes after the verb (*is, 's, are, 're*, and so on), and the verb must agree with it.

> NOT THIS:   **There's** stacks of mail.

> BUT THIS:   **There're** stacks of mail

> OR THIS:   **There's** a stack of mail.

**Exception:** When the real subject is the singular *a lot* followed by a prepositional phrase with a plural object, the verb is plural:

SUBJECT: SINGULAR

PREPOSITIONAL PHRASE

| VERB: PLURAL | | OBJECT: PLURAL | |
| --- | --- | --- | --- |
| There were | a lot of | people | at the party. |

(2) Sometimes a cause of wordiness. (See **CONCISION**.)

NOT THIS:    **There are** three contracts in the file.

BUT THIS:    Three contracts **are** in the file.

(See **EXPLETIVE PRONOUNS; NUMBER; PREPOSI-
TIONAL PHRASES; and SUBJECTS**.)

**these (those) kind of things**    NonSAWE.

NOT THIS:    I don't recommend **these kind of things.**

BUT THIS:    I don't recommend **this kind of thing.**

OR THIS:    I don't recommend **these kinds of things.**

**THESIS SENTENCES**    A **thesis sentence** states the main point
or thesis of an article or essay (*The mayor is corrupt; The death
penalty ought to be abolished*). Not every article or essay contains a
thesis sentence. But, when one does, that sentence is usually in the
first paragraph, the last paragraph, or both.

**the way**    Prefer *in the way* in sentences such as *Do it (in) the way
I say.*

**they**    Avoid using as an indefinite pronoun because vague.

NOT THIS:    **They** say that the President will sign the bill.

BUT THIS:    Some commentators say that the President will
sign the bill.

OR THIS:    The President will sign the bill.

**they're**    See **their, there, they're.**

**they, them, their, theirs**   As a plural pronoun *they, them, their,* or *theirs* often has a plural antecedent:

PLURAL ANTECEDENT          PLURAL PRONOUN
If  **interest rates**   rise,   **they**      produce inflation.

But it is now also SAWE, in both speech and writing, to use a plural pronoun with a singular antecedent, provided that the antecedent is generic and human—either a singular indefinite pronoun (*anyone, each, everyone, someone,* and so on) or a singular, generic, human phrase (*a friend, a person, every student, the average American*):

SINGULAR ANTECEDENT                    PLURAL PRONOUN
Show     **a friend**     you care about     **them.**

**Caution:** Nevertheless, some readers object to this use because it constitutes a grammatical error.

NOT THIS:   **Every student** has **their** troubles.

BUT THIS:   **Every student** has **his or her** troubles.

**thing**   A useful word, as in *a thing to remember, the thing I forgot,* and *for one thing.* But prefer a more specific word when you can think of one.

NOT THIS:   The **thing** I remember best is being hit by a semi.

BUT THIS:   The **event** (or **calamity**) I remember best. . . .

**thinking**   For a noun, prefer *opinion* or *view.*

NOT THIS:   What is your **thinking** about the immigration problem?

BUT THIS:   What is your **opinion** of the immigration problem?

**this, that**   Make sure that the antecedent of *this* or *that* is clear to your reader (see **ANTECEDENTS; VAGUENESS;** and **AMBIGUITY**).

> NOT THIS:   She wanted to travel often, but **that** [*travel? frequent travel?*] was not possible.

> BUT THIS:   She wanted frequent travel, but **that** was not possible.

**this/these here, that there**   NonSAWE and wordy for *this, these,* and *that.*

> NOT THIS:   **These here** books are expensive.

> BUT THIS:   **These** books are expensive.

**thrash, thresh**   Sometimes confused, perhaps because similar in pronunciation. *Thrash* means "beat" or "flog": *He **thrashed** his attacker.* *Thresh* means "separate by beating": *He **threshed** the wheat.*

**throughout**   Such words as *all, entire,* and *whole* are wordy. (See **CONCISION.**)

> NOT THIS:   **Throughout** the **entire** summer he worked in the garden.

> BUT THIS:   **Throughout** the summer he worked in the garden.

**thrust**   Usually a source of wordiness. (See **CONCISION.**)

> NOT THIS:   The **thrust** of my proposal is. . . .

> BUT THIS:   My proposal is. . . .

**thus, thusly**   Synonymous. Prefer *thus* because shorter. *Thusly* is probably a hypercorrection of *thus* (see **HYPERCORRECTION**). Not every adverb must end in *-ly.*

**tight, tightly** Synonymous as adverbs: *close the door tight* (or *tightly*). *Tight* is also an adjective: *a tight fit.*

**till, until, 'til** Synonymous. Not only *till* but, even more, *'til* may seem a bit folksy or poetic to some readers.

**timber, timbre** Sometimes confused. *Timber* means "trees": *a large tract of timber. Timbre* means "quality given to a sound by its overtones": *the timbre of a Stradivarius.*

**time frame** Prefer *period* because shorter and unpretentious.

> NOT THIS:   the **time frame** for the invasion.

> BUT THIS:   the **period** for the invasion.

**'tis** Folksy or poetic. Prefer *It is.*

**TITLES OR HONORIFICS** Abbreviations, words, or phrases that confer honor upon their bearers. Be careful how you use them. A Chief Justice of the United States is reported to have been offended when called *Justice* rather than *Chief Justice.* A Ph.D. may be offended if called *Miss, Mrs., Ms.,* or *Mr.* rather than *Dr.* On the other hand, many Ph.D.'s find *Dr.* pretentious. It is not easy to know what to say, though there is agreement that physicians must be called *Dr.* Perhaps the best advice when you are in doubt is to err on the side of too much rather than too little honor. To avoid giving almost certain offense, get titles and honorifics right.

> NOT THIS:   **Judge** Rehnquist.

> BUT THIS:   **Chief Justice** Rehnquist.

**to** Sometimes a source of wordiness. (See **CONCISION**.)

> NOT THIS:   Where is she going **to?**

> BUT THIS:   Where is she going?

**to be** Often a source of wordiness. (See **CONCISION.**)

NOT THIS:   The work week needs **to be** shortened.

BUT THIS:   The work week needs shortening.

**together** Often a source of wordiness. (See **CONCISION.**)

NOT THIS:   collaborate or cooperate **together.**

BUT THIS:   collaborate or cooperate.

**TOKENS VS. TYPES** The distinction between **tokens** and **types,** best explained by an example, is useful in describing counts—word counts, for instance. In the sentence *The last in is the first out,* there are seven tokens but only six types, because there are two tokens of the type *the.* Thus, a person of few words may actually be garrulous: a person of few types but many tokens, saying the same thing over and over.

**TONE** Anything about a written or spoken utterance—words, word order, capitalization, voice quality—that reveals, but does not actually describe, the writer or speaker's beliefs or feelings either about readers or listeners, about his or her subject, or about himself or herself. The **tone** of most utterances is, of course, relatively neutral: the utterances reveal little or nothing about anything they don't actually describe. But the tone of some utterances is unmistakably friendly (*Like our other friends and patrons, you . . .*), or obsequious (*I hesitate to offer my opinion to an expert, but . . .*), or condescending (*As every schoolchild knows, you ought to . . .*), or contemptuous (*"No compromises,"* Mr. Herkimer piously *intoned*), or ironic (*On the sumptuous buffet were shards of cheese, an elderly smoked sturgeon, a despondent chicken salad, and a decanter of anonymous fluid*). Often the tone of your utterances is at least as important as their content.

**tony**   NonSAWE as a word of praise.

> NOT THIS:   a **tony** neighborhood.
>
> BUT THIS:   an **upper-class** neighborhood.

**too**   Do not use *too* unless you qualify it.

> NOT THIS:   too small, too large, too expensive.
>
> BUT THIS:   too small **for comfort,** too large **to maintain,** to
> expensive **to be affordable.**

**TOPIC SENTENCES**   A topic sentence either announces the topic of a paragraph or summarizes the paragraph. Typically, it is the first sentence in the paragraph. It is one means of making a paragraph coherent. (See **COHERENCE** and **PARAGRAPHS AND PARAGRAPHING.**)

**tortuous, torturous**   Sometimes confused. *Tortuous* means either (1) "twisting and turning" (*a **tortuous** road*) or (2) "devious" (*a **tortuous** opponent*). *Torturous* means "painful" or "pertaining to torture": *a **torturous** hernia.*

**total**   SAWE but informal to mean "completely destroy": *They totaled the building.*

**total of**   Unnecessary.

> NOT THIS:   a **total of** $300.
>
> BUT THIS:   $300.

**to, too, two**   Often confused, because identical in sound. *To* is a preposition (***to** her surprise*); *too,* an adverb (***too** cold*); *two,* an adjective (***two** people*) or a noun or pronoun (*the **two** of us*).

**toward, towards** Synonymous.

**tragedy, tragic** Use sparingly except in reference to drama.

NOT THIS: a **tragic** decline in profits.

BUT THIS: an **unfortunate** decline in profits.

**TRANSFERRED EPITHETS** An adjective modifying a noun in a text but, by implication, actually modifying another, closely associated noun not in the text. The adjective, that is, is transferred from the former noun to the latter. An example is *guilty* in the phrase *guilty secret*. It is not the secret that is guilty but the (unnamed) person who keeps it.

A transferred epithet is a special case of metonymy. (See **METONYMY.**)

**TRANSITIONS** Transitions are like signposts. They are words, phrases, or sentences that point back to where readers have been and forward to where they are going. Coming at or near the start of a new sentence or paragraph, a transition tells readers how what lies ahead will relate to what has gone before. Here are some relationships that transitions can express.

**Addition:** and, also, or; besides, furthermore, likewise, moreover, similarly; for another thing, in addition; what's more

**Cause or logical connection:** because, for, since; consequently, hence, so, therefore; as a result, for this reason, in conclusion, it follows that

**Chronology:** first, second, finally; before, earlier, hitherto, previously; after, afterwards, later, next,

> soon, then, thereupon; meanwhile, simultaneously, while; at once, at the same time, on another occasion
>
> **Contrast:** but, despite, however, instead, nevertheless, nonetheless, rather, though, yet; at the same time, by contrast, in fact, on the contrary, on the other hand
>
> **Exemplification:** as, like, say; for example, for instance, such as
>
> **Explanation: paraphrase, restatement, or summary:** namely; in a word, in other words, in short, in sum; put differently, that is, that is to say, to make the same point in another way; to summarize

**transpire**  Pretentious to mean "happen."

NOT THIS:  It **transpired** that both of us were in Honolulu.

BUT THIS:  It **happened** that both of us were in Honolulu.

**-trix**  See -ess, -ette, -trix and **SEXIST LANGUAGE.**

**troop**  A *troop* is a collection of things or people, usually of soldiers. **Caution:** Do not use *troop* to mean "soldier."

NOT THIS:  Yesterday, the I.R.A. ambushed three British **troops.**

BUT THIS:  Yesterday, the I.R.A. ambushed three British **soldiers.**

**try and, try to**  Prefer *try to: Try to remember.* (See **be sure and, come and, try and.**)

**two**   See **to, too, two.**

**tycoon**   SAWE to mean "powerful businessperson or industrialist": *a ruthless tycoon.*

**type**   See **kind, sort, type.**

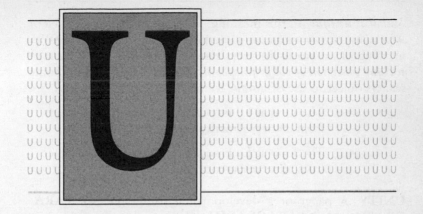

unaware, unawares  Similar in meaning. But *unaware* is an adjective (*unaware of the danger*); *unawares*, an adverb (*acted unawares of the danger*).

under the auspices of  Prefer the shorter and less pretentious *sponsored by*.

unexceptionable, unexceptional  Sometimes confused. *Unexceptionable* means "incapable of being taken exception to" or "beyond reproach": *unexceptionable conduct*. *Unexceptional* means "ordinary" or "routine": *an unexceptional performance*.

uninterested  See **disinterested, uninterested**.

unique  The oldest meaning of *unique* (from *unus*, the Latin word for *one*) is (a) "being the only one of its kind": *The Taj*

*Mahal is unique.* In this meaning, nothing can be *more* or *less* or *most* unique or *so* unique as something else. A newer, but SAWE, meaning of *unique* is (b) "very rare or unusual": *This is the most unique collection of old gramophones in the world.* **Caution:** Some readers object to use of *unique* to mean (b).

> NOT THIS:   The food at Le Français is so **unique** that diners from all over America go there.

> BUT THIS:   The food at Le Français is so **unusual** that diners from all over America go there.

**UNITY** A paper or a developmental paragraph (see **PARA-GRAPHS AND PARAGRAPHING**) has **unity** if it sticks to its subject or topic, resisting the temptation to include a fact or an idea that, however interesting, is irrelevant. (See also **COHER-ENCE.**)

**UNIVERSAL GRAMMAR** (1) Scrutiny of languages shows not only how different they are from one another but also, more important, how much they are alike. Indeed, there is good reason to believe that there is a **universal grammar,** consisting not just of all the characteristics that all languages happen to share but of the ones that they must share if humans can learn them, speak or write them (few of the thousands of languages, dead or alive, have been written as well as spoken), and understand one another's speech and writing. If, then, there is a universal grammar, it is rooted in the human mind.

(2) In any case, every language has, for example, a means for referring to things and predicating qualities of them or relation-ships among them, a means for negating, a means for making requests, and a means for transforming a statement into a ques-tion. But no language makes this transformation by making the question a mirror image of the statement (the last sound first, the next to the last second, and so on), presumably because no human could make that transformation (though a computer could). Every

language, moreover, is as good for lying as for telling the truth. Languages are as useful to the wicked as they are to the virtuous.

**universal, universally**  SAWE to mean "everywhere on earth," not "throughout the universe": *a universal belief.*

**unless and until**  Wordy for *unless* or *until.* (See **CONCISION.**)

> NOT THIS:   **unless and until** the governor gives permission.

> BUT THIS:   **unless** (or **until**) the governor gives permission.

**unprecedented**  Use it only to mean "without precedent," never to mean "rare."

**unthinkable**  Everything, of course, is thinkable. But *unthinkable* is SAWE to mean "not to be considered": *Postponing the reunion is unthinkable.*

**up**  Often a source of wordiness. (See **CONCISION.**)

> NOT THIS:   Clean **up** the storeroom.

> BUT THIS:   Clean the storeroom.

**upcoming**  Prefer *forthcoming* because more widely accepted.

> NOT THIS:   the **upcoming** directory.

> BUT THIS:   the **forthcoming** directory.

**USE AND MENTION**  Linguistics and the philosophy of language distinguish between the **use** and **mention** of an expression. The distinction is best shown by examples:

> Paris is a city. [*Paris* is used.]
> *Paris* is a five-letter word. [*Paris* is mentioned.]

A chiropodist treats the human foot. [*Chiropodist* is used.]
*Chiropodist* and *podiatrist* mean the same. [*Chiropodist* and
*podiatrist* are mentioned.]

If he comes in, I'll see him. [The adverb clause *if he comes in*
is used.]
*If he comes in* is an adverb clause. [The adverb clause *if he
comes in* is mentioned.]

Usually, an expression that is mentioned is set off either by italics
(or underlining), as in the examples above, or by a pair of double
quotation marks. (See **METALANGUAGES AND OBJECT
LANGUAGES.**)

**use to, used to**   Write *use to* after *did*.

NOT THIS:   Did he **used to** work at the cafeteria?

BUT THIS:   Did he **use to** work at the cafeteria?

But write *used to* otherwise.

NOT THIS:   I am **use to** Bill's ravings.

BUT THIS:   I am **used to** Bill's ravings.

(See also **-ed, -d.**)

**utilize**   Prefer the shorter synonym *use*.

NOT THIS:   **Utilize** the services of an investment counselor.

BUT THIS:   **Use** the services of an investment counselor.

**VAGUENESS** Indeterminacy of meaning. In one kind of **vagueness,** what is indeterminate is just what things an expression refers to. Take the words *book* and *booklet*. How small must a book be to be called a booklet? How large must a booklet be to be called a book? The answers to these questions are indeterminate: both words are vague.

In the other kind of vagueness, what is indeterminate is what the boundaries are of the thing a word refers to. The word *Midwest,* for instance, is vague. Iowa and Wisconsin are certainly in the Midwest. But what about Michigan? Or Ontario? The word is vague.

**valuable, valued** Sometimes confused. *Valuable* means either "worth a considerable amount of money" (*a valuable ring*) or "very useful" (*a valuable tool in an emergency*). *Valued* means "prized" (even if not valuable): *a valued keepsake*.

**various**   NonSAWE as a pronoun.

NOT THIS:   **Various** of the gifts were displayed.

BUT THIS:   A **variety** of the gifts were displayed.

**vastly**   Now SAWE to mean "very greatly" even in contexts not involving measures or weights: *vastly amused*.

**venal, venial**   Sometimes confused. *Venal* means "capable of being bought or bribed," "corrupt or corruptible": *a venal politician*. *Venial* means "excusable" or "forgivable": *a venial sin* (contrasted with a *mortal* sin).

**verbal**   See **oral, verbal**.

**VERBALS**   A **verbal** (a gerund, an infinitive, or a participle) combines characteristics of a verb with those of an adjective or a noun. (See **GERUNDS; INFINITIVES;** and **PARTICIPLES.**)

**VERBS**   A **verb** is a word or phrase that expresses an action or a state of being, that can occupy certain positions in a sentence or clause, and that changes its form for different purposes. Verbs occupy a unique niche in grammar. Like nouns and adjectives, they are a part of speech. And, like subjects and direct objects, they are a function. (See **FORMS AND FUNCTIONS.**)

How can you spot the verb in a sentence or clause? One way is by its position. Usually, though not always, the verb (V) is the first part of the predicate (PRED), just to the right of the subjects (S):

The man with the gun was making trouble.

Sometimes the verb *is* the predicate:

S        PRED

V

The woman in the sable coat screamed.

But a better way to spot a verb is to look for a word or phrase that can change its form in one or more of these three ways for one or more of three purposes:

(1) Change in tense to indicate the time of the action or state expressed by the verb—by use of the suffix *-ed* or *-ing* or of the auxiliary *be* (*be/is/are/was/were/been/ being*), *have* (*have/has/had*), *shall* (*shall/should*), or *will* (*will/would*) (see **AUXILIARIES**):

| | |
|---|---|
| scream/screams | has/have screamed |
| is/are screaming | has/have been screaming |
| screamed | had screamed |
| was/were screaming | had been screaming |
| shall/will scream | should/would scream |
| shall/will be screaming | should/would be screaming |
| shall/will have been screaming | should/would have been screaming |
| shall/will have been being screaming | should/would have been being screaming |

**Note:** See the note following (3) below.

(2) Change either in the mode of the action or state being expressed by the verb or in the writer's attitude toward that action or state—by use of the auxiliary *can* (*can/could*), *do* (*do/does/did*), *may* (*may/might*), *must, ought to,* or *would* (see **AUXILIARIES**):

*capability:* can/could scream

*certainty:* do/does/did scream

*choice or consent:* would scream (if he or she could)

*contingency:* (if here, he or she) would scream

*custom or habit:* would (often) scream

*desire, intention, or wish:* (those who) would scream

*doubt, possibility, uncertainty:* may/might scream, would
   seem (to be screaming)

*necessity or obligation:* must scream, ought to scream

*permission:* may/might scream

*request:* would (you please) scream?

(3) Change in number (singular, plural) or person (first,
   second, third) to make the verb agree with its
   subject—use of the suffix *-s* or the auxiliary *be*
   (*am/are/is/was/were*) or *have* (*have/has/had*).

| SUBJECT | VERB (AND PREDICATE) |
|---------|----------------------|
| I | am screaming [singular, first person]. |
| We | are screaming [plural, first person]. |
| You | are screaming [second person]. |
| He/She | is screaming [singular, third person]. |
| Jim | was screaming [singular, third person]. |
| The boy | screams [singular, third person]. |
| The boys | scream [plural, third person]. |
| They | are screaming [plural, third person]. |
| Jim and Mary | were screaming [plural, third person]. |
| Jim | has been screaming [singular, third person]. |
| Jim and Mary | have been screaming [plural, third person]. |

and so on.

**Note:** English has two special verbs: the linking verb *be* and the transitive verb *have* (both of which are also auxiliaries). These two verbs change number, person, and also tense, not by use of suffixes or auxiliaries but by use of different words, at least for the simple present and the simple past tenses. The simple present tense of *be* uses three words:

am [singular, first person]

are [plural, first and third persons; and singular and plural second person]

is [singular, third person]

The simple past tense uses two words:

was [singular, first and third persons]

were [plural, first and third persons; and singular and plural second person]

The simple present tense of *have* uses *has* for the singular of the third person and uses *have* for all the other numbers and persons. The simple past uses *had* for both numbers and all persons.

(See **LINKING VERBS; MOOD; SEQUENCING VERBS; VERBALS;** and **VOICE.**)

**VERBS: TRANSITIVE AND INTRANSITIVE** (1) A **transitive verb** (*like* or *give*, for instance) takes at least one object, a direct object (*John likes books*) and sometimes an indirect object as well (*John gave Marcia books*).

(2) An **intransitive verb** need not take an object but may: *John lives, swims; John lives a life of ease, swims ten lengths daily.*

(3) Some verbs—the linking verbs *be* and *seem*—are neither transitive nor intransitive: *John is fat, is a fatty; John seems fat, seems to be a fatty.* (See **FORMS AND FUNCTIONS; LINKING VERBS;** and **VERBS.**)

**via**   Use only to mean "by way of" (*to the Pacific via Panama*), never "by means of."

> NOT THIS:   became wealthy **via** hard work.

> BUT THIS:   became wealthy **by means of** hard work.

**viable**   Avoid using to mean anything other than "capable of survival": *The infant was premature but viable.*

> NOT THIS:   a **viable** plan for reducing overhead costs.

> BUT THIS:   a **practical** plan for reducing overhead costs.

**VIRGULE**   Use a **virgule** (/):

(1)  To divide one line of verse from the next in a run-on quotation:

Spenser writes of his "long fruitless stay / In princes' court. . . ."

(2)  To separate alternative expressions:

and/or      parent/guardian

(3)  To separate parts of a date:

12/25/94

(4)  To mean "per" or "a" in an abbreviation:

$1.89/lb.    200 r.p.m.

(5) To set off a phoneme in a phonemic transcription (a phoneme is the smallest meaningful linguistic unit):

/b/

**vis-à-vis**  (Note the grave accent mark above *a*.) Use only to mean "face-to-face with" or "compared with," not to mean "about": *steel file cabinets* **vis-à-vis** *cardboard.*

**visually challenged**  A euphemism for *astigmatic, blind, near-sighted,* and so on. (See **EUPHEMISMS** and **POLITICAL CORRECTNESS.**)

**viz**  Avoid this abbreviation of Latin *videlicit* because pretentious.

> NOT THIS:   Refer all inquiries to the manager, **viz** Clyde Monroe.

> BUT THIS:   Refer all inquiries to the manager, Clyde Monroe.

**VOICE**  In English, most transitive verbs have two **voices:** the active voice (AV) and the passive voice (PV). In the *active voice*, the verb (V) describes the action, its subject (S) names the actor, and its direct object (DO) names the person or thing acted upon:

> S                 V (AV)            DO
> Jack (actor)   **loves**   (action)   Meg (acted upon).

In the *passive voice*, however, the subject names the acted-upon, and the object of the preposition *by* names the actor:

> S                 V (PV)                 OBJECT OF *BY*
> Meg (acted upon)   **is loved**   (action) by Jack (actor).

Notice that, in the passive voice, both *by* and its object may be left out: *Meg* **is loved.**

**Caution:** Use the passive voice only when the actor is unknown (*The ambassador* **was assassinated**) or unimportant (*I* **was inoculated** *against smallpox*), or when the use of the active voice would cause an awkward shift in subject (*She has high standards but is* *admired by her students*). Be especially careful not to let the passive voice conceal important information about the actor.

> NOT THIS:   A teacher **was shot** yesterday in her classroom.

> BUT THIS:   A drug dealer **shot** a teacher yesterday in her classroom.

> OR AT LEAST THIS:   A teacher **was shot** yesterday in her classroom by a drug dealer.

(See **VERBS; TRANSITIVE AND INTRANSITIVE VERBS; SUBJECTS; DIRECT OBJECTS; PREPOSITIONS;** and **SHIFTS.**)

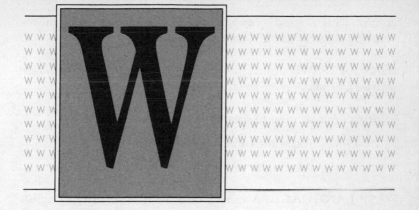

**wages** Counted as a plural in modern SAWE.

> NOT THIS: The wages of sin **is** death.

> BUT THIS: The wages of sin **are** death.

**wait on** NonSAWE for *wait for*.

> NOT THIS: I stood at the door for a half hour, **waiting on** him.

> BUT THIS: I stood at the door for a half hour, **waiting for** him.

**waive, wave** Sometimes confused. *Waive* means "give up a claim to": *he **waived his right to silence**. Wave* as a verb means "make a

---

gesture with a hand" (*wave goodbye*); as a noun *wave* means "moving ridge of water" (*crest of the wave*).

**wants for**  SAWE deletes *for* in such sentences as *The manager wants (for) you to check the accounts.*

**want to**  Avoid using to mean "ought to" or "should."

NOT THIS:  You **want to** be kind to animals.

BUT THIS:  You **ought to** (or **should**) be kind to animals.

**WASP LANGUAGE**  A variety, or dialect, of American English spoken or written by many WASPs—that is, white Anglo-Saxon Protestants, often rich, primarily educated people.

The chief features of **WASP language** are the use, in referring to something, of the oldest word or phrase for it that is still correct in the language and the avoidance of all euphemisms and any expressions that are faddish or trendy. It prefers *fat* to *stout*, for example, *rich* to *wealthy*, *old people* to *senior citizen*, *poor* to *disadvantaged*, *crippled* to *handicapped*, *nice house* to *lovely home*, *sick* or *ill* to *indisposed*. See **EUPHEMISMS.**

**way**  Avoid using to mean "away."

**ways**  NonSAWE as a substitute for *way.*

NOT THIS:  a long **ways.**

BUT THIS:  a long **way.**

**well**  See **good, well.**

**well and good**  *All is well and good* is wordy (see **CONCISION**) for *All is well* or *Everybody looks good.*

**were**    *Were* has two uses. (1) It is, in the indicative mood, the third-person plural, past-tense form of the verb *to be: They* **were** *there.*

(2) It is, in the subjunctive mood, the only form of the verb *to be* in an adverb clause or a noun clause that makes a statement contrary to fact: *If Janet* **were** *mayor, she would fire the chief of police; he wishes that he* **were** *rich.* Use (2) of *were* occurs chiefly in formal writing; informal writing substitutes *was.* **Caution:** Some readers object to use of *was* in contrary-to-fact clauses in any writing. **Another caution:** Do not use *were* in an *if*-clause that is not contrary to fact (this use of *were* is hypercorrection).

NOT THIS:    If John **were** blushing, Mary didn't notice it.

BUT THIS:    If John **was** blushing, Mary didn't notice it.

NOT THIS:    I will cancel the picnic if it **were** to rain.

BUT THIS:    I will cancel the picnic if it rains.

(See **HYPERCORRECTION; MOOD; NUMBER; PERSON;** and **VERBS.**)

**we, us**    Use *we* as a subject or a subject complement, *us* as an object: *We the people protest. They deceived* **us** *the people.*

**what**    SAWE counts *what* as either singular or plural, depending upon context. Singular: *What* **is** *the case?* Plural: *What* **are** *often problems. . . .*

**what all, who all**    Emphatic or intensive forms of *what* and *who. What* **all** *did you do?* and *What did you do?* are synonymous, but the former is not emphatic.

**whereabouts**    Often wordy for *where.* (See **CONCISION.**)

NOT THIS:    **Whereabouts** is he?

BUT THIS:    **Where** is he?

**where . . . at, where . . . to**  Wordy for *where*.

NOT THIS:    **Where** is the dean's office **at?**

BUT THIS:    **Where** is the dean's office?

NOT THIS:    **Where** is the flight going **to?**

BUT THIS:    **Where** is the flight going?

**who (whoever), whom (whomever)**  *Who* functions either as subject (*the person who loves you; who minds the store?*) or as subject complement (*Who is she?*). *Whom* functions only as object (*the person whom you love; whom are you speaking for?*). In informal writing, however, *who* functions not only as subject or subject complement but also as object—*unless* the object is object of a preposition *and* the preposition precedes it: *To whom am I indebted?* (but: *who am I indebted to?*). **Caution:** Some readers object to the use of *who* as an object in any writing, formal or informal.

NOT THIS:    a source **who** he declined to name.

BUT THIS:    a source **whom** he declined to name.

**Another caution:** Do not hypercorrect *who* to *whom*. (See **HYPERCORRECTION.**)

NOT THIS:    Give it to **whomever** is there.

BUT THIS:    Give it to **whoever** is there.

*Whoever* is not the object of the preposition *to;* it is the subject of the clause *whoever is there.* The object of the preposition is that whole clause.

NOT THIS:    The government may not tell universities **whom** they may admit and **whom** should be denied admission.

BUT THIS:    The government may not tell universities **whom** they may admit and **who** should be denied admission.

The first *whom* is correct: it is the direct object of the verb *may admit*. The second, however, should be *who:* it is the subject of the clause *who should be denied admission*. What may have encouraged hypercorrection of *who* to *whom* was a—usually commendable—desire for parallelism. (See **PARALLELISM**.)

**wide range of**    Wordy for *many*. (See **CONCISION**.)

NOT THIS:    a **wide range of** pundits.

BUT THIS:    **many** pundits.

**window of opportunity**    A cliché. (See **CLICHÉS**.) Prefer *opportunity*.

**-wise**    A SAWE combining form added to a noun to make an adverb and meaning either (a) "in the manner of" (*snakewise*), (b) "in the position or direction of" (*clockwise*), or (c) "with regard to" (*fashionwise*). **Caution:** Many readers object to use of *wise* to mean (c), especially if the resulting adverb has commercial connotations (*dollarwise, pricewise, saleswise*) or cannot be justified as less wordy or more graceful (*an improvement humanrightswise* for *an improvement in human rights*).

**without**    Always a preposition, never a conjunction, in SAWE.

NOT THIS:    I cannot go **without** she says so.

BUT THIS:    I cannot go **without** her saying so.

(See **but, hardly, scarcely**.)

**with regards to**    See **regard, regards**.

**witness** As a verb, usually pretentious for *see*.

NOT THIS:   Sam **witnessed** the opening of the World Series.

BUT THIS:   Sam **saw** the opening of the World Series.

**wont** SAWE but a bit old-fashioned to mean "habit": *He had a cocktail with lunch, as is his wont.*

**world of** Wordy for *many* or *much*.

NOT THIS:   a **world of** opportunities

BUT THIS:   **many** opportunities

**worsen** Now SAWE to mean either "become worse" or "make worse": *The crisis worsened last week.*

**worthwhile, worth while** (1) Before a noun, use *worthwhile: a worthwhile project.* As a predicate adjective, use *worth while: The project is worth while.*

(2) Both forms are vague as words of praise. Prefer a more descriptive term such as *productive, profitable,* or *well-researched.* (See **DESCRIPTIVE AND EVALUATIVE WORDS.**)

**would** Usually a source of wordiness (see **CONCISION**) in descriptions of a customary or habitual activity.

NOT THIS:   Every morning he **would** sort the mail.

BUT THIS:   Every morning he **sorted** the mail.

**wreak, wreck** Often confused. *Wreak* means (among other things) "to cause": *The explosion **wreaked** great confusion in the shopping center. Wreck* as a verb means "to ruin or damage by breaking up": *The tornado **wrecked** the pavilion.*

NOT THIS:   The fire **wrecked** havoc.

BUT THIS:   The fire **wreaked** havoc.

**WRITER'S BLOCK**   Perhaps all writers, however good or prolific, have at some time suffered from **writer's block**—paling at the sight of a blank sheet that they must fill with prose.

Probably the best way to cope with writer's block is to size up your writing task. What is your subject? What do you know about it? What do you need to find out? Who are your readers? What do you know about them, and what do you need to find out? What's your intention, purpose, or goal in writing for them? What constraints does your mode or genre of discourse—personal letter, letter to an editor, informal essay, learned article—impose upon you? What is the maximum number of words you may use, for instance? What's the appropriate tone? The appropriate vocabulary?

**WRITING AND CREATIVITY**   Perhaps the most important point to make about writing is this: writing an essay or novel or just a letter to a friend is not like baking a cake or manufacturing aspirin tablets. Writing is a creative activity like inventing a recipe or a medication.

When you bake a cake or manufacture aspirin tablets, however well or poorly, you follow a recipe or standard procedure that tells you, step by step, just what to do. But there are no recipes or standard procedures for writing anything. For every essay, novel, or letter is unique. Never before has anyone put those words in that very order down on paper, and no one ever will, except perhaps to copy them.

Consequently, before baking a cake, you know just what it will look and taste like—barring mistakes and accidents, of course. And so with manufacturing aspirin tablets. But you never know what an essay will look like, what it will say, until you have written it. If you did, you wouldn't have to write it. Writing consists of deciding—word by word, sentence by sentence, paragraph by paragraph—just what it will look like.

Everything you write, then, is a result of your creativity. But your creativity is guided by two things. One is your intentions, purposes, or goals in writing—usually to inform your readers or to persuade them to do something. The other is your knowledge—of your subject, of course, but also of the English language, your readers, and rhetoric. Rhetoric—the act of adapting your writing to your subject, your intentions, purposes, and goals, and to your readers—is the subject of this book.

**WRITING PROCESS**    For some time, the term **writing process** has been much used in discussion of teaching writing. But the term is misleading. In the usual sense of *process,* a process is a step-by-step procedure or recipe for doing something: *the process of manufacturing gum drops.* Because writing, however humble, is always a creative activity, there are no recipes or procedures for doing it. At best, there are guidelines and suggestions of the sort that this book provides. (See also **WRITING AND CREATIV-ITY.**)

**Xmas**  Prefer *Christmas.*

**ye** Never use as a substitute for *the*. Even in Old English, the word meaning "the" was not spelled *ye*. It was spelled *þe* (*þ* is a letter called a *thorn*).

**year around, year round** Prefer the latter.

**YEARS SPELLED OUT** *Nineteen hundred and ninety-eight* is wordy for *nineteen ninety-eight*. (See **CONCISION**.)

**yon, yonder** Though neither word is archaic or obsolete, they appear rarely in SAWE. *Yon* survives chiefly in the phrase *hither and yon*. And yonder seems to survive only in the song (by Henry Creamer and J. Turner Laytu) "Way Down Yonder in New Orleans."

**your's, yours** Only *yours* is SAWE.

**you was** NonSAWE for *you were*.

>NOT THIS:  **You was** right.

>BUT THIS:  **You were** right.

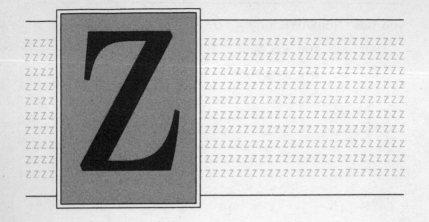

**zeal, zest** Sometimes confused. *Zeal* means "ardent, enthusiastic, fervent, passionate interest in doing something": *a **zeal** to right social wrongs.* *Zest* means "gusto, keen enjoyment, relish": *a **zest** for life.*

**ZEUGMA** A figure of speech (see **FIGURES OF SPEECH**) using a verb with two subjects, objects, or modifiers, or an adjective with two nouns, only one of which is appropriate or both of which are appropriate but in different ways: *Not only John but the girls are happy; He took his medicine and his time; She kept her appointment and her temper; They walked in good spirits and the rain.*

**zip** SAWE but informal to mean "great energy or vigor": *she did her work with **zip**.*

---

348